# ALMSHOUSES
## A Social & Architectural History

# ALMSHOUSES
## A Social & Architectural History

Brian Howson

Also by Brian Howson:
*Houses of Noble Poverty* (Belle View Books, 1993)

First published 2008
Reprinted 2013

The History Press
The Mill, Brimscombe Port,
Stroud, Gloucestershire, GL5 2QG
www.thehistorypress.co.uk

© Brian Howson, 2008

The right of Brian Howson to be identified as the Author of this work has been asserted in accordance with the Copyrights, Designs and Patents Act 1988.

All rights reserved. No part of this book may be reprinted or reproduced or utilised in any form or by any electronic, mechanical or other means, now known or hereafter invented, including photocopying and recording, or in any information storage or retrieval system, without the permission in writing from the Publishers.

British Library Cataloguing in Publication Data.
A catalogue record for this book is available from the British Library.

ISBN 978 0 7524 4258 7

Printed in Great Britain

# CONTENTS

| | |
|---|---|
| List of Colour Plates | 7 |
| List of Black and White Illustrations | 7 |
| List of Almshouse Plans | 8 |
| | |
| Introduction | 10 |
| Chronology | 11 |
| | |
| *Part One: Social Context* | 13 |
| Charitable Giving | 13 |
| Hospitals in Antiquity | 14 |
| The Hospital Orders | 15 |
| The Military Orders | 16 |
| Monastic Affiliations | 17 |
| The Incidence of Leprosy | 20 |
| Founders and Benefactors | 22 |
| The Reformation | 27 |
| Elizabethan Almshouses and the Old Poor Laws | 30 |
| The Elizabethan Settlement | 31 |
| The Rise of the Merchant Classes | 31 |
| The Emergence of the Gentry | 34 |
| The Stuarts | 34 |
| James I and Charles I | 37 |
| The Civil War | 42 |
| The Restoration | 43 |

| | |
|---|---:|
| The Glorious Revolution | 48 |
| Queen Anne | 51 |
| Georgian Almshouses | 52 |
| Victorian Almshouses | 59 |
| The Workhouse | 59 |
| The Charity Commission | 61 |
| The Present Day | 68 |
| The Almshouse Association | 72 |
| Hospitals and Almshouses in Other Countries | 73 |
| | |
| *Part Two: Architectural Context* | 77 |
| Great Hall with Chapel Attached | 77 |
| Great Hall with Chapel Detached | 84 |
| The Cruciform Layout | 88 |
| The Courtyard Design | 92 |
| | |
| *Part Three: Gazeteer* | 109 |
| Bibliography | 151 |
| Appendix | 153 |
| Index | 155 |

# ILLUSTRATIONS

## COLOUR PLATES

1. St Nicholas' Hospital chapel, Harbledown, Kent (1084)
2. Hospital of St Mary BV, Canterbury, Kent (1225)
3. St Edmund's Hospital chapel, Gateshead, Tyne and Wear (1247)
4. Merchant Venturers' Hospital, York, North Yorkshire (1280)
5. Trinity Hospital (the Newark), Leicester, Leicestershire (1351)
6. The Bedehouse, Higham Ferrers, Leicestershire (1423)
7. Hospital of St John the Baptist/ St John the Evangelist, Sherborne, Dorset (1437)
8. St Leonard's Hospital, Tickhill, South Yorkshire (1470)
9. Forde's Hospital, Coventry, West Midlands (1529)
10. Long Alley Almshouses, Abingdon, Oxfordshire (1553)
11. Lord Leycester's Hospital, Warwick, Warwickshire (1571)
12. Lord Leycester's Hospital, Warwick, Warwickshire (1571)
13. Beamsley Hospital, Craven, North Yorkshire (1593)
14. Browne's Hospital interior, Stamford, Lincolnshire (1610)
15. Moretonhampstead Almshouses, Moretonhampstead, Devon (1639)
16. Sir William Turner's Hospital, Kirkleatham, Cleveland (1676)
17. Holy Jesus Hospital, Newcastle-on-Tyne, Tyne and Wear (1682)
18. Shireburn Almshouses, Stydd-under-Langridge, Lancashire (1728)
19. Shireburn Hospital, Hurst Green, Lancashire (1706)
20. Tyne Master Mariners' Asylum, Tynemouth, Tyne and Wear (1836)
21. Aberford Almshouses, Aberford, West Yorkshire (1844)
22. Sir Francis Crossley's Almshouses, Halifax, West Yorkshire (1855)
23. Roebuck Memorial Homes, Huddersfield, West Yorkshire (1928)

## BLACK AND WHITE ILLUSTRATIONS

*Page no.*

- 15 Cluny Abbey, Burgundy, France
- 18 The Beguinhof, Bruges, Belgium (1235)
- 18 Santo Spirito in Sassia, Rome, Italy (1204)
- 18 Central courtyard, St John's Hospital, Rhodes
- 19 Hospitum, St Mary's Abbey, York, North Yorkshire (1400)
- 19 St Leonard's Hospital, York, North Yorkshire (986)
- 21 Hospital of St Mary BV, Newcastle-upon-Tyne, Tyne and Wear (1189)
- 21 A leper
- 22 God's House, Southampton, Hampshire (1197)
- 24 St Mary Magdalene's Hospital Chapel, Ripon, North Yorkshire (1130)
- 25 Ruins of St Ann's Hospital Chapel, Ripon, North Yorkshire (1438)
- 25 Sherburn Hospital gatehouse, Durham, County Durham (1181)
- 26 St Wulston's Hospital Worcester, Hereford and Worcester (1298)
- 28 Hospital of St Cross, Winchester, Hampshire (1136)
- 29 St Saviour's Hospital, Wells, Somerset (1424)
- 29 Bablake's Hospital, Coventry, West Midlands (1507)
- 33 Interior, Merchant Venturers' Hospital, York, North Yorkshire (1280)
- 33 Sir William Turner's Hospital, Kirkleatham, Cleveland (1676)
- 35 Sir William Moyles' Almshouses, St Germains, Cornwall (1583)
- 35 Lord Leycester's Hospital, Warwick, Warwickshire (1571)
- 36 Jesus Hospital, Rothwell, Northamptonshire (1591)
- 37 Waldron's Almshouses, Tiverton, Devon (1579)
- 38 Greatham Hospital, Greatham, Cleveland (1810)

38 Greatham Hospital, Greatham, Cleveland (drawing 1995)
39 The Charterhouse, London (1611)
40 Hull Charterhouse, Humberside (1649)
41 Napper's Mite, Dorchester, Dorset (1615)
41 Almshouses, Mapledurham, Oxfordshire (1613)
42 Ingram's Hospital, York, North Yorkshire (1640)
43 Henry Cornish's Almshouses, Chipping Norton, Oxfordshire (1640)
43 Fauconberg Hospital, Coxwold, North Yorkshire (1662)
45 Les Invalides, Paris, France (1674)
45 Chapel, Les Invalides, Paris, France (1674)
46 Kilmainham Hospital, Dublin, Republic of Ireland (1686)
47 Royal Hospital, Chelsea, London (1692)
49 Morden College, Blackheath, London (1695)
49 Royal Naval Hospital, Greenwich, London (1705)
50 College Matrarum, Salisbury, Wiltshire (1682)
50 Berkeley Hospital, Worcester, Hereford and Worcester (1666)
52 Trinity Hospital, Mile End Road, London (1695)
53 Holy Jesus Hospital, Newcastle-upon-Tyne, Tyne and Wear (1682)
53 Fountain's Hospital, Linton-in-Craven, North Yorkshire (1721)
55 Alnut's Hospital, Goring Heath, Oxfordshire (1726)
55 Shireburn Hospital, Hurst Green, Lancashire (1706)
55 Christ's Hospital, Abingdon, Oxfordshire (1553)
56 Twitty's Almshouses, Abingdon, Oxfordshire (1707)
57 Tomkins Almshouses, Abingdon, Oxfordshire (1733)
58 Mary Wandesford Hospital, York, North Yorkshire (1739)
58 Mary Lowther's Hospital, Ackworth, West Yorkshire (1741)
59 Well Hospital, Well, North Yorkshire (1758)
61 Goldsmith's Almshouse, Acton, London (1811)
62 Lady Hewley's Almshouses, York, North Yorkshire (1840)
62 Dr Caleb Crowther's Almshouses, Wakefield, West Yorkshire (1840)
63 Saltaire Almshouses, Saltaire, West Yorkshire (1855)
64 Joseph Crossley's Almshouses, Halifax, West Yorkshire (1863)
64 Seamen's Houses, Whitby, North Yorkshire (1842)
66 St Anne's Bedehouse, Lincoln, Lincolnshire (1847)
69 New Earswick, York, North Yorkshire (1904)
70 Durham Aged Mineworkers' Cottage Homes
73 *Hotel-Dieu*, Beaune, Burgundy, France (1443)
74 Neukoop Hospital, The Hague, Holland (1608)
74 Meulenaer Almshouses, Bruges, Belgium (1613)
76 Cook County Almshouse, Chicago, USA (1835)
76 Tewksbury Almshouse, Tewksbury, Massachusetts, USA (1852)
78 Model of the Farmery, Fountains Abbey, North Yorkshire (1240)
79 St Nicholas Hospital, Salisbury, Wiltshire (1214)
82 Sint Jan's Hospitaal, Bruges, Belgium (1188)
85 Gateway St John's Hospital, Canterbury, Kent (1089)
86 Hospital of St John the Baptist, Northampton, Northamptonshire (1327)
90 Hospital Royale, Grenada, Spain (1504)
90 The Savoy Hospital, London (1519)
92 Bond/Bablake Hospital, Coventry, West Midlands (1507)
94 Ewelme Hospital, Ewelme, Oxfordshire (1437)
98 Spence's Hospital, Carleton-in-Craven, North Yorkshire (1698)
100 Browne's Hospital, Stamford, Lincolnshire (1493)
106 Frieston Hospital, Kirkthorpe, Wakefield, North Yorkshire (1595)

## ALMSHOUSE PLANS

78 Fig.1 The Farmery, Fountains Abbey, North Yorkshire (1240)
79 Fig.2 Hospital of St Mary, Chichester, West Sussex (1229)
80 Fig.3 Hospital of St Mary, Chichester, West Sussex, section (1229)
80 Fig.4 Hospital of St Nicholas, Salisbury, Wiltshire (1214)
81 Fig.5 Hospital of St John the Baptist, Winchester, Hampshire (1290)
81 Fig.6 Hospital of St Saviour, Wells, Somerset (1424)
81 Fig.7 The Bedehouse, Higham Ferrers, Northamptonshire (1423)
81 Fig.8 Hospital of St Mary Magdalene, Glastonbury, Somerset (thirteenth century)
82 Fig.9 Hospital of St John the Baptist/John the Evangelist, Sherborne, Dorset (1437)
83 Fig.10 Tonnerre Hospital, France (1300)
83 Fig.11 Tonnerre Hospial, France, section (1300)
84 Fig.12 *Hotel-Dieu*, Paris, France, woodcut (1260)

| | | | |
|---|---|---|---|
| 85 | Fig.13 Hospital of St John, Canterbury, Kent (1089) | 100 | Fig.26 Browne's Hospital, Stamford, Lincolnshire (1493) |
| 86 | Fig.14 Hospital of St Mary Magdalene, Winchester, Hampshire (1158) | 101 | Fig.27 Forde's Hospital, Coventry, West Midlands (1529) |
| 86 | Fig.15 Hospital of St John the Baptist, Northampton, Northamptonshire (1327) | 102 | Fig.28 Kilmainham Hospital, Dublin, Republic of Ireland (1680) |
| 87 | Fig.16 Hospital of St John the Baptist, Northampton, Northamptonshire, elevation (1327) | 102 | Fig.29 Lord Leycester's Hospital, Warwick, Warwickshire (1571) |
| 87 | Fig.17 The Great Hospital, Norwich, Norfolk (1249) | 103 | Fig.30 The Royal Hospital, Chelsea, London (1692) |
| 89 | Fig.18 *Ospidale Maggiore*, Milan, Italy (1546) | 103 | Fig.31 Sir William Turner's Hospital, Kirkleatham, Cleveland (1676) |
| 89 | Fig.19 Hospital of Santa Cruz, Toledo, Spain (1540) | 104 | Fig.32 Cobham College, Cobham, Kent (1598) |
| 91 | Fig.20 The Savoy Hospital, London (1519) | 104 | Fig.33 Coningsby Hospital, Hereford, Hereford and Worcester (1615) |
| 93 | Fig.21 Bond's Hospital, Coventry, West Midlands (1507) | 105 | Fig.34 Whitgyft's Hospital, Croydon, London (1596) |
| 95 | Fig.22 Ewelme Hospital, Ewelme, Oxfordshire (1437) | 106 | Fig.35 Trinity Hospital, Mile End Road, London (1696) |
| 96 | Fig.23 St Cross Hospital, Winchester, Hampshire (1136) | 108 | Fig.36 Beamsley Hospital, Craven, North Yorkshire (1593) |
| 99 | Fig.24 The Charterhouse, London (1611) | 108 | Fig.37 Frieston Hospital, Kirkthorpe, Wakefield, West Yorkshire (1595) |
| 99 | Fig.25 Spence's Hospital, Carleton-in-Craven, North Yorkshire (1698) | | |

# Introduction

The care of elderly people in the United Kingdom is becoming of increasing significance as more and more people are living well beyond retirement age, and a goodly number are surviving into their eighties and nineties.

Changing lifestyles over the years since the Second World War has meant that many children in this country no longer look after their parents in their old age, as do their opposite numbers in other parts of the world. In order to pay for all the trappings of modern life, often both partners in a marriage or relationship must work, leaving no time for the day-to-day care of their elderly parents. When their relatives get too frail to look after themselves, they must either pay for specialist care or rely on the local authority to provide it. This latter solution is, however, becoming increasingly unattractive, as EU directives place more onerous financial burdens on publicly funded care, which must be passed on to the council taxpayer; in many cases this is not politically acceptable. Many local authorities have almost ceased providing direct care for the elderly, seeing their role rather as controllers and co-ordinators of private-sector provision.

The current preoccupation with geriatric care is, however, by no means new. We have in this country a well-established and well-documented tradition of provision for our old folk, predominantly charitable in origin, and reaching back over a thousand years. The organisations proving this care are known generically as almshouse charities.

This work aims to outline the development of almshouses, from their origins as medieval hospitals, adjuncts of the monastic system, through the Tudor and Stuart periods, when the concept of the almshouse as a self-contained dwelling emerged, to Georgian and Victorian times when the system became more urban than rural in character and philanthropic in provision.

It has been estimated that over 2,000 separate groups of occupied almshouses in England have survived to the present day, with an unknown additional number of former almshouse buildings now used for non-residential purposes. Altogether there are thought to be some 25,000 separate almshouses, generally in groups of four to ten dwellings. Most towns of any size, and a great number of villages, have one or more groups, in many cases quite unnoticed by the general population, still housing the less well-off in society, though thankfully, not, as in the past, those in absolute penury. This present study is concerned primarily with English almshouses, although some reference is made to examples elsewhere, both in the main text and in the Appendix.

Part One, by far the longest section, considers almshouses in their social context from medieval times to the present day. Part Two looks briefly at their architectural context, and Part Three consists of a gazetteer of some 500 of the most significant almshouse groups in the country, setting out their characteristics and location. It will be appreciated that with so many groups in existence, space does not permit the inclusion of them all, and the author apologises in advance to trustees whose groups are not included.

With such a large number of almshouse groups, it has not been possible for the author to visit each and every one. It has been necessary therefore to rely to a great extent upon research by others who have gone before, together with help from those in the present day who have given generously of their time and experience.

Acknowledgement must firstly be made to the pioneers of almshouse lore; the Victorian architect F.T. Dolman's *Hospitals of the Middle Ages*, published in 1858, Miss Rotha Mary Clay's *The Medieval Hospitals of England*, published in 1909 and Walter H. Godfrey's *The English Almshouse*, published in 1955. Their seminal research formed the armature upon which the body of this book is wound.

Two other recently published works also stand out as being major contributors to the current body of knowledge: Brian Bailey's *Almshouses*, published in 1988, with its comprehensive list of charities both great and small, in town and village, and Clive Berridge's *The Almshouses of London*, published in 1987, which covers almshouses past and present in the metropolis.

Many individuals have assisted during the several years which led to the preparation of this volume, and it would be difficult, if not impossible, to acknowledge each and every one's contribution. However, one individual and one organisation must be singled out for special mention. David Scott OBE, the erstwhile director of the Almshouse Association, together with its current director and staff at Wokingham, gave unstinting help and support. Their detailed knowledge of and care for all the almshouses of the United Kingdom, together with their comprehensive database of charities registered with the Association, has been invaluable. David Scott's own extensive knowledge, not only of the buildings, but also of many of the personalities, almsfolk and trustees, has been an inspiration.

The author is conscious of the fact that the study covers mainly the largest and best-documented institutions. Hundreds of small local charities remain scattered throughout the land whose trustees, often in the prime of life themselves, give freely of their time and resources, keeping alive the traditions of service and care which have been fostered during a thousand years of almshouse history. It is to those largely unsung and unrewarded philanthropists that this volume is dedicated.

## CHRONOLOGY

| | |
|---|---|
| 816 | Synod of Aix, France. |
| 986 | Hospital of St Peter, York, North Yorkshire (later refounded in 1350 by King Stephen as St Leonard's Hospital). |
| 1089 | Harbledown Hospital, Canterbury, Kent by Archbishop Lanfranc. |
| 1123 | St Bartholomew's Hospital, London by Rahere. |
| 1136 | Hospital of St Cross, Winchester, Hampshire by Henry de Bois. |
| 1200 | St John's Hospital, Northampton, Northants by William Sancte Clere. |
| 1249 | The Great Hospital, Norwich, Norfolk by Walter de Suffield. |
| 1331 | Trinity (Newarke) Hospital, Leicester, Leicestershire by Henry, Earl of Lancaster. |
| 1437 | Hospital of St John the Baptist and Evangelist, Sherborne, Dorset. |
| 1437 | Ewelme Hospital, Oxfordshire by William de la Pole. |
| 1485 | William Browne's Hospital, Stamford, Lincolnshire. |
| 1517 | Hospital of the Savoy, London by King Henry VII. |
| 1539 | Dissolution of the monasteries. |
| 1571 | Lord Leycester's Hospital, Warwick, Warwickshire (conversion from guildhall). |
| 1592 | Forde's Hospital, Coventry, West Midlands. |
| 1596 | Holy Trinity Hospital, Croydon, London, by Archbishop Whitgift. |
| 1611 | The Charterhouse, London (converted to almshouses from a Carthusian monastery by Thomas Sutton). |
| 1639 | Almshouses at Moretonhampstead, Devon. |
| 1670 | Les Invalides, Paris, France. |
| 1684 | Kilmainham Hospital, Dublin, Ireland. |
| 1686 | The Royal Hospital, Chelsea, London. |
| 1694 | The Royal Naval Hospital, Greenwich, London. |
| 1695 | Morden College, Blackheath, London. |
| 1695 | Trinity Almshouses, Mile End Road, London. |
| 1707 | Twitty's Almshouses, Abingdon, Oxon. |
| 1733 | Sarah, Duchess of Marlborough's Almshouses, St Albans, Hertfordshire. |

1826   Licensed Victuallers' Homes, Peckham, London.
1836   Tyne Master Mariners' Asylum, Tynemouth, Tyne and Wear.
1840   Dr Caleb Crowther's Almshouses, Wakefield, West Yorkshire.
1844   Arberford Almshouses, Aberford, near Leeds, West Yorkshire.
1856   Bradford Tradesmen's Homes, Bradford, West Yorkshire.
1881   United Westminster Almshouses, Westminster, London.
1897   Diamond Jubilee Almshouses, Whippingham, Isle of Wight.
1898   Durham Aged Mineworkers' Homes, County Durham.
1900   Linen and Woollen Drapers' Homes, Mill Hill, London.
1919   North-east Railway Cottage Homes, Darlington, Co. Durham.
1921   Whiteley Village, Surrey.
1946   Foundation of The National Association of Almshouse.
1986   Service in Westminster Abbey to commemorate 1,000 years of almshouses.

# PART ONE
# SOCIAL CONTEXT

## CHARITABLE GIVING

Charitable giving has been part of the British way of life for many centuries. The Victorian era is considered by many to have been the most prolific in charitable and philanthropic works, but really one has to look much, much further back in history to find its true origins. The practice of aiding the poor and feeble has been carried out in all countries from time immemorial. In the Bible, when the patriarch Job was justifying himself, he spoke of his charitable acts in words that can today be used to describe the ideal philanthropist:

> When the ear heard me, then it blessed me; and when my eye saw me, it gave witness to me: because I delivered the poor that cried and the fatherless, and him that had none to help him. The blessing of him that was ready to perish came upon me: and I caused the widow's heart to sing for joy. I put on righteousness and it clothed me: my judgement was as a robe and a diadem. I was the eyes of the blind, and the feet of the lame. I was the father to the poor: the cause which I knew not I searched out.
>
> (Job 29 v.11-16)

Before Christianity was properly established, the instinct of sympathy for those in distress prompted acts of kindness which philosophers commended and religious leaders endorsed. An imposing array of texts exhorted people to charitable works. The beggar is a figure in almost all schools of literature with which we are familiar, and where there are beggars, there must be those who gave to them. In China, long before the Christian era, there were refuges for the aged and the sick who, for some reason or other, could not be cared for by the family as was the usual custom. There were also schools for poor children, free eating houses for labourers and societies for paying the expenses of marriage and the burial of the dead.

From the first though, the altruistic instinct seems to have been reinforced by egotistical instincts, originating in educational, political or religious considerations. The first of these motives was doubtless the weakest of the three. The desire to promote self-satisfaction by development of the benevolent impulses is largely a modern form of selfishness, and yet we can find traces of it among the ancients.

Formerly, just as now, political considerations frequently led to acts of charity. Free or greatly cheapened corn for the Roman people was in fact a mischievous gratuity; and while sympathy for the people undoubtedly motivated many who favoured charity, the principle cause of their largess was political self-seeking. Accordingly, the legislation of the later Roman Empire for the better care of infants and the support of young women with children resulted partly from sympathy for the needy, but mainly from a wish to fill up the depleted ranks of the population.

The commonest and most powerful incentive to benevolence has, everywhere and at all times, been that supplied by religion. Any impulse or habit that was for the good of the people was likely to have been fixed or at least intensified by religious considerations. Almost all customs, including the organisation of the family and of the government, and even habits of dress, diet and cleanliness, have been dictated by religious doctrine. To whatever source we may trace the sentiment of pity and the desire to help the destitute, it certainly had not been in existence for long before it was cultivated, almost hijacked, by religious authority.

But religion, like motives based on educational or political considerations, has too frequently substituted self-seeking for self-sacrifice as the main reason for aiding the poor. The charity of antiquity was very largely a means of obtaining merit. 'The riches of the infinite God,' says the *Vendidad*, 'will be bestowed upon him who relieves the poor'. According to a Hindu epic, 'He who giveth without stint food to the fatigued wayfarer, never seen before, obtaineth merit that is great.' It was, after all, in order to justify himself that Job enumerated his works of mercy.

On the other hand, while rewards were offered for benevolent work, punishments were promised for the hard-hearted. The grim threat of the *Talmud* – 'The house that does not open to the poor shall open to the physician' – is typical of many passages that might be quoted from early religious writings. Under the influence of such threats, or of more direct ones, believers felt constrained to aid the poor for purely selfish reasons; to do some act that seemed to have been prescribed, in order that it might be accounted to them as altruism. Really, the act itself was not one of charity at all but of penance; its motive was not a desire to aid the distressed as much as to placate a more-or-less unreasonable deity or fate.

## HOSPITALS IN ANTIQUITY

We use the term almshouse now to describe a whole range of residential charitable institutions, but in antiquity, and indeed in medieval times, it was just one of several functions that could be applied to a single building. Actually, the appellation 'almshouse' was not much used before the fourteenth century, when the principal refuge for the poor and sick was the hospital. Hospital, hospice, hostel, and hotel are all derived from the Latin *hospes*, meaning a guest. The term hospital, in the sense we know it today, covered almshouse, asylum, orphanage, foundling home, guest house for travellers and particularly pilgrims, and poor house. A document of 1232 tells us that Esslingen received 'the poor, pilgrims, transients, pregnant women, abandoned children, the halt and the lame – in fact every one'. A name often given to hospital is *domus dieu*, and frequently *domus pauporum*.

When and where the first hospital was established is not known for certain. According to some authorities, a certain Zoticus built a hospital in Constantinople during the reign of the Emperor Constantine, and it is clear that the early Christians in the east founded hospitals soon after Julian the Apostate came to the throne in 361, as is evidenced by a letter sent by him to the high priest of Galatia directing him to establish a *xenodochium* in each city, to be supported by public revenues. The fact that the first hospitals were founded in the east accounts for the use, even in the west, of the names of various kinds of charitable institution derived from Greek, which was, of course, the principal language used throughout the Mediterranean. *Nosocomium* was used for the sick, *Brephotrophium* for foundlings, *Orphanotrophium* for orphans, *Ptochium* for the poor who were unable to work, *Gerontochium* for the aged and *Xenodochium* for poor or infirm pilgrims. The declared aim of the Emperor was to rival the philanthropic work of the Christians who cared for pagans as well as for their own.

One of the most famous foundations of this era was that of St Basil, who established a hospital in Caesarea in Cappodocia, present-day Turkey, in 369. This *basilias*, as it was called, was enormous, like a small town, with buildings for different kinds of need. St Basil's example was followed throughout the east, although not on the same scale; at Alexandria by St John the Almsgiver, at Ephasus by Bishop Brassianus, at Constantinople by St John Chrysostan and St Pulcheria, sister of Theodosius II, who founded a '*multa publica hospitum et pauporium domicilia*' – a public hospital and home for the poor. Among later institutions in Constantinople were an orphanage founded by Alexius, built in 1118, and the Hospital of Forty Martyrs, founded in 1190.

The first establishments in France date from the sixth century, when the pious King Chuldebert founded a *xenodochium* at Lyons in 549. Other foundations were those of King Sigibert at Autun in 598 and at Athis, near Paris in 630, Caesarius at Arles and a hospice to which Hinemar of Reims assigned considerable revenues between 806 and 882. The establishment of the famous, or infamous,

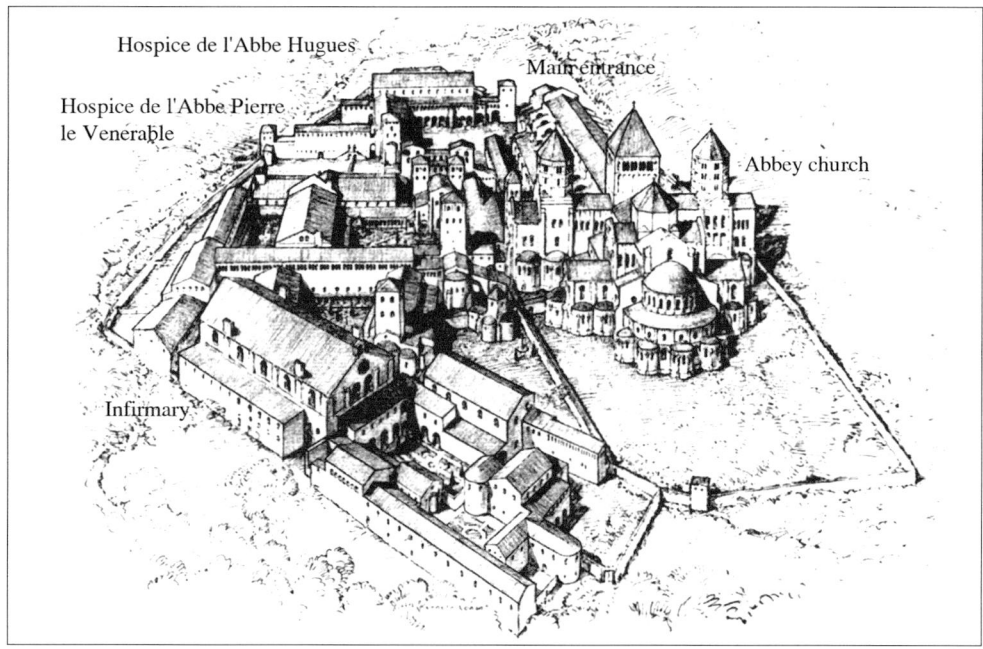

Cluny Abbey, Burgundy, France.

institution which later became known as the Hotel-Dieu in Paris was attributed to Landry, Bishop of Paris, in around 660. In Spain, the most important institution for the care of poor, sick people was founded in 580 by Bishop Masona at Merida in the province of Badajoz.

The Holy Roman Emperor Charlemagne decreed that hospitals which had been neglected before his reign should be restored in accordance with the needs of the time, and, further, ordered that a hospital should be attached to each cathedral and monastery. Following Charlemagne's death in 814, many hospitals were neglected and their revenues misappropriated. But even under those unfavourable conditions, many bishops were distinguished by their zeal and charity. Ansgar, Archbishop of Hamburg, who died in 865, founded a hospital at Bremen; and the Benedictine abbey at Cluny, founded in 910, set an example, which was copied throughout France and Germany, of providing hospitals in which poor people from outside the monastery were cared for. The monk charged with overseeing this hospital was enjoined to search out the needy in the neighbourhood. Among the monasteries notable for this relief were those Benedictine houses at Corbie in Picardy, Hirschau, Braunweiler, Deutz, Liesborn, Baumgarten, Eberbach, Volkenrode and Walkenreid.

Diocesan clergy were not exempt, and under directions emanating from the Council of Aachen in 817, each collegiate church was requested to maintain a hospital and was obliged to contribute towards its upkeep and support. Hospitals of this type were founded at Cologne in 1021, at Hildesheim in 975 and at Ausburg in 973. More provision was made by major churches; thus at Trier the hospitals of St Maximus, St Matthew, St Simeon and St James took their names from the church to which they were attached. During the period 1207 to 1570, no fewer than 155 hospitals were founded in Germany alone.

## THE HOSPITAL ORDERS

The establishment of confraternities and special religious orders for the purpose of ministering to the sick and infirm was one of the most important developments in the history of hospitals. The first of these appeared in Siena, Italy, towards the end of the ninth century. This was the famous hospital of Santa Maria della Scala, founded in 898. The management of the hospital was, surprisingly enough, in the hands of the citizens of Siena, though subject to the control of Pope Celestine III. Similar institutions, governed by the rule of St Augustine, sprang up throughout Italy, but by the thirteenth century they had passed from ecclesiastical control into the hands of the magistrates. The loose religious orders of Beguines and Beghards, established in the latter part of the twelfth century in the northern countries of Belgium, France and Germany, included in their charitable works the care of the sick and the feeble. The most important of the new orders to emerge at this time was that of the Holy Spirit or Holy Ghost. In the middle of the twelfth century, Guy de Montpellier opened a hospital in that city dedicated to the Holy Ghost and prescribed the rule of St Augustine for its administration. Approved in 1198 by Pope Innocent III, branches of the institution spread rapidly throughout France and in 1204 the same pontiff caused to be built a hospital at Sassia near to Rome dedicated to St Maria. Responding to the Pope's command, Guy de Montpellier moved to Rome to take charge of the hospital, bringing with him his system of hospital administration. The hospital was thereafter was known as Santo Spirito in Sassia. The Pope's example was imitated throughout Europe where nearly every city of any size had a hospital of the Holy Ghost. In Rome the hospital of St Andrea was founded in 1216, not far from the Lateran, and the hospital of St Giacomo in Augusta was founded in 1339. Thus Holy Spirit or *Heilig-geist* became a favourite dedication for hospitals.

## THE MILITARY ORDERS

The Crusades, amid much religious fervour, gave rise to various orders of chivalry which combined military service with the care of pilgrims, the sick, and the infirm. Of these orders, three – the Teutonic Knights, the Knights Templar and the Knights of Malta, or St John, also known as the Knights Hospitaller – are the best known.

The Teutonic Knights first established a hospital under the walls of the city of Acre, in which Count Adolf of Holstein, together with knights from the cities of Bremen and Lubeck, cared for the sick and the wounded. The hospital was named *domus hospitalis S Mariae Teutonicorum,* and was approved by Pope Clement III in 1191. The members of the order dedicated themselves to caring for the sick, and their rule prescribed that they should build a hospital wherever the order was introduced. However, soon afterwards, the centre of the order's activities was transferred from the Holy Land to Europe, where they were called in 1225 to fight the heathen Prussians. They were especially active in Germany where, because of its strict military discipline, the order was given control over many hospitals.

By comparison, the Knights Templar were more warlike. They were established in 1119 in Jerusalem by nine knights, calling themselves The Poor Fellow Soldiers of Jesus, who took up arms to protect pilgrims journeying to the Holy Land. Their headquarters were in the mosque built on the site of the Temple of Solomon, hence their more usual name, the Knights Templar.

The Order of St John of Jerusalem, or, as they have become known, the Knights Hospitaller, are thought to have emanated from the hospital connected with the Benedictine abbey of St Maria Latina in Jerusalem in the year 1065. When the first Crusaders arrived in Jerusalem in 1099, Gerhard, the abbot of St Maria, caused a new hospital to be built to replace the old one. He dedicated it to St John the Baptist, from which the new order, which was approved by the Pope in 1154, took its name. The order's original brief was the care of the sick and the feeble, but as the Crusades bore on, the care of wounded knights was added to its tasks and it became more military-orientated.

Other hospitals were established by the Order at Acre, Cyprus, Messina, Vechio and Villefranche. After the Turkish conquest of the Holy Land in 1309, the Order took over the island of Rhodes, and when Rhodes itself fell in 1530, the order transferred to the island of Malta where it remained until 1798, when the island was annexed by Napoleon. The order is still extant today, with its headquarters in Rome.

There are many documents emanating from Rome which testify to the interest and indeed zeal shown by successive popes in the provision of hospitals in these early days. They granted permission for a hospital to have a chapel, a chaplain and cemetery of its own, and exempted it from Episcopal jurisdiction, making it immediately answerable to the Holy See. They approved statutes and intervened to correct abuses, defended its property rights and compelled restitution where the hospital's property had been unjustly appropriated. Indulgences were granted to founders and patrons, to those who prayed in the hospital chapel and to all who made a contribution to the support of the hospital and its inmates.

## MONASTIC AFFILIATIONS

Modern, Western charitable giving began with the formulation of the Rule of St Benedict, which stated that, 'every arriving guest must be welcomed as if he were Christ'. At the Synod of Aix en Provence in France in AD 816, Pope Stephen V declared that it was the duty of every bishop to ensure that a hospice was provided for travellers, and of every canon to allocate one-tenth of his income for charitable purposes. He also laid down the Seven Corporal Works of Mercy, guidelines for the conduct of monks and canons in their daily lives, and particularly in their relations with the public at large. They were:

    Visiting the sick
    Ministering meat, drink and clothing to the needy
    Lodging the miserable poor
    Burying the dead
    Keeping the mad safe
    Nourishing orphans and widows
    Caring for lying-in women until they are delivered, recovered and churched

The Corporal Works of Mercy were generally known as almsgiving, which took its name from the Greek word *eleemonsune*, meaning compassion, which had been translated into the Old English *aelmysse,* from which the word alms is obviously derived. Almsgiving was not confined solely to Europe; the Islamic world, and particularly Mogul India, had for many centuries provided care and hospitality for their poor, aged and sick. And their *caravanserai* fulfilled the same function as the hospital for travellers in the West.

These requirements, particularly the obligation to give alms daily to the sick, the aged, the infirm and the needy, involved a whole range of activities, from the doling out of food and clothing to the provision of education and shelter.

The official in charge of almsgiving was the almoner, whose name has survived down the centuries and is now used to describe the person in charge of patients' welfare in a modern hospital. The almoner's window was usually situated in the outer wall of the monastery, adjoining the main gateway into th*e curi*a or great quadrangle. Remains of the almoner's window can still be seen at Dorchester and Evesham. It was through this window that alms were administered to the queuing poor. In addition, as has been indicated, it was the practice in some orders to educate the poor children of the town. Durham had its 'Children of the Almonry' school and many nunneries taught young girls, a practice which laid the foundations for modern convent education.

As time went by, the more infirm elderly poor, who needed domiciliary care, rather than merely being given alms, were taken into the *curi*a and housed in the *Hospitum* – literally, the place of hospitality. However, in due course these same elderly became something of a nuisance, placing greater demands on the brethren and interfering with the sedentary life of the monastery. Accordingly, at some time around AD 900 it was decided to remove them from the precincts of

*Almshouses: A Social and Architectural History*

The Beguinhof, Bruges, Belgium (1235).

Santo Spirito in Sassia, Rome, Italy (1204).

Central courtyard, St John's Hospital, Rhodes.

Social Context

*Above:* Hospitum, St Mary's Abbey, York, North Yorkshire (1400).

*Right:* St Leonard's Hospital, York, North Yorkshire (986).

the monastery proper and build special mini-monasteries for them, called hospitals. In some cases they wiould be close to the parent houses, or, just as likely, many miles away.

Each hospital was staffed by monks seconded from the main site, assisted by lay brothers, *conversi*, or, in the case of sisters, *oblate*. They were endowed with sufficient land and tithes to provide an independent income for the good works. By the time of the English Reformation in the sixteenth century there were some 800 of these hospitals, spread throughout the length and breadth of England and Wales. The oldest known hospital in England was that dedicated to St Leonard in York, founded by the Saxon King Athelstan in 986.

Tradition has it that the hospital's origins lay in the canons' responsibility for the welfare of the poor servants of York Minster, to which King Athelstan gave support by requiring every plough operating in the diocese of York to contribute each year twenty sheaves of corn as alms towards the upkeep of the needy. A small hospital was built on royal land to the west of the Minster, and given the same dedication as the cathedral. In 1246 an inquisition jury identified the recipients of hospitality as the poor, sick and infirm who had no homes but slept in the streets at night. William Rufus (1087-1100) moved the hospital a little further west, and on this growing site King Stephen (1135-1154) constructed a church dedicated to St Leonard, from which the hospital henceforth took its name.

The charitable functions of the hospital were to distribute daily alms at its gates to thirty poor people, give alms to prisoners in the city and to leper houses, and maintain 206 sick, poor folk within the hospital until they had convalesced sufficiently to be able to return to work. The hospital was staffed by thirteen brethren and eight sisters (who had special responsibility for tending to the sick and poor) pursuing a quasi-monastic lifestyle, involving chastity and renunciation of worldly goods; those with an aptitude for learning were placed in theological schools in York. Beds in the hospital might be endowed by private benefaction, with benefactors (or their heirs) nominating persons to be maintained by the hospital. In the building housing the infirmary, whose chapel still survives as a ruin, the lower floor was allocated to nursing exposed infants and looking after orphans and poor children. It was required that the chimney here functioned well, to avoid the children being harmed by smoke.

The extensive lands accumulated by the hospital were carefully cultivated and their crops, along with the sheaf alms, sold to finance the hospital's work. However, this income proved increasingly insufficient to support the hospital's needs and the number of residents had declined by the early fourteenth century. By the end of the century, due partly to mismanagement by the masters of the hospital, as well as delinquency on the part of many in paying the sheaf-alms, the hospital was in a parlous condition. Fire had destroyed the church's bell-tower, and the roofs of the infirmary and dormitory needed urgent repair, as did the other buildings of the hospital, its manors, and the rentable properties it owned in the city. The foundation alms had been pilfered and church ornaments and vestments pawned to pay the hospital's debts, while the master's personal household had run up high expenses. The hospital's debt was £543. Despite this, the hospital managed to survive until the Dissolution.

## THE INCIDENCE OF LEPROSY

From the eleventh century to the fourteenth, the need for refuge and care for the elderly, the sick and the infirm was increased substantially by the incidence of leprosy, which spread like the plague throughout Western Europe. Leprosy has been known since the dawn of history and is mentioned in Exodus 4, 6, and described in detail in Leviticus:

> … when a man shall have in the skin of his flesh a rising, a scab, or bright spot, and it be in the skin of his flesh like the plague of leprosy then he shall be brought unto Aaron the priest, or unto one of the sons of the priests: and the priest shall look on the plague in the skin of the flesh; and when the *hair* in the plague is turned white, and the plague in sight be deeper than the skin of his flesh, it is a plague of leprosy; and the priest shall look upon him, and pronounce him unclean.
>
> (Leviticus 13 v.2)

*Social Context*

*Above:* Hospital of St Mary BV, Newcastle-upon-Tyne, Tyne and Wear (1189).

*Right:* A leper.

In the Middle Ages some saintly characters strove to alleviate the suffering of lepers. The physician St Gregory of Tours endowed a hospital with 500 beds for lepers, and by his example St Francis of Assisi taught his disciples to nurse lepers. St Elizabeth of Thuringia was depicted in the painting by Durer, 'Feeding the Lepers', and Santa Caterina da Siena, a Dominican nun who, in 1366 bathed and dressed the sores of lepers in the Hospital Della Scala, appears in paintings by Bazzi and Vanni and in a sculpture by Gofa. The Sovereign Military Order of Malta, founded in Jerusalem by the Blessed Gerard in the eleventh century, was renowned for its charitable and humanitarian works for the succour and care of lepers.

Leprosy is generally considered to have been introduced by Crusaders returning from the Holy Land. Indeed, Voltaire phlegmatically observed that: 'All that we gained in the end by engaging in the crusades was leprosy; and of all that we had taken, that was the only thing that remained with us.'

That was not entirely true, for lepers were known to have existed in England in Saxon times, and at least two lazer-houses, as leper hospitals were known, had been established within twenty years of the Norman Conquest, long before the first crusade was mounted.

*Almshouses: A Social and Architectural History*

God's House, Southampton, Hampshire (1197).

The two earliest lazer-houses, founded in England before 1100, were at Harbledown near Canterbury, and at Rochester, also in Kent. Harbledown was founded by Abbot Lanfranc (1005-1087), William the Conqueror's first Archbishop of Canterbury, and was dedicated to St Leonard. Rochester's was founded by Bishop Gundolph and dedicated to St Bartholomew. Of the two, only Rochester's hospital building remains, much enlarged and changed beyond recognition, standing in Chatham High Street and now used as a church. Harbledown's original hospital chapel remains, but the lepers' living accommodation, originally thatched huts, has of course long since gone.

Burton Lazars, originally called Burton St Lazarus, the village near Melton Mowbray in Leicestershire, takes its name from St Lazarus, one of several patron saints of lepers. It was St Lazarus to whom the hospital situated there, of the Blessed Virgin and St Lazarus, founded during the reign of King Stephen in 1146, was dedicated. By tradition, St Lazarus was Bishop of Marseilles and in Western Europe was the principal patron of lepers. In central Europe, St James was more popular, whilst in England Mary Magdalene was supreme. A 'Maudlin House' was another popular name for a leper hospital in medieval England.

## FOUNDERS AND BENEFACTORS

Monks were not, however, the only providers of hospitals in those early days. In medieval Europe, travel between towns was an inconvenient, hazardous and time-consuming business. Decent roads were few and far between and accordingly only short distances could be covered each day, generally on foot or, if one were fortunate or wealthy, by coach or on horseback. As travel became more common for business and administrative purposes, the need for frequent stopping-places along the principal routes developed, and with the absence of what we now know as hotels or inns, hostels or hospitals were established, close to the main gateways to important towns and cities.

Above all though, the early medieval period was a time of pilgrimage, with sufferers from various diseases making long journeys to the principal shrines of Europe in the hope that some miracle would transform their lives. These hopeful wayfarers constituted an increasingly important element of the travelling public, and were the principal users of hospital accommodation in certain towns. Towns and cities which grew to become regional centres each had a number of wayfarers' hospitals, including York, Beverley and Newcastle in the north of England, and St Albans, Exeter, Bristol, Southampton and of course London in the south, to mention only a few.

It was also the practice for certain men and women, some great, some not so great, to provide hospitals as a charitable act, in many cases on condition that the inmates prayed every morning and evening for the soul of their benefactor (or benefactrix) and his or her family. The occupiers of such hospitals were often called Bedesmen, since in saying their prayers, they tolled their rosary beads; the hospital itself in such circumstances would be called a Bedehouse.

At the top of the list of these individual benefactors were, of course, the clergy; mainly bishops and archbishops, who saw it as an essential part of their spiritual duty to set an example. Most cathedral cities had a clutch of hospitals and almshouses, such as St Leonard's, York, as already mentioned. Ripon in North Yorkshire is another good example, having three which have survived to the present day. The hospital of St Mary Magdalene, a one time lazer-house in Stonebridgegate, survives as an almshouse with Victorian cottages and two chapels, one built in a style to match the cottages, and the other built of stone and dating from the foundation of the hospital in 1139. The other two hospitals lie within walking distance of the town's Early English cathedral, and are dedicated to St John the Evangelist and St Anne. Both, like St Mary Magdalene, have relatively modern accommodation for almspeople, although the hospital of St Anne in High St Agnesgate, retains the ruins of the original twelfth-century chapel in its grounds. All three hospitals are of ecclesiastical foundation. Indeed, the chairman of the trustees of the hospital of St Mary Magdalene is still the Dean of Ripon Cathedral, the post-Dissolution equivalent of the Abbot of Ripon Monastery.

Durham City, another monastic settlement in the north of England, has several hospitals in its vicinity, all founded by clerics. Sherburn Hospital, lying approximately two miles to the south of the city, was founded in 1181 by Bishop Hugh de Puiset as a lazer-house for sixty-five occupants in five convents of thirteen. Each convent was ministered to by a chaplain, the whole hospital being controlled by a master. The hospital was endowed with extensive lands and properties and was the principal leper hospital in the north. It was extensively damaged during the Battle of Neville's Cross in 1346, the year of the Battle of Crécy, but survived as a lazer-house until 1434 when, thankfully, the need for its specialist accommodation diminished and it was appropriated for other, more general uses. Buildings were variously erected and demolished during its 800-year history and today a representative sample of each major period remains – the Norman church, medieval gatehouse, Elizabethan range, Georgian master's house and Victorian hospital block, which was, until the advent of the National Health Service after the Second World War, used for medical geriatric care. Now it houses some one hundred and fifty men and women in modernised accommodation in near-idyllic surroundings.

Worcester was another cathedral city with hospitals founded and endowed by the clergy. Of the three medieval hospitals which existed prior to the Reformation, only one has survived to the present day, and that only as a museum rather than as a religious institution.

The Hospital of St Wulston, the last Saxon bishop in England, has an uncertain foundation date, although it must have been prior to 1095, the date of Wulston's death. It was certainly known as St Wulston's Hospital a few years after 1203, when the bishop was canonised.

The hospital was established as an almshouse for the aged and was situated outside the Sidbury (the south gate of the city), just a few hundred yards or so from the cathedral precincts. Wulston endowed the hospital with lands for its upkeep, and in subsequent years, gifts of land and tithes

St Mary Magdalene's Hospital chapel, Ripon, North Yorkshire (1130).

of property were donated in the city of Worcester, as well as elsewhere in Worcestershire and the surrounding counties.

In its early days the hospital was administered by a master (who did not necessarily have to be a priest), assisted by two chaplains and certain poor brethren, all living under the Rule of St Augustine. There is no accurate record of the number of inmates, although it has been ascertained that certainly in 1294 there were twenty-two feeble residents in the infirmary. In the same year the hospital received a handsome gift of sixty marks and ten pounds sterling from one William de Molendis, a clerk in holy orders. In return he was to have the benefit of masses and prayers in the chapel, together with the right to nominate three poor chaplains in the infirmary with beds 'in a decent place'. This practice of granting board and lodging to poor people, not necessarily poor and aged people, in return for a cash payment was known as a *corrody*. It was continued at St Wulston's as late as the fourteenth and early fifteenth centuries by the master, William Dylew. There is a record that in 1396 Thomas Croke was granted 'to the end of his life one chamber built recently near to the gate of the hospital', and again in 1403 Nicholas and Sybil Baily were allocated 'a good chamber with a fireplace and privy'. The system was rather similar to that of the present-day nursing home, the difference being that a lump sum was paid upon entry, instead of being paid weekly.

The granting of *corrodies* was frowned upon as an abuse of the charitable role of the hospital, and in 1441, Bishop Bourchier drew up new ordinances which stated that henceforth the master should be a priest in holy orders, that there should be two chaplains, five brethren and two poor sisters only, and that the granting of *corrodies* should cease. The chaplains were each to have an allowance of four marks annually, a chamber to themselves, and three-and-a-half yards of cloth for a gown. The brethren and sisters, who were to join in daily prayers for the souls of their predecessors, and the founder, patrons, and benefactors, were each to have seven pence per week. The hospitals affairs were to be conducted under seal, and the renting out of any of the endowed land or property was not to be undertaken without the consent of the brethren and sisters. In effect, the hospital became a corporate body.

*Social Context*

*Left:* Ruins of St Ann's Hospital chapel, Ripon, North Yorkshire (1438).

*Below:* Sherburn Hospital gatehouse, Durham, County Durham (1181).

In 1298 the hospital had become known as The Preceptory (or Commandery) of St Wulston, in imitation of the military religious orders of the Knights Templar and Hospitallers. But there is as yet no proof of any connection with the Hospitallers either at Worcester or nearby Dinmore and the origins of the name remain a mystery. However it has been known as The Commandery ever since.

Along with many monasteries and other hospitals, the Commandery was suppressed by Henry VIII (1509-47) following his break with Rome in 1534, and was purchased by its last master, Richard Morysyne, for just £14 3s 5d. He sold it five years later to a clothier 'in consideration of four hundred and fourscore and eighteen pounds of good and lawful money of England'. Quite a profit! Subsequently, it reverted to residential use and, during the English Civil War, it served as the headquarters of Charles II (1630-85) in the 1651 Battle of Worcester. It survives to this day as a museum and tourist centre.

The Hospital of St Cross at Winchester, Hampshire, was established in 1136 by Henry de Blois, the brother of King Stephen (1135-54) and Bishop of Winchester. Originally thirteen 'impotent' men were to be maintained permanently in the hospital and provided with lodgings, suitable raiment and sufficient food. The hospital was the subject of many changes in the following centuries; these will be described in detail in Part Two.

St Wulston's Hospital Worcester, Hereford and Worcester (1298).

# THE REFORMATION

Many other hospitals of note were founded in this early period, some of which we shall look at in detail later. Meanwhile, we must consider the dramatic changes that were wrought by the English Reformation and particularly the Dissolution of the monasteries by Henry VIII and the suppression of the chantries and hospitals by his son Edward VI (1547-53).

By the middle of the 1530s there were some 800 medieval hospitals, more or less evenly distributed throughout the whole of England. When the Reformation had finally run its course, by around 1560, only a handful remained and those that had survived had been re-founded on secular lines and rebuilt in the new collegiate style.

The Reformation proper, as compared with Henry VIII's excuse for the rape of much of England's architectural heritage, began in the Germany of Martin Luther (1483-1546). Luther, an Augustinian friar, was professor of theology at the University of Wittenberg in Saxony. He clashed with the ecclesiastical establishment of the day, particularly over the matter of indulgences, and, following a long and bitter series of disputes, was excommunicated from the Catholic Church.

Indulgences had originated as the commutation of penances stipulated by priests at Confession; in effect, one would pay a fine rather than carry out the penance itself. Gradually, however, this was extended far beyond the purpose for which indulgences were intended, and became a payment not only to save a sinner in this life, but also from Purgatory, that place in the afterlife where the departed souls were tormented before being allowed into God's presence. The living were encouraged to make payments to the church to save the souls of their dead relatives, but what had started as being a reasonable alternative to minor humiliation and discomfort on the part of the sinner soon became part of the church's mainstream fundraising. Bishops sold indulgences to raise money for their own personal expenditure, and it was alleged that much of the cost of building St Peter's in Rome was funded in this way.

The aristocracy could insure themselves against an uncomfortable afterlife by the endowment of a charity, a special chapel, or indeed, just an altar within a parish church where prayers could be offered regularly for the souls of the departed benefactor and his family. Usually the prayers were accompanied by the burning of incense and candles, with the light burning continually.

Ordinary folk could not afford their own chantries; they could scarcely afford a decent burial. So, in early medieval Europe they banded together to form fraternities or confraternities; the titles are interchangeable, and are otherwise known as religious or parish guilds.

These guilds should not be confused with craft or merchant guilds, although they did have some elements in common with them. The parish guilds were primarily burial clubs, the precursors of the Victorian Friendly Societies, providing monies out of aggregated subscriptions for a decent interment, plus regular prayers for the soul of the departed, either as part of an annual requiem mass or in the form of *obits*, special prayers offered on the anniversary of the death of the parishioner.

Every parish, however small, had its fraternity under the patronage of a particular saint or saints; the Trinity, the Blessed Virgin Mary, Corpus Christi, St John the Baptist, St John the Evangelist and so on. Its principle function, as mentioned above, was to provide individual members with a good funeral, as solemn and well-attended a send-off as possible, together with regular prayers thereafter. But like all social organisations, many guilds grew and in time were able to provide other facilities, such as material help to younger members. They provided food, clothing and shelter in the form of hospitals and almshouses for the poor, sick and elderly brethren, as well as interest-free loans to provide dowries for daughters. They also provided help for members who fell on hard times because of fire or flood, offering a kind of insurance service; and they acted as executors of wills of deceased members.

At their most primitive level, a guild's members would gather together on the patronal feast day to offer masses for past and present brothers and sisters at the altar, or, if the fraternity could afford one, at the the chantry chapel. All living members had to contribute at least one mass penny to help with the upkeep of the altar and the payment of the priest, but many guilds expected that

Hospital of St Cross, Winchester, Hampshire (1136).

members should bequeath a certain amount of their worldly goods to the fund – one shilling in every pound's worth of chattels up to maximum of forty shillings, in the case of the Fraternity of St Mary and the Holy Cross in Chesterfield – as well as annual collections for alms.

Many of the larger fraternities, such as those at Aylesbury, Banbury, Coventry, Chester, Chesterfield, Derby, Hull, Maidstone, Newcastle-on-Tyne, Taunton, Warwick, Wells and Worcester, ran schools and almshouses for their members, and there is evidence that they provided much-needed help for their less-fortunate brethren right up to their dissolution in 1547, and even afterwards. Many owned guildhalls or guild houses, as well as tenements providing rent-free accommodation for destitute members. Some guilds looked after bridges (there is a famous example in Wakefield), highways, sluices and sea walls. Birmingham's Holy Cross Fraternity maintained a chiming clock and employed a midwife. Guild money built towers and spires at Louth in Lincolnshire and even whole churches as at Coventry and Bodmin.

These larger, city fraternities were dominated by local dignitaries. Indeed, upon the suppression of the guilds under Edward VI, many guild masters formed the nuclei of the town councils which were afterwards incorporated.

The larger guilds, centred upon the major towns, went far beyond the services provided by the local fraternities; indeed they provided services which could not be classed as charitable by any stretch of the imagination, such as banking, insurance and cultural and religious patronage. They were major property owners, had splendid guildhalls and formidable rent rolls as a result of handsome endowments by wealthy benefactors, as well as regular subscriptions from thousands of members. They derived rents from lands, tenements, mills and barns, and their members included dignitaries from England and, surprisingly enough, from the continent of Europe. And, of course, there were similar systems in France, Germany, Italy and Catholic Holland, with similar reciprocal arrangements.

Boston's St Mary's guild had an income of over £900 in 1520; Coventry's Holy Trinity fraternity was probably the biggest single landlord in the city. Great institutions had aldermen, wardens, chamberlains to prepare the accounts, stewards to collect subscriptions from a far-flung membership, almoners to administer the charitable works, together with cupbearers, macebearers, choristers and organists and umpteen clergy. Coventry's Holy Trinity fraternity at Bablake with its Bablake Hospital, had thirteen full-time priests and the fine church of St John.

*Social Context*

St Saviour's Hospital, Wells, Somerset (1424).

Bablake's Hospital, Coventry, West Midlands (1507).

As might be expected, Luther was highly critical of these practices, particularly the notion that forgiveness would ensue from penance. He maintained that penitence not penance was the only antidote for sin, and nailed his famous ninety-five theses on the subject to the door of Wittenberg Cathedral. He formulated the *Doctrine of Justification by Faith* and published several tracts which were highly critical of the established Church's powers. In one addressed to 'the Nobility of the German Nation' he claimed that the state actually had authority over the Church rather than vice versa, a notion which was subsequently taken up by Henry VIII of England as justification for breaking with Rome. The German princes accepted Luther's teaching enthusiastically; the

Church had dominated their lives for centuries, not only through the Pope, but also through the office of the Holy Roman Emperor. They eagerly latched onto a concept which would rid them of the Church's control, and give them the autonomy which they had craved for so long.

Meanwhile in England, King Henry, at odds with his wife, Catherine of Aragon, and besotted with Anne Boleyn, petitioned the Pope for an annulment to his marriage, on the grounds that as Catherine had been married previously to his dead brother, Arthur, the union was incestuous. Pope Clement declined to grant the annulment and, as a result of Henry's persistent refusal to accept this decision and his marriage to Anne in 1533, excommunicated him from the Catholic Church.

Henry's response was to enact a spate of legislation which weakened the Pope's influence in England, culminating in the Act of Supremacy of 1534 which declared:

> Albeit the King's Majesty justly and rightfully is and oweth to be supreme head of the Church of England, and so is recognised by the Clergy of this realm in their Convocation, yet nevertheless for corroboration and confirmation thereof, and for the increase of virtue in Christ's religion within this realm of England, and to repress and extirp all errors, heresies and other enormities and abuses heretofore used in the same, be enacted by the authority of this present Parliament that the King our Sovereign Lord, his heirs and successors, Kings of this realm shall be taken accepted and reputed the only Supreme Head on earth of the Church of England.

Upon obtaining control of the Church in England, Henry began to tap its great wealth. The Act of Supremacy had directed that all annates – that is, yearly sums of money amounting to one-tenth of the clergy's income – which had previously been paid to Rome should in future be paid to the Crown. Moreover, Henry was not content with the assessments based upon values in 1292, as the Pope had been. He wanted the full up-to-date value, and to ensure this, appointed as his Vicar General one Thomas Cromwell, the son of a Putney blacksmith, who had a particular genius for administration. He produced the *Valor Ecclesiasticus*, a valuation of all the Church's assets, which showed just how wealthy the Church had become over the years, and it was not long before the idea occurred him to confiscate all the Church's lands for the King's use. Unfortunately many hospitals were included, particularly so if they were of monastic foundation or housed bedesmen whose principal purpose was praying for the souls of their dead benefactors.

There then followed six years of persecution, blackmail, extortion and judicial murder, during which all the monasteries in the kingdom were closed, their buildings torn down, their lands sold off and their plate melted down for bullion. All the proceeds went to the Crown. Moreover, of the 800 or so hospitals which had existed prior to 1540, most of which had been associated with the monastic system, only a handful survived into the reign of Henry's daughter, Elizabeth, and those that did lost the direct support of the Church of England and had to rely in future on other institutions and individuals for patronage.

## ELIZABETHAN ALMSHOUSES AND THE OLD POOR LAWS

The Elizabethan period marked England's transition from medieval to modern times, in both a political and a social sense. England, whilst still predominantly a rural country, enjoyed a fast-improving standard of living for the rank and file, with a much more comfortable existence than their counterparts across the channel. But of course, as always, the very poor found life difficult.

However, a series of disastrous harvests, which had affected the whole of Europe during the 1590s, encouraged Queen Elizabeth I (1558-1603) and her ministers to introduce legislation which influenced social conditions, particularly for the relief of poverty and the control of the economy. Prior to the Poor Law Act of 1597, poor relief had been administered in a somewhat haphazard manner by the parishes. An Act of 1536 had limited the receipt of alms to friars, shipwrecked mariners, the lame and the blind, although ordinary folk were permitted to continue to solicit 'broken meats' and 'refuse [waste] drink'. Parish funds were established as obligatory 'by gathering of such charitable and voluntary alms every Sunday, Holy Day and other festivals'. Parish councils were fined for default and non-resident clergy had to contribute at least one-fortieth of their income in alms, and churchwardens saw to it that they did. The Vagabond Act of 1547, enacted during the reign of Henry VIII, invited parishes to erect houses for the accommodation of the disabled poor, and a similar Act of 1552 set up parish registers of the poor. Since it was feared that the plague, still endemic in Europe, was spread by beggars, a system of licensing was introduced, together with measures to confine them to their homes.

Lincoln opened a poor relief fund in 1550 to which all citizens of any substance contributed. London, Norwich, Exeter, Cambridge and Ipswich soon followed suit, making contributions compulsory for all households of a certain size. There was thus established a system of indoor and outdoor relief which, when modified by the Act of 1597, lasted until the great Poor Law Act of 1834. Also, between 1570 and 1600 several charity hospitals, in the modern sense of the word, were established, together with many groups of almshouses which by this time were endowed not by the clergy, but by the laity. Three elements contributed directly or indirectly to the foundation of these almshouses; the Elizabethan Settlement, the rise of the merchant classes and particularly the rise of the gentry.

## THE ELIZABETHAN SETTLEMENT

When Elizabeth ascended the throne in 1558, the country was at war with both France and Scotland. The religious divisions which had beset it since her father's death had weakened the authority of the state and had created deep divisions in society. What was needed was a new religious settlement which would reach out to both factions, Catholic and Protestant, and impose some semblance of order and harmony in religious affairs.

In choosing new members of her council, Elizabeth retained the moderate elements of the predominantly Catholic faction, supplementing them with Protestants. She appointed no Vicar General as her father had done, but instead exercised her authority as head of the Church of England through a Court of High Commission, staffed by lay members and lawyers as well as clerics. Many of the strict rules which the clergy had, up to that time, had to observe were relaxed, most importantly the rule of celibacy. From henceforth clergymen could marry and many of the young ones availed themselves of the opportunity straight away. During subsequent decades their offspring were to form the very backbone of Tudor and Stuart society.

## THE RISE OF THE MERCHANT CLASSES

The rise of the merchant classes was allied to the general increase in living standards throughout the country, and in no small part to the increase in trade with foreign parts which was such a feature of Elizabethan economics. The process of industrialisation was continuing apace. With the religious settlement which granted much more equality to dissenters than was experienced on the Continent, persecuted artisans from all over Europe migrated to England bringing with them new skills. Textile workers from the Low Countries imported new ways of producing fine cloth, and French Huguenots followed them, together with German metalworkers who were persuaded to share their secrets in exploiting indigenous metals, such as tin, copper, iron and lead.

As tradesmen imparted their skills, so too did entrepreneurs and financiers. Markets were needed for surplus manufactured goods and a new breed of businessman, the merchant adventurer, emerged. This in its turn spawned a breed of explorer-privateer, which led in turn to the foundation of the great trading companies, the East India Company, the Company of Merchant Adventurers and the Russia Company. As trade grew, particularly in the mercantile centres such as London, Bristol, Norwich and York, so did the merchant classes, and it was natural that they should form themselves into trade associations or guilds. It was equally natural that they should look after their aged, sick and less-fortunate colleagues in times of need by way of charity, and in particular, by the provision of schools and almshouses.

Of course, the nobility continued as they had done in the past to build dwellings for their retired retainers. Lord Burleigh built almshouses at his home town of Stamford. Bess of Hardwick built a similar group at Derby and Lord Northampton built Trinity House, Greenwich. Generally speaking though, the lesser gentry were concerned with direct poor relief, and in their wills made bequests for straightforward charity, either as doles or endowments.

The City Livery Companies in particular made prodigious provision for their decayed members and in this endeavour London far outdid the rest of the country. Between 1480 and 1660, more than one-third of all charitable giving in the country derived from the capital, although at no time during that period did London's population amount to much more than five percent of that of the whole realm. Skinners, leather-sellers, drapers and haberdashers all made generous provision for their members and for the poor in general, as did the companies dealing in the more exotic commodities, such as goldsmiths, silversmiths and clockmakers. They all contributed generously, establishing almshouses, hospitals, schools and orphanages, both inside the city proper and in the innumerable towns and villages from which their members had originally come.

One or two merchants stood out for their remarkable acts of generosity. Sir Martin Bowes, a Yorkshireman who made his fortune as a goldsmith, left a large bequest, one half for poor relief, the other for charitable purposes. Sir Thomas Owe, a rich merchant tailor, left a similar bequest. Sir James Lancaster was another who left all his money to charity, the greater part to the Skinners' Company of which he was a member. Most of the bequest was for the training of apprentices and for the dowries of young maids.

The almshouses of the City Livery Companies were spread throughout Greater London together with those provided by the parishes themselves. Within a stone's throw of Bishopgate and Broad Street there were the almshouses of the parish clerks, those of the leather-sellers, the tailors, and the linen-armourers, as well as several groups built by individual benefactors.

Bristol was second only to London in philanthropic works, although it had a population of only 17,000. It was led by a merchant class 'of great vitality, boldness and magnitude', making the most of the opportunities after the Dissolution, buying ex-monastic properties for £1,790, to which the parishes contributed £500 from the sale of church plate. The merchants were principally concerned with poor relief schemes for the unemployed and the founding of grammar schools. Robert Thorne left more than £6,000 for the founding of a school and for poor relief. Sir John Gresham left £2,000, and even Henry VIII gave his doctor, George Owen, a parcel of land originally owned by the Order of St John of Jerusalem, which was used for the support of ten almsmen. William Chester purchased Black Friars which was turned into almshouses. The Society of Merchant Venturers established their own almshouses for aged seamen with endowments which, by 1600, produced £100 a year.

A famous example in the north of England is the hospital founded by Sir William Turner – the Lord Mayor of London who supervised the rebuilding of the capital after the Great Fire of 1666 – at the place of his birth, Kirkleatham, near Redcar in Cleveland. It is thought that Sir Christopher Wren had a hand in the design, since he and Sir William were friends and had obviously collaborated in the planning of many of the new buildings in the City after the catastrophe.

Turner's Hospital was originally founded in 1676, although it was completely remodelled by Sir William's great-nephew Cholmley Turner in 1742, in the then-fashionable Classical style. The whole composition echoes Wren's much larger works at Chelsea and Greenwich, which we shall come to later, and is laid out as a rectangular courtyard, open on the northern side, and separated from the rest of the village by a magnificent wrought-iron screen and entrance gates, with the founder's arms in the arched overthrow. We shall consider the architectural features of this, perhaps the most important of the northern almshouses, in Part Two.

*Social Context*

*Above:* Interior, Merchant Venturers' Hospital, York, North Yorkshire (1280).

*Right:* Sir William Turner's Hospital, Kirkleatham, Cleveland (1676).

## THE EMERGENCE OF THE GENTRY

Possibly the most significant social change in seventeenth-century England was the emergence of the gentry as a distinctive class. This was brought about for several reasons. Firstly, as already mentioned, the decision to allow the clergy to marry produced in due course a class which, although somewhat impoverished when compared to the aristocracy, nevertheless was well educated and provided the raw material for country doctors, lawyers, schoolmasters, and of course further clergy. Secondly, with the availability of ex-monastic lands, the *nouveaux riches* in the emerging mercantile centres were able to purchase large estates and establish themselves as country gentlemen. They in turn spawned their own dynasties and in due course made provision in their wills, not only to house their own retired retainers, but also, as acts of charity, provided almshouses for the public at large.

Several important foundations date from this late Elizabethan period. Perhaps the most important, particularly in the Midlands, is Lord Leycester's Hospital at Warwick, founded by the Queen's favourite, Robert Dudley in 1571 as a refuge for retired soldiers. It used as its nucleus buildings previously occupied by religious guilds; the Guild of St George, the Holy Trinity Guild and the Guild of St Mary the Virgin. These buildings form what must surely be the most picturesque group of almshouses in the whole country. Steeply roofed with shingles, timber-framed and leaning rather drunkenly in places, and loosely arranged around a cobbled courtyard, the hospital is entered through an archway, itself surmounted by Dudley's crest – a bear and ragged staff. The buildings are still in use for the same purpose today, housing eighteen retired servicemen, who, on ceremonial occasions, wear a medieval cap and gown, the uniform provided for them as part of the bequest of the founder over four hundred years ago.

Jesus Hospital, Rothwell in Northamptonshire was founded in 1591 by a local schoolmaster, Owen Ragdale, who asked in return for the endowment that the inmates should have:

> … special care and regard that his tomb in Rothwell church and the epitaphs, superscriptions, walls, pavements and other things therewith annexed, should be kept whole, safe, bright and clean.

The buildings, housing originally some thirty men, enclose a small quadrangular court, entered through a sturdy gateway.

Waldren's Almshouses, Tiverton, Devon were also built in 1579, in the middle of of Elizabeth I's reign. Situated in Wellbrook Street, this picturesque set of almshouses was erected by John Waldron, a wealthy merchant, for the support of eight aged, poor men who received 2s each per week, 8s yearly for milk, and 12s 6d on New Year's Day. The building has a little open gallery or arcade along the front, and is festooned with plaques and shields, all making reference to the founder and his family. Unfortunately, Waldron did not live to see the building's completion, as recorded on one of the inscriptions:

> John Waldron and Ann his wife built this house in the time of his life, at such a tyme as the walls were fourteyne foot hye, he departed this worlde, on the eighteenth of July [1579].

## THE STUARTS

If the Elizabethan age marked England's transition from a medieval to a modern state, the period during which the Stuarts reigned, from 1603 to 1714, marked the country's transformation from a minor European kingdom into arguably the most powerful nation on earth, both economically and militarily. At the beginning of the period, King James I (1603-1625) ruled by divine right; at the end, King George I (1714-1727) owed his throne to an Act of Parliament. James expected to 'live on his own', financing his affairs out of his own personal resources, rents from Crown lands, feudal dues and customs levies. By 1714 Queen

*Social Context*

Sir William Moyles' Almshouses, St Germains, Cornwall (1583).

Lord Leycester's Hospital, Warwick, Warwickshire (1571).

Jesus Hospital, Rothwell, Northamptonshire (1591).

Anne (1702-1714), the last of the Stuarts, received a stipend and control of the country's finances was vested in Parliament.

In 1603 England was really a second-rate power with very few territories overseas. In 1714 she held a substantial empire in America, Africa, India and further east. This massive expansion, achieved in just over a century, was brought about by the need to trade; to find an outlet for the products of the burgeoning economy, which was itself the product of the Elizabethans' development of the country's industries, particularly in metal, pottery and textiles. As seen already, some of Britain's great trading companies had been formed during the previous century. In 1607 the East India Company made a profit of no less than 500 per cent; in 1611 and 1612 the Russia Company paid a dividend of 90 per cent! Membership of these largely speculative organisations was restricted to the seriously rich. The cost of buying into the East

Waldron's Almshouses, Tiverton, Devon (1579).

India Company was £50, that for the Merchant Adventurers £200 – enormous sums by the standards of the day.

During this period, earthenware and glass replaced wood and pewter at table. Calico and linen replaced leather and silk for clothing, and the modern male attire of coat, waistcoat and breeches was introduced. Diet was transformed too; root crops were introduced during this period both as foods in themselves and, most importantly, as a means of keeping cattle alive during the winter. Potatoes, tea, coffee and chocolate were all introduced, although only the first proved capable of being grown here. Agriculture was transformed by the first Enclosure Movement and by the invention of specialised machinery. Output rose astronomically, creating great wealth for many landowners although, conversely, it created hardship for the dispossessed peasants who began the long exodus from the country to the towns. This itself culminated in the Industrial Revolution of the nineteenth century.

The Stuart period can be divided into four distinct phases; the rule of James I and Charles I prior to the English Civil War (1603-1642); the Civil War and Commonwealth (1642-1660); the Restoration of Charles II and his son James II (1660-1688); and the Glorious Revolution (1688-1714), embracing the reigns of William and Mary and Queen Anne.

## JAMES I AND CHARLES I

James VI of Scotland succeeded Elizabeth I as James I of England in 1603, and his son succeeded him as Charles I. Both their reigns were marked by chronic inflation brought about by a burgeoning agricultural economy, itself the result of two related phenomena. Firstly, there was Charles' disposal, in his insatiable search for money, of land acquired by Henry VIII following the Dissolution of the monasteries. Secondly, and somewhat related, was the enclosure of the open-field system, which had been in existence since Norman times, to create large agricultural

*Above:* Greatham Hospital, Greatham, Cleveland (1810).

*Left:* Greatham Hospital, Greatham, Cleveland, drawing 1995.

estates. The increases in wealth that the improved agricultural methods brought about – although enjoyed directly only by the landowners – did allow them to provide charitable relief in the form of grammar schools and almshouses, although significantly it was generally those new landowners who were to back the Puritan cause in the power struggle to come.

In 1610 at Greatham – originally in County Durham, now in Cleveland – Bishop Stichell refounded the thirteenth-century Hospital of God, St Mary and St Cuthbert, although it was rebuilt yet again in 1803 by James Wyatville, under the patronage of the Duke of Bridgewater. The hospital to this day houses a wide range of almspeople, both within the hospital proper and in the village of Greatham, ranging from elderly gentlemen, the objects of the original charitable trust, to whole families in need. Recently, the main hospital buildings have been supplemented by a new residential home for elderly couples, with the dwellings built around a courtyard with cloisters, as in traditional almshouse design.

In 1611 Thomas Sutton, Queen Elizabeth's Master of Ordnance in the north of England, acquired the buildings of the Charterhouse in the Clerkenwell area of London. The Charterhouse,

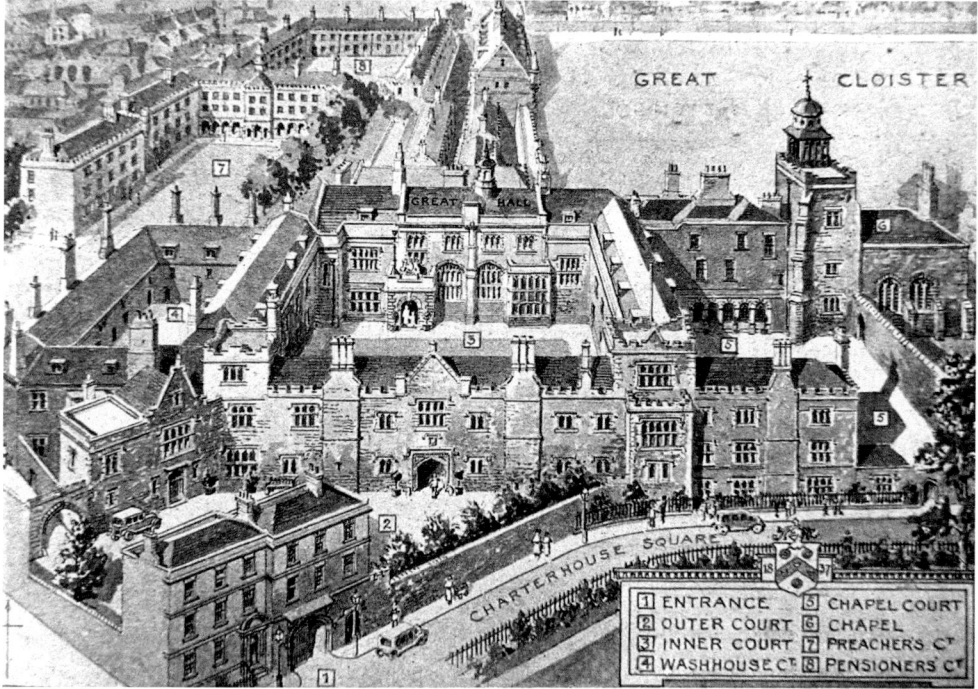

The Charterhouse, London (1611).

as all Carthusian monasteries were called, had been founded in 1371 by Sir Walter de Manny, a friend of the Black Prince, on land previously owned by St Bartholomew's Hospital. During the traumatic events surrounding the Dissolution, the monks of the Charterhouse were obdurate in their opposition to Henry's changes and were treated cruelly before the monastic buildings were sequestered and sold, firstly to Lord North and later to the Duke of Norfolk. He destroyed the great cloister and the old chapel, and used the stone to construct Master's Court and other buildings. Both Elizabeth I and James I spent the first days of their reigns at Charterhouse. The Ridolfi Plot in support of Mary Queen of Scots was hatched in Charterhouse in 1571, as a result of which the Duke of Norfolk lost his head.

Thomas Sutton endowed the buildings as a school and almshouse for old men, originally housing eighty souls. The twin establishments survived side by side until 1872, when the school was transferred to Godalming in Surrey. Today, the number of elderly residents has been reduced to just forty. As well as occupying the converted monastic buildings, the almshouse uses several purpose-built blocks in what was the Great Cloister.

The interiors of many of the rooms are of national if not international importance, particularly the Elizabethan Great Chamber with its painted ceiling and chimney piece. Oliver Cromwell attended many Governors' meetings there, as did several monarchs, since all kings and queens of England and their consorts have been Royal Governors since 1611. The great gates giving access from Charterhouse Square are monastic, and one arm of the executed last prior of the monastery, John Houghton, was once fastened to these gates. The house above dates from 1716, replacing an earlier one. Washhouse Court still looks very much as it did in the early years of the late sixteenth century, and Master's Court now shows its original stonework again, having been restored following damage sustained during the Second World War.

There were several Carthusian monasteries established in the country during the medieval period. The first was founded at Witham in Somerset in 1173 and the second one at Hinton, also in Somerset,

*Almshouses: A Social and Architectural History*

Hull Charterhouse, Humberside (1649).

in 1232. There were no more for over a century, but then no less than seven Charterhouses were founded within seventy years, among them the one at London, already referred to, and one at Hull in Humberside. Associated with the Hull Charterhouse from the very beginning was a hospital or college for thirteen poor men and thirteen poor women, of whom one man was to preside over the rest, under the title of master. This hospital, or *Maison Dieu* as it was then known, stood on the eastern boundary of the priory which was suppressed by Henry VIII in 1535. However, following a great deal of discontent locally, Henry re-established the priory in the following year, in consideration of a payment of 400 marks, only to suppress it yet again in the aftermath of the Pilgrimage of Grace in 1539, when the convent was forced to surrender to the king its house, lands and endowments. In return, the prior, Randolph Malevorer, received a pension of 50 marks and six monks received 10 marks each per annum for life. The hospital continued unmolested, principally because its patronage had been transferred by Henry's son Edward VI to the Mayor and Corporation of Hull. It was rebuilt in 1649, just after the Restoration of Charles II and again in 1780, and to this day has the formal title of The Master, Brethren and Sisters of God's House Hospital of Kingston upon Hull, although it is still known locally as the Charterhouse.

In 1613, two years after the founding of the London Charterhouse, Edward Alyn, the actor/manager of the Fortune Playhouse in London, founded his College of God's Gift, later to be known as Dulwich College. It was not opened until 1619, when it provided accommodation for six poor men and six poor women, together with a school for the education of twelve boys. The school has long since disappeared but the almshouse is still there, a beautiful cream-coloured building at the corner of Gallery Road with College Road, Dulwich, south London.

Henry Howard, Earl of Northampton, built three groups of almshouses in 1614, all quadrangular in plan, at Clun in Shropshire, at Castle Rising in Norfolk and at Greenwich.

Sir Thomas Conningsby, a friend of Sir Philip Sydney, founded a hospital for twelve old men and a chaplain at Hereford in 1614. The accommodation, half for retired soldiers or marines and half for Sir Thomas' own retainers, was built round a small courtyard which utilised the chapel and dining room buildings which originally belonged to the Knights of St John of Jerusalem. The inmates had quaint military-style uniforms which they wear to this day on ceremonial occasions, the senior man being known as the Corporal of Conningsby's Company of Servitors.

*Social Context*

*Right:* Napper's Mite, Dorchester, Dorset (1615).

*Below:* Almshouses, Mapledurham, Oxfordshire (1613).

*Almshouses: A Social and Architectural History*

Ingram's Hospital, York, North Yorkshire (1640).

Perhaps the most delightfully named of the complexes built during this early Stuart period is that known as Napper's Mite, in the centre of the Dorset town of Dorchester. Provided for in the will of Sir Robert Napier in 1615, the almshouses originally provided seven single-storey cottages around a small courtyard. The upper storey at the front, set over an arcaded walkway, is the audit room. The central gable supports a large clock on iron brackets, which is a later addition. The accommodation has proved to be far too small for modern standards, and the old folk are now housed in more suitable homes elsewhere. However, the buildings now live on as a café. Members of the public can now sit out in the courtyard, as did many generations of almsfolk during the past 350 years.

Finally in this early Stuart period, mention must be made of two picturesque groups, typical of everyone's idea of the English almshouse. The first group, at Mapledurham in Oxfordshire, was founded in 1613 by a certain John Lister for six poor persons of the parish. Constructed of rustic brick under a steep red roof, the six dwellings match almost exactly in architectural detailing the adjoining manor house. Modern standards of accommodation have dictated that they be converted into two larger dwellings, but thankfully – externally at least – they remain quintessential almshouses.

The second group, in the little village of Moretonhampstead on the edge of Dartmoor, was built in 1637 by a long-forgotten benefactor. They are contstructed from square blocks of granite at the front under a thatched roof, with mullioned windows at the eaves level. Like Napper's Mite mentioned earlier, they have a loggia with turned stone columns, supporting the eleven semi-circular arches of the arcade. The dwellings no longer house almspeople, who have been rehoused in more modern accommodation across the way. However, the buildings are well looked after, since they are now in the ownership of the National Trust.

## THE CIVIL WAR

With the Civil War and its aftermath came the rise of the Puritans, and the suppression of any extraneous church activities. Only two new parish churches are known to have been built during the Commonwealth, in Leeds and Berwick-on-Tweed. Very few almshouses were built either. Ingram's Hospital in Bootham, York was built in 1640 by Sir William Ingram, using material

*Social Context*

Henry Cornish's Almshouses, Chipping Norton, Oxfordshire (1640).

Fauconberg Hospital, Coxwold, North Yorkshire (1662).

from the nearby Holy Trinity Priory which had been suppressed by Henry VIII. Also in 1640, Henry Cornish built his set of picturesque almshouses at Chipping Norton in Oxfordshire. Multi-gabled, of Cotswold stone, the almshouses are enclosed within a substantial stone wall with a wrought-iron gateway. Fauconberg Hospital in Coxwold, North Yorkshire, is a similar example built during this period.

## THE RESTORATION

For Charles II, the Commonwealth had not existed; he discounted the eleven years of the Interregnum and dated his reign from the death of his father, 30 January 1649. Various Acts of Parliament were speedily passed, mainly to provide him with an income in lieu of the Purveyance and revenue from the Court of Wards. He received an income of £100,000, mainly from an excise on beer, cider and tea, and a further £1 million was voted by Parliament to pay for the army. An Act of Indemnity was passed, pardoning all offences arising from the Civil War and its aftermath, apart from the signatories to Charles I's death warrant. But of the fifty or so arraigned for that, just over half were condemned and only eleven actually executed. Confiscated lands of Royalist supporters were in the main restored, although several thousand Catholic landowners were disappointed, particularly in Ireland.

Throughout the reign of Charles the country was more or less at war with Holland, although, surprisingly enough, a marriage was arranged between William, Prince of Orange (1650-1702) and Mary (1662-94), the daughter of James, Duke of York, Charles's younger brother. In the closing years of the reign, local government was remodelled to produce parliamentary electorates and juries favourably disposed to the king. Under the new order, Charles imposed upon the City of London the particular rule that no Lord Mayor, Sheriff or Recorder could be appointed without royal approval. As a result of this, after Charles' death in 1685, James II succeeded peacefully. Indeed, the two risings which took place soon after – those of the Earl of Argyll in Scotland and the Duke of Monmouth, Charles' illegitimate son, in Dorset – had little or no support and were quickly put down. Both leaders were executed and savage reprisals followed. Judge Jeffreys' Bloody Assizes in the South West after Monmouth's defeat at Sedgemoor became particularly notorious.

During his brief reign, James II (1685-88) tried every avenue to install Catholics into high office, ignoring the Test Act of 1673 which sought to test office-holders' allegiance to the Church of England. Opposition was fierce, fuelled by news of Louis XIV's persecution of French Protestants, but despite that, James installed the Papist Earl of Tyrconnel as Lord Lieutenant of Ireland, Sir Roger Strickland, also a Papist, as Lord High Admiral, Lord Arundell of Wardour as Lord Privy Seal, and Edward Petre, a Jesuit, as a member of the Privy Council. The chief minister, Sunderland, also declared himself to be a Catholic, although not until June 1688. Further 'remodelling' of local government was planned, and the Court of Commissioners for Ecclesiastical Causes imposed Catholics upon the colleges of Oxford and Cambridge.

In 1687 James issued a Declaration of Indulgences, which suspended the Test Acts and allowed freedom of religious practice to Protestants and Catholics, and followed it a year later with a reaffirmation, sending dissenting bishops to the Tower.

The last straw came when his queen bore him a son, James Edward, which ensured that the king's attempts to restore the Catholic religion to the state would be continued indefinitely. As a result, an invitation asking William of Orange to come to England was sent, signed by seven Englishmen, including the Bishop of London, the Earl of Danby, a Sydney, a Russell and a Cavendish.

James backpedalled immediately, replacing Catholic appointees with Protestants, and annulling all municipal charters granted since 1679 which had favoured the Catholic cause; but to no avail. William landed at Brixham in November 1688 with 11,000 foot soldiers and 4,000 horse, and the whole of the country went over to his side, led by James' younger daughter, Princess Anne. James fled to France with his wife and his son Charles Edward, who was to provide, over the next fifty years or so, some colourful interludes in English history.

Royalty's contribution to the provision of almshouses during this period was specialised and monumental; specialised because provision was made for aged servicemen only, and monumental because the buildings provided were first and foremost prestigious reminders of the munificence of the Crown. They were architectural masterpieces, the Crown's tangible contribution to civic design. Charles II's sojourn on the Continent during the years of the Commonwealth had of course exposed him to the influence of the court of Louis XIV (1643-1715) with its lavish lifestyle, and the emerging Renaissance architecture carried out on a scale which, although relatively common on mainland Europe, had never been experienced in England because of the Puritan regime.

Louis' contribution to the building of Paris was a spectacular achievement, brought about not so much by the genius for design of the newly emerging architectural profession, but by its ability

*Social Context*

Les Invalides, Paris, France (1674).

Chapel, Les Invalides, Paris, France (1674).

Kilmainham Hospital, Dublin, Republic of Ireland (1686).

to organise the construction of large, complex structures, together with the total control of the environment of the city. Prior to that, the guilds of builders and carpenters had a stranglehold on all new construction, which was consequently on a scale which reflected the relatively modest resources of individual members. It took the breadth of vision and resources of the Sun King and his cohorts to produce architecture on a scale which previously had been experienced only in the building of the great cathedrals during the Gothic period.

Royal patronage in France during this period took the form of several large institutions for the poor. Two notable ones were the Hopital de la Salpetriere, begun in 1656 and completed in 1668, and L'Hotel de Mars ou des Invalides, commenced in 1674, with the first inmates moving in in 1676. Both buildings were designed by Liberal Bruant, son of Sebastian Bruant, 'Général de Bâtiments [buildings], Ponts [bridges] et Chaussees [roadways] de France'. The Hôpital de la Salpetrière was an asylum or workhouse, which was actually in use until the twentieth century and housed over 7,800 persons during its heyday.

In 1663 Bruant succeeded his father as 'Maistre des Oeuvres de Charpentiers pour avoir l'oeil sur tous les charpentiers des maisons royales', and 'Architecte du Roi', and eleven years later was entrusted with the building of L'Hôtel de Mars ou des Invalides which the king had commissioned for 'les estropiez, vieux et caducs soldats' [crippled, old and decrepit soldiers] who had until then been housed in monasteries. The edict for the foundation of the hospital, dated 1674, recites:

> qu'il estoit bien raisonable que ceux de cette monarchie ... jouissent du repos qu'ils ont assuré a nos autres sujets, et passaient le reste de leurs jours en tranquillité.

The design took the form of a central court known as La Cour Royale, 290ft by 190ft, and flanked by two smaller courts on either side, each 138ft by 120ft. Within La Cour Royale, opposite the main entrance, Bruant placed his chapel, the Soldiers' Church, a considerable building some 192ft by 72ft. Later, Mansard attached his Church of the Dome at the farthest end, separated from the chapel proper by the high altar. On either side of the chapel, separated from it by long, narrow courts, were large projecting enclosures of long buildings, with the one to the east containing the infirmary and the one to the west a priest's garden and cloister-garth, with miscellaneous administrative buildings.

*Social Context*

Royal Hospital, Chelsea, London (1692).

Les Invalides was one of the great improvements to Paris made by Louis XIV and had a profound influence on the court of Charles II, both in England and, as it turned out, in Ireland too.

With the precedent of Les Invalides in mind, the idea of an asylum for aged and disabled veterans was first considered in the 1670s by the Earl of Grenard and the Earl of Essex. James Butler, the Duke of Ormonde, spent the years of exile with Charles II in Paris, and upon the Restoration was made firstly Lord Lieutenant and later Viceroy of Ireland, based in Dublin. In 1679 the king agreed to a levy on Irish military pay, the proceeds of which were to be devoted to the erection of a building to be used as an asylum for those: '… who by reason of age, wounds or other infirmities since their first coming into Our army, are grown unfit to be any longer continued in Our service'. Ormonde wished the hospital, his first venture in Ireland, to be on a grand scale, classical in layout and Continental in style, for although he needed a home for pensioners, he also wanted a building of distinction which would mark Dublin's debut as a city of European standing.

William Robinson, the Surveyor General of Ireland, was consulted, and a site in the village of Kilmainham near Phoenix Park on the outskirts of the city was selected, on which were the ruins of the Preceptory of the Knights Hospitaller. The design was duly approved by Ormonde and the foundation stone laid in April 1680. The new building was to be so spectacular that it was suggested that Trinity College in the city should move there and the hospital be transferred to the college's existing buildings in College Green, as '… the Hospital would make a magnificent college and being out of town would be free from those mischiefs that now attend it'. The Hospital was completed at the end of 1686 at a cost of £23,500, and dedicated to the martyr Charles I.

Kilmainham Hospital, originally housing 300 old men, is much smaller than Les Invalides, having only one courtyard, instead of seven as in Paris. The courtyard is surrounded on three sides by arcades, the fourth originally having been arcaded except for the central five bays of the dining room. The enlarged master's lodge and the passage adjoining the chapel encroach onto the loggia in the north-west and north-east corners.

With the examples of Les Invalides and Kilmainham in mind, and whilst the latter was under construction, in 1682 Charles commissioned the building of the Royal Hospital at Chelsea, although owing to mismanagement by Lord Ranelagh, the hospital treasurer, the buildings were not completed until 1692. Christopher Wren, Charles' Surveyor General of Works, was entrusted with the original design, although extensions were added in later centuries by Robert Adam, Sir John Soane and Sir John Vanbrugh. Like Louis XIV, Charles founded the hospital for veterans of the regular army who had become unfit for duty, either because of old age (they had to have served at least twenty years with the colours) or as a result of wounds. Originally the asylum was provided with only one quadrangle, but with the increase in the size of the standing army effected by James II and William III, provision had to be made in later years for a greater number of in-pensioners, and further accommodation was provided in two other courts.

Charles himself had very little money to spare, and received no support from his Government. A notable exception was the Paymaster General, Sir Stephen Fox, who as well as providing substantial funds out of his own pocket, organised a subvention of army pay, as in Ireland, which was the hospital's main source of revenue until 1847, since when it has been supported by Parliamentary votes. The site chosen comprised some thirty acres upon which had once stood the Chelsea College, an intended theological institution founded by James I. Three open courts were provided, mainly by Wren. The principal one, Figure Court, with the statue of Charles I in the centre, is the most important architecturally, containing as it does the Great Hall and Chapel, together with the principal pensioners' wards.

## THE GLORIOUS REVOLUTION

Following the flight of James II to France, William and Mary were declared joint rulers by Act of Parliament in February 1689 and, under the Act of Settlement of 1701, the succession was fixed, failing heirs, to Mary's sister Anne, and after that to the House of Hanover, descendants of Charles I's sister Elizabeth and the Elector Palatine.

Almost the first of William's priorities was the subjugation of Ireland which, with the exception of Londonderry, had briefly been liberated from British rule following the revolt of Irish Catholic peers. Starting with the Battle of the Boyne in July 1690, William's campaign was as successful as Cromwell's had been fifty years earlier. The upstart Catholic Patriot Parliament was annulled, and all but a handful of the Irish population was excluded from all public offices.

Following Charles II's example of building hospitals for soldiers at Kilmainham and Chelsea, William and Mary perceived a need to provide for their retired seamen. The Queen's House at Greenwich had been designed by Inigo Jones (1573-1652) in the Palladian style for Charles I's queen, Henrietta Maria. After the Restoration, the Queen Mother again took up residence there and Greenwich became one of Charles II's favourite haunts. So fond was he of it that he decided to build a residence there, and commissioned John Webb, Inigo Jones' pupil and nephew to pull down the medieval Palace of Placentia, overlooking the River Thames, and build a replacement on the site. When his niece Mary was looking for a site for her new hospital for retired seamen, Webb's building, now known as the King's House, seemed ideal.

The Royal Naval Hospital, Greenwich, was founded by Royal Charter in October 1694, and at first, as its charitable status indicates, only had modest pretensions. Its purpose was entirely related to the relief of aged seamen and their dependants. Like Les Invalides, the building acquired a quality which had not been anticipated when it was commissioned. Sir Christopher Wren became the Surveyor of Works and was so enthusiastic that he gave his services free of charge. His first design had a magnificence never seen before in secular English architecture. The plan had a Baroque arrangement of narrowing courts leading to its central feature, a vast, domed chapel in the style of St Paul's. Queen Mary was overwhelmed by its monumentality and was unhappy because it obscured the Queen's House. Moreover, she wished that the King's House should remain intact. She decreed that a corridor of land be left some 115ft wide between the Queen's House and the river.

Wren's final design compromised on the central chapel by dividing it. Two smaller chapels were built, each with its own dining hall and cupola and facing one another across a narrow court, with the Queen's House further up the hill on the central axis.

*Social Context*

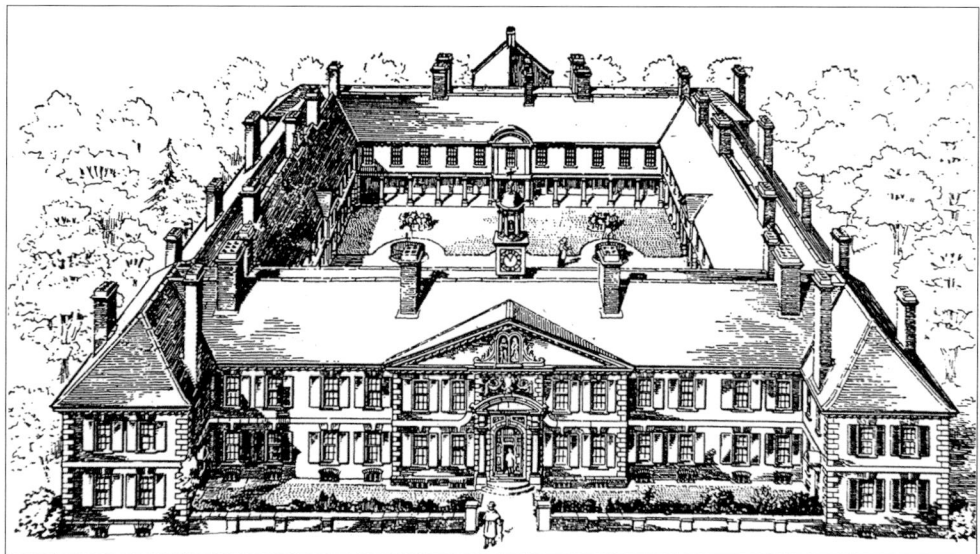

Morden College, Blackheath, London (1695).

Royal Naval Hospital, Greenwich, London (1705).

Wren was succeeded as Surveyor of Works by Sir John Vanbrugh (1664-1726). Unusually, the foundations of all the blocks were laid at the same time, in 1696. The King's House, renamed King Charles' House, was refurbished as the chapel and its twin, the King William Block – which was the refectory – was the first new building to be completed. It contained the Painted Hall, perhaps the most famous Baroque room outside Italy. Both buildings had smaller brick-built blocks alongside, but they were caught up in the growing monumentality of the composition and were eventually rebuilt to match the Webb design, giving added emphasis to the Palladian Court.

John Evelyn was the hospital's first treasurer and raised £7,000 within a month of taking office. Athough Queen Mary died shortly after the Royal Charter was proclaimed, King William was

*Above:* College Matrarum, Salisbury, Wiltshire (1682).

*Left:* Berkeley Hospital, Worcester (1666).

determined to see the project through and, as well as donating the royal buildings and the grounds to the hospital, gave £2,000 to the building fund.

The first pensioners took up residence in 1705, some eleven years after the original charter was granted, although their numbers did not reach 1,000 for a further generation. Its full capacity of 3,000 was not reached until the later eighteenth century.

From the outset, there were complaints that the needs of the pensioners were being subjugated to the visions of the architects. Both Vanbrugh and Nicholas Hawksmoor considered that the hospital should not be completed until it had a central feature and repeatedly produced amendments to the plan, each one more extravagant than the last. Indeed, a minute of the Fabric Committee dated sometime in 1717 complained:

> … the Board, taking notice that the Managers of Works do contrive and execute designs, as well in the outward buildings as in the disposition of the inside, without consulting or advising with the Board. Resolved that whoever shall for the future undertake any schemes or proceed in any work without the approval of the Board first, shall defray the charge of all the works at their own expense.

The distinguished members of the Board were originally chosen with a view to their fundraising abilities, but their influence on the increasingly grandiose design was more noticeable. Hardly had Hawksmoor finished the inside of the Hall than James Thornhill was appointed to paint it – and it took him nineteen years to complete the project! Even after having waited such an inordinately long time for their refectory, the poor pensioners were banished to the floor below. The room was considered to be much too grandiose for them to use. Indeed, Dr Johnson, after a visit to Greenwich in 1763 commented that the buildings of Greenwich were 'too magnificent for a place of charity', and Peter the Great is reputed to have suggested to King William that he convert St James' into a hospital and move his court to Greenwich.

In the 1860s, over a century and a half after its foundation, when its numbers had again decreased to less than half its capacity, a Royal Commission was set up to inquire into the many allegations of corruption and maladministration. It decided to close the institution, and in 1873 the Royal Naval College was transferred from Portsmouth to the magnificent hospital buildings of Greenwich.

Another of Wren's masterpieces, again an almshouse, lies less than two miles from the Royal Naval Hospital. Morden College is approached from a narrow footpath leading from the southeast corner of Blackheath. Founded in 1695 by Sir John Morden to accommodate 'poor honest, sober and discreet merchants who shall have lost all their estates by accidents and perils of the seas, or by any other accidents, ways or means, in their honest endeavour to get their living by way of merchandising', the college accommodates forty-four pensioners in four ranges around a beautifully proportioned courtyard with the usual refectory and chapel. The chapel contains woodcarvings by Grinling Gibbons, fine stained glass and a six-sided pulpit. The design is all that one would expect of Wren, its brick and tile with stone dressings and the colonnades to the courtyard quite reminiscent of Chelsea.

Salisbury is particularly well-endowed with almshouses, as might be expected from a cathedral city, having no less than fourteen separate groups dating from medieval times until the present day. Two stand out as masterpieces of the Renaissance: the Trinity Hospital of 1702, typical of the courtyard design, and the magnificent College Matrarum, built for the widows of the clergy in 1682. Standing just within the cathedral precincts, this is Sir Christopher Wren at his best in the domestic scale, with classical proportions, a fine pediment and cupola over.

## QUEEN ANNE

William and Mary died without heirs and were succeeded by Mary's younger sister Anne (1702-1714). During the twelve years of her reign, very few almshouses of note were built.

However, Berkeley Hospital, Worcester and the Fishermen's Hospital, Great Yarmouth were both completed during her reign, having been begun during the reign of her sister and brother-in-law. Two London almshouses of this period stand out as being exceptional. The Ironmongers' Almshouses in Kingsland Road, Shoreditch, were built by Sir Richard Geffrye in 1710. The twenty-eight two-storey almshouses form three sides of an open square, with the chapel occupying the centre of the main range. It has a pediment, bell tower and a statue of the founder in a niche over the entrance hall. Although no longer used as almshouses, the old London County Council preserved the buildings as a museum of London domestic architecture, and as the Geffrye Museum it is now a well-known centre for the study of building materials and methods from bygone ages.

Trinity Almshouses, Mile End Road, which were actually founded in 1695, are attributed to Wren and were built for the Corporation of Trinity House as a home for retired seamen, like so many others throughout the country. Two rows of single-storey almshouses, twelve on one side, eleven on the other, face each other across a narrow, slightly tapering, grassed courtyard with a delightful little chapel with pediment, clock tower, cupola and weather-vane closing the vista at the narrow end. At the other, the Mile End Road frontage, the difference between the odd and even number of dwellings is made up by a serpentine brick wall with wrought-iron gates between the pedimented gables of the cottages, each with sundry commemorative plaques and maritime artefacts, including two model ships carved out of marble. Holy Jesus Hospital, Newcastle-upon-Tyne is an example of northern almshouses of this period.

## GEORGIAN ALMSHOUSES

The principal social problem facing the Georgians, or more properly, the Hanoverians, was how to deal with poverty in the light of the social changes brought about by industrialisation on the one hand, and the enclosure of common land on the other.

Trinity Hospital, Mile End Road, London (1695).

*Social Context*

*Above:* Holy Jesus Hospital, Newcastle-upon-Tyne (1682).

*Right:* Fountain's Hospital, Linton-in-Craven, North Yorkshire (1721).

England was almost unique in having a poor law at all. Elsewhere in Europe, especially in Catholic countries such as Ireland, relief was still looked upon as something that should operate outside the state, either as almsgiving to be administered by the church, or as care by the extended family. As noted previously, an administrative system had existed since Elizabethan times which, particularly since the Act of Settlement and Removal of 1662, confirmed that the relief of poverty was to be the duty of the smallest unit of local administration, the parish. The 1662 Poor Law set out the responsibility for a pauper's relief, which would be administered with regard to 'settlement'. Everyone was deemed to have a 'settlement' in one – and only one – parish. Such a settlement, a typically English property right, could be established in one of several ways: a) by being born in a particular parish, b) by having a father settle there, c) by marrying a husband there, d) by being hired as a servant for at least one year there, e) by being apprenticed there, or f) by renting a dwelling-house there.

A person looking for relief by reason of illness, destitution or incapacity for work could only look to the parish in which he or she had a settlement, and no other. This policy had the obvious merit of defining responsibility for relief in a clear way. However, it also had the flaw of keeping workers in or near their settlement parish. Strictly speaking, a person needed a certificate to leave his parish to seek work elsewhere. Paupers wore a 'P' badge on their clothing and officers in charge had the right – in fact, the duty – to drive vagrants and all those without relief back to their native parishes.

On the other hand, this exclusive policy had its benefits. Paupers who hailed from the parish engendered some sympathy from their neighbours and from the overseers of the poor, who made sure that they did not actually starve, and indeed in many ways made life as comfortable as could be expected for those who had fallen on hard times.

Those who had no settlement were relentlessly driven from the parish. The poor, the old and the sick were all ejected or, in some cases, bribed to move on. Unmarried, pregnant women were treated particularly badly; if they gave birth in the parish then their offspring would immediately be entitled to settlement.

The cost of poor relief accelerated at an alarming rate during the eighteenth century. In 1700 it was estimated to be £600,000; by 1776 it had risen to £1.5m and by 1803 it was a staggering £4.2m. Part of these funds went towards relief for the sick, the old and the unemployed. But increasingly, it went to topping up the income of workers on rock-bottom wages, to support their families or to help out during periods of only seasonal employment. The Speenhamland ruling of 1795 linked topping-up to inflation and imposed an intolerable burden on those responsible for raising the cash – who were usually the magistrates.

The ratepayers resented the poor, considering them to be feckless, naturally idle and having little inclination to work. Spare cash would be spent on drinking and debauchery. Defoe complained:

> When wages are good they won't work any more than from hand to mouth; or if they do work they spend it in riot or luxury, so that it turns to no account to them. Again, as soon as trade receives a check, what follows? Why, then they grow clamorous and noisy, mutinous and saucy another way, and in the meantime they disperse, run away and leave their families upon the parishes to wander about in beggary and distress.

As previously, magistrates believed that wages should be kept low to keep labourers at work longer; to make them more industrious is to 'lay them under the necessity of labouring all the time they can spare from rest and sleep'. Keeping the workers only an inch or two from penury meant that as soon as they became ill or there was a downturn in the economy, they and their families were on the parish. They were never able to save anything that would tide them over bad times. Furthermore, there was but a whisker, in financial terms, between working and being on the parish. Indeed, institutionalised paupers generally ate better than families where the breadwinner was in work.

The answer, first tried in 1697 in Bristol, was the poorhouse, described by Jeremy Bentham as 'a mill to grind rogues honest and idle men industrious'. The poorhouse was based on the principle that 'if you don't work you don't eat'. There, the poor could be taught useful skills and at the same time earn their keep, thus sparing the ratepayers the responsibility of providing for them. The Knatchbull Act of 1723 endorsed at national level the policy which hitherto had been pursued at local level, giving discretion to magistrates to refuse outdoor relief to those who would not enter a house of industry. The management of the poorhouse was, more often than not, put in the hands of private contractors who exploited the inmates unmercifully for their own ends.

*Social Context*

*Above left:* Alnut's Hospital, Goring Heath, Oxfordshire (1726).

*Above right:* Christ's Hospital, Abingdon, Oxfordshire (1553).

Shireburn Hospital, Hurst Green, Lancashire (1706).

Twitty's Almshouses, Abingdon, Oxfordshire (1707).

A certain Matthew Marryat of Buckinghamshire was, in the 1730s, running as many as thirty houses. Children had a particularly hard time, and the infant mortality rate in London workhouses was very high. Out of 2,340 children put into workhouses in 1750, only 168 were still alive by 1755. But in spite of the theory, poorhouses proved to be totally uneconomic and had to be continuously supported from the rates. By definition, the inmates were the most unproductive people in society; generally women and young children abandoned by their menfolk, the aged, the sick, and, increasingly, the mentally defective. Moreover, the unscrupulous private contractors who ran them were siphoning off any surpluses. In due course, it was realised that the parish was really too small a unit to support a workhouse. So parishes were joined together to form Poor Law Unions, with joint houses of industry. Bigger poorhouses incurred bigger losses and only a few hundred were founded.

These responses to poverty failed because they tried to cure the symptoms rather than the root cause, and in any case, were local in scope rather than part of any national policy. Thus poverty was seen by many economists as a necessary concomitant to progress. Indeed, Malthus observed that poverty was the fault of the indigent, since they bred too quickly. And, as Henry Fielding wrote, 'so very useless indeed is this heavy [Poor Law] tax and so wretched its disposition, that it is a question whether the poor or the rich are more dissatisfied since the plunder of one serves so little to the real advantage of the other.'

But what of the almshouses during this period? Generally speaking, Georgian almshouses were modest in size and scale compared to their predecessors, although usually beautifully proportioned, as might be expected in this age of elegance. There were a few exceptions, but none to match the Royal Hospital at Greenwich or St Cross at Winchester.

Despite its small size – there were only six dwellings – few almshouses during this period were more impressive than Fountaine's Hospital at Linton-in-Craven in the Yorkshire Dales. This almshouse was founded in 1721 by Richard Fountaine, a local lad made good, who was the timber merchant supplying materials for the building of Castle Howard. The design is reputed to have been prepared by Sir John Vanbrugh himself whilst working in Yorkshire. It is certainly in his style; massive proportions to otherwise small dwellings, with a central chapel, tower and cupola.

Tomkin's Almshouses, Abingdon, Oxfordshire (1733).

Alnut's Hospital at Goring Heath in Oxfordshire was built, as in previous centuries, around three sides of a courtyard with the fourth side having the usual screen wall with entrance gate. The eight single-storey dwellings are arranged symmetrically – four on either side of the chapel – with, as at Linton, a tower and cupola.

Perhaps the most curiously built block in the country is situated at Stidd-under-Langridge in Lancashire, where John Shireburn, the local squire, built a small block of six cottages in 1728. The stone building consists of five short bays, the central three having semi-circular arches under a curious Dutch gable. The upper floor is approached by a grand central staircase which arrives at a balustraded balcony, the whole composition giving the illusion of a much larger building than is actually the case.

Not far away, at Mitton in Lancashire, a relative, Sir Michael Shireburn, built a much more imposing group of ten almshouses, each of two rooms. The group consisted of five dwellings on either side of the usual chapel, with the pediment surmounted by classical urns. The almshouses and the chapel formed three sides of a square; the fourth is closed off by a low balustrading, with the entrance in the centre reached by a semi-circular array of fifteen stone steps. The doors of the almshouses bore the names of the local parishes which benefited from the charity. Unusually, this group of almshouses was demolished stone by stone, and rebuilt in the centre of the nearby village of Hurst Green in 1947.

Abingdon, in Oxfordshire, has a major group of almshouses in its churchyard. The earliest, originally known as St Helen's Hospital, was founded in 1417 and suppressed in 1546. It was refounded in 1553 and named Christ's Hospital, with thirteen occupants. Known locally as

Mary Wandesford Hospital, York, North Yorkshire (1739).

Mary Lowther's Hospital, Ackworth, West Yorkshire (1741).

The Long Alley, the sixteenth-century building has a long wooden gallery running its whole length on the elevation which faces the parish church. In 1707, Charles Twitty added six more single-storey cottages, three for men and three for women, the classical design having a large central pediment with plaques, surmounted by a timber lantern. Then, eleven years later in 1718, Christ's Hospital was extended by the addition of the so-called Brick Alley almshouses to form the third side of the square, with the parish church of St Helen in the centre. These, the latest almshouses, were a bricklayer's tour de force, with classical arches and pediments and balustrading to the first-floor walkway.

Nearby, in 1733, Benjamin Tomkin, another local worthy, provided a further group of eight brick-built almshouses with a Dutch influence. There were four on either side of a narrow alley, at the end of which a classical gateway, with a pediment and plaque set above, led to a garden beyond.

Social Context

Well Hospital, Well, North Yorkshire (1758).

The city of York, as we have already seen, has several groups of almshouses, with three or four added during the Hanoverian period. Mary Wandesford founded an almshouse in 1739 in Bootham for ten poor spinsters 'who shall retire from the hurry and noise of the world into a Religious House of Protestant Retirement'. The single building is attributable to John Carr of York. It has seven two-storey arched bays, with the central three surmounted by a large pediment with a statue of the foundress in a niche in its centre.

In 1741, fifty miles or so away to the south, in the village of High Ackworth near Pontefract, Mary Lowther endowed a low, single-storey row of stone almshouses. Recently renovated, they are similar in date to Well Hospital in North Yorkshire, although the latter is more vernacular in style.

## VICTORIAN ALMSHOUSES

With the Victorian era came the last great age of almshouse building. Of the two thousand or so groups of almshouses currently occupied, it has been estimated that more than 30 per cent were built during the sixty-nine years of the great queen's reign.

Housing emerged as one of the great social problems of the period, as thousands of former agricultural labourers and their families migrated to the towns to look for work in industry. Row upon row of squalid terrace houses were thrown up in the streets surrounding the new factories, with, in many cases, several families occupying one house. Crime and disease were rife as these 'rookeries', as they were termed, became the forerunners of the emerging urban phenomenon: the classic slum.

## THE WORKHOUSE

For the sick, the aged, and those who had neither home nor work, there remained only the poorhouse. With the emergence of the austere Victorian ethic, the benevolent if somewhat despotic system which had prevailed in previous centuries was replaced by a much more repressive and cruel regime. In 1832, two years after the Swing Riots had been put down, with nineteen men hanged and nearly 500 transported, a Royal Commission was set up to inquire into the workings of the Poor Law. The report, instead of concerning itself with paupers and vagrants, concentrated on inadequately paid labourers in counties where the poor rates were being used to supplement wages. As mentioned previously, this had become known as the 'Speenhamland system' after the Berkshire parish where, in 1795, the magistrates pegged the level of 'outdoor' relief to the price of bread. In 1832, however, the Commissioners condemned the system, arguing that paupers did not respect their employers if their wages were enhanced by relief. They were discouraged from providing for their families and elderly parents when they knew that they could be thrown on the rates. They were convinced that the Poor Law was undermining the economy by interfering with 'natural' laws.

The Commissioners suggested that the administration of the system, with its perceived inefficiencies and corruption, should be replaced by a more unified, efficient system, regulated by a locally appointed board, with direction from central government. The centre of the new system was not to be the old, local poorhouse, the receptacle for the helpless, poor and aged, but the workhouse, a new, purpose-built institutional building which had the aim simultaneously to 'relieve the helpless, deter the idle, set children on the right path, encourage thrift and temperance, reduce crime, improve agriculture, raise wages and heal the growing divisions in the social order'.

Because it was thought that many parishes were too small to maintain a workhouse of adequate size, several parishes were grouped together to form a Workhouse Union, with one central facility administered by professional staff. Outdoor relief was formally abolished – although in certain parts of the country, this was ignored – and all people claiming relief were forced to enter the workhouse where, as a deterrent, the living conditions were deliberately made far worse than those of the lowest-paid worker outside. The Workhouse Test ensured that only the 'deserving' cases were admitted, and in truth, only the really desperate availed themselves of the privilege.

The new workhouses – so much like prisons that they were termed 'bastilles' – were architect-designed on the so-called 'panopticon' principle. This design was generally cruciform in shape, with a central observation tower over the master's quarters. A rectangular boundary wall enclosed the whole building, interacting with the wards to produce four courtyards rather like the cruciform hospitals of medieval times, each for a different class of pauper – male, female, young and old. Families were separated upon entering, with even husbands and wives kept apart, and all their worldly possessions including their clothes were taken from them, to be replaced by the workhouse uniform. Alcohol and tobacco were banned and a vicious regime of hygiene imposed, not just to ensure good health but as a discipline in itself. The pauper could not leave the building without the express approval of the master, unless of course he wished to discharge himself, which would of course deprive him of relief.

Able-bodied paupers were set to work breaking stones, grinding corn, or picking oakum. The punishment regime was severe, and in some cases inhuman. In the Warwick workhouse, a two-and-a-half-year-old child was punished for dirtying itself by having its excrement forced into its mouth; at the Hoo Union workhouse, teenage girls were flogged by the master; and at the notorious Andover workhouse, the paupers were so hungry that they fought amongst themselves for the gristle and marrow in the bones they were set to crush.

Dickens' most famous character, Oliver Twist, epitomised in the popular imagination the Victorian workhouse, although it is significant that the novel was published in 1837, only three years after the Poor Law Amendment Act of 1834, and so could only have described the old-style poorhouse. There was, nevertheless, a great deal of opposition to the new workhouses, not just from the poor themselves, but from the enlightened few in the more fortunate classes of society, who were becoming more and more concerned at the plight of the lower orders.

The scandal of the Andover workhouse – which broke in 1845 – brought down the Poor Law Commission, and from 1847 until 1871 responsibility was passed to the Poor Law Board,

Goldsmith's Almshouse, Acton, London (1811).

although the Board never actually met. From 1871 until 1919, the Local Government Board had responsibility for Poor Law administration, and from 1919 until 1929 the Ministry of Health was the responsible department.

## THE CHARITY COMMISSION

What the Poor Law Commission was to the workhouse, the Charity Commission was to almshouses. The Charity Commission was set up under the Charitable Trusts Act of 1855, following a series of scandals which rocked mid-Victorian society.

Until then, corruption had been endemic in the management of charitable undertakings, particularly long-established hospital and almshouse charities, which usually vested the ownership of the assets in its master or warden. As seen in previous chapters, many foundations dating from medieval times had large landholdings which, as time went by, produced huge incomes – far more than was really necessary for the maintenance of the inmates. The fictitious Hiram's Hospital in Anthony Trollope's *The Warden*, the opening novel in the *Chronicles of Barsetshire*, deals with just such a situation, where the kindly Revd Septimus Harding, the hospital's warden, lives in a degree of comfort on the income derived from the foundation, oblivious to the fact that under the terms of the bequest, the income should have been spent on the eleven old men who comprised the brotherhood. The remorse experienced by the gentle old man, and the subsequent gutter-press vilification which leads to his resignation, form the opening scenes in Trollope's evergreen series.

The real-life scandal which is thought to have given Trollope the plot for *The Warden* was centred on Winchester's Hospital of St Cross, referred to earlier. Revd Francis North was the son

*Almshouses: A Social and Architectural History*

Lady Hewley's Almshouses, York, North Yorkshire (1840).

Dr Caleb Crowther's Almshouses, Wakefield, West Yorkshire (1840).

of the Bishop of Winchester and a nephew of the then Prime Minister, Lord North, when in 1808 he was appointed by his father to the hospital's mastership. He did not live in, having a much more comfortable home in the Rectory of old Alresford, the living of which had also been given to him by his father. He was accused of pocketing most of the income from the foundation over the forty years that he was master. When the story broke, the press had a field day and the affair was the subject of debate in the House of Commons, following which the Attorney General instituted an inquiry in the Court of Chancery. By this time Revd North, an old man of seventy-seven, had been made Earl of Guildford. At first he defended himself vigorously and ultimately tried to resign, although the then bishop refused to accept his resignation until the inquiry had reported.

*Social Context*

Saltaire Almshouses, Saltaire, West Yorkshire (1855).

This it did in 1853, finding the Earl guilty of misappropriation of the hospital funds. He was ordered to repay certain monies, but in the event only repaid about £4,000, compared with the estimated £300,000 which he received during his tenure. He resigned in 1855, the year that *The Warden* was published.

The Charity Commission was set up soon after to safeguard charities and in particular the income from their endowments. This was especially so in the case of educational charities where available money was not being used to best effect. For instance, they found that in the case of Dulwich College, a combined almshouse and school, the bedesmen were growing fat at the expense of the scholars. As a result of the Charity Commissioners' intervention, the educational establishment was hived off as a separate entity with its own endowment.

The basic law relating to charities dates from 1601, from the Charitable Uses Act of that year. The definition of what constitutes a charity is found in the Act's preamble:

> Relief of aged, impotent and poor people, the maintenance of sick and maimed soldiers and mariners, schools of learning, free schools and scholars in universities... the repair of bridges, ports, havens, causeways, churches ... and others.

This definition was refined in 1891 by Lord MacNaughten in what has since been known as the Pemsel Case, as follows:

> Charity in its legal sense comprises four principal divisions – trusts for the relief of poverty, trusts for the advancement of education, trusts for the advancement of religion, and trusts for other purposes beneficial to the community, not falling under any of the previous heads.

The powers of the Charity Commission have evolved over the years, with the current relevant legislation being the Charities Act 2006. Most of the older charities are governed by Trust Deed, but from its earliest days, the principal instrument used by the Charity Commissioners for newly formed charities and for control and supervision has been 'the scheme'. A charitable scheme is nothing more than a formal statement of what the charity's purpose is, who its trustees are, what their duties and responsibilities are, and what its assets, and particularly its income, are.

*Almshouses: A Social and Architectural History*

*Left:* Joseph Crossley's Almshouses, Halifax, West Yorkshire (1863).

*Right:* Seamen's Houses, Whitby, North Yorkshire (1842).

The law of trusts is complex, but a fundamental premise affecting all trusts is the principle that no change may be made to the purpose or benefit for which the trust was originally set up. This is referred to as the doctrine of *cy-pres* – derived from the Norman French, meaning roughly 'close to'. Since 1857 there have been repeated attempts to relax the doctrine because, it was argued, it often gave rise to confusion among trustees and was seen as stifling new initiatives and inhibiting change, particularly in the case of parochial charities. The latest consideration of this matter followed the Woodfield Report on Charities, published in 1988, but the view taken by the Charity Commissioners and endorsed by the government was that the doctrine of *cy-pres* was very flexible, and that to bind it by legislation would inhibit its evolution and narrow its scope.

Day-to-day control of the 165,000-odd present day charities is administered through 'the scheme' and whenever a charity having a Trust Deed approaches the Commissioners to effect some change or other, such as the mortgaging of property, the opportunity to replace it with a scheme is usually taken. This and the submission of an annual return and accounts is usually sufficient to maintain control, although since 1988 it has been the practice to amalgamate, under a new scheme, certain local charities with incomes of less than £200.

From 1836, a change in attitude was discernible among some members of the Church of England. 'Slum Parsons' emerged with sympathy for the Chartist reforms and an increased fervour for parochial work, particularly in industrial areas. There was an insistence in many quarters, born perhaps out of guilt, that the middle, lay and clerical classes had a duty to the labouring classes which resulted in the provision of clothing clubs, soup kitchens, parochial schools and almshouses.

In the industrial North, particularly the West Riding of Yorkshire, Nonconformist dissent predominated. Mainly a layman's religion, which encouraged participation through preaching,

Sunday School work and the collective control of committees of elders, it fitted many emerging young industrialists for a future career, whether in business or, after the Reform Acts, as Members of Parliament. William Lovett, one of the Chartists' leaders, encapsulated the mood of many of his contemporaries when he stated that, 'we must come to look upon practical Christianity as a union for the promotion of brotherly kindness and good deeds to one another'.

Believer and unbeliever alike – and there were many unbelievers in the emerging ruling classes – shared then an ethical standard which was almost puritanical in its outlook, with a rectitude and devotion to duty as fervent as any which had preceded it. This code of ethics, since termed 'evangelicalism', found its outlet in philanthropy and schemes of social reform calculated to mitigate the evils of the new industrial society without changing them. Out of this, the last great period of almshouse building emerged.

By and large, the vast majority of Victorian almshouses were provided in modest groupings of between five and twelve dwellings, generally single-storey with unexceptional architectural features. Most towns and many villages throughout the country had at least one such grouping; some more, with as in previous centuries, a predominance in Yorkshire and the London area.

Lady Hewley's Almshouses of 1840, situated off St Saviourgate in York, is just such a group; twelve stone-built cottages with a tiny chapel built into the corner where the street changes direction. Only a plaque on the St Saviourgate frontage betrays the presence of this unpretentious, unobtrusive home for retired ladies from York and the surrounding district. Slightly more flamboyant are the eight Tudoresque almshouses built twenty miles or so to the south in Wakefield, provided for under the will of Dr Caleb Crowther, who died in 1840. Standing at the junction of George Street with Thornhill Street, the predominantly single-storey cottages have a central two-storey feature housing a boardroom over one of the cottages. Each entrance doorway has a five-centred arch with dripstone over, as do the windows, with tall stone chimney-stacks and picturesque barge-boarding to the gable ends. The almshouses were to be occupied only by 'Christian dissenters from the Church of England, of any denomination except Roman Catholics'. This policy was extended to the twelve governors who were recruited from the largest dissenting churches situated within a mile of Wakefield's market cross. No Roman Catholic, attorney-at-law, or solicitor was ever to be elected as governor and those chosen had to affirm that they had never in the past been or would ever in the future be a member of the Church of England or 'profess or act in support of those opinions or politics which are commonly called Tory or Conservative'.

The growth of London, over the years, brought about the relocation of many almshouse groups, partly because of disasters such as the Great Fire, partly because their sites became more valuable, particularly those near to the centre, and partly because new land uses became necessary as a result of progress in housing and public health. St Martin-in-the-Fields Almshouses were affected by such changes. They stood originally, before 1681, near Charing Cross, but in that year they were relocated in Charing Cross Road, housing sixty old ladies from the parish of St Martin-in-the-Fields. By the close of the eighteenth century a need was established for a new burial ground on land occupied by the almshouses. As they were considered to be in need of replacement anyway, they were relocated again in 1818, this time to Camden Town, at the junction of Bayham Street and Pratt Street. Two-storey, of brick with stone dressings, the original chapel at the rear has since been converted into dwellings. The Camden Town and Kentish Town Almshouses of about the same date, founded by Mrs Esther Greenwood of Regent's Park, stand in Rousden Street off Camden Road. Tudoresque, of brick with cream render, they are typical of residential property in the heart of the densely packed metropolis. By contrast, the St Pancras Almshouses of 1850, situated not far away in Southampton Road, are surrounded by a leafy garden where in the summer the occupants can sit out to enjoy the flowers.

Most of the nineteenth-century almshouse groups described so far have little to commend them from the architectural standpoint, but, as might be expected in this age of exuberance, there were many more throughout the country which demonstrated the best of the Victorians' sense of dignity and monumentality.

St Anne's Bedehouse, Lincoln, Lincolnshire (1847).

In the North East, at Tynemouth, the Tyne Master Mariners' Asylum of 1836 displays a sense of dignity and repose which is the very epitome of the almshouse tradition. Constructed of tooled stone, with Dutch gables and an Italianate campanile, the Asylum occupies an elevated position amongst landscaped grounds which set the building off to its best advantage. Recent renovation and improvement works have left the building unimpaired architecturally and fit for its purpose for another 150 years.

Moving further south, to the West Riding of Yorkshire, a spate of building during the middle and later years of the nineteenth century produced a whole series of architecturally important almshouses. Sir Titus Salt, having made his fortune spinning the wool of the alpaca from South America, in 1853 started to build what became the most famous model village in England at Saltaire, a few miles to the north of Bradford, now a World Heritage Site The village, complete with shops, churches and chapels, parks, a school, a hospital, a club, a library, a laboratory, a billiards room, an assembly hall, a gymnasium, an art school, a chess room and a lecture theatre, but no public houses, was laid out around an enormous spinning mill. It was as long as St Paul's Cathedral with a chimney 250ft high, modelled on the bell tower of St Maria Gloriosa in Venice. The public buildings, built of stone, were also designed in the Italianate style, as were the 850 or so dwellings, of which forty-five were almshouses. Erected around Alexandra Square, the almshouses were built to resemble miniature Italian villas, mainly single-storey, although two at each side opposite one another were two-storey. On the roof of the two-storey houses was placed a bell turret, whilst under each gable, which were supported by decorative acanthus leaf foliage carved in stone, was carved the initials T.S. and C.S. in monogram, to commemorate Sir Titus and his wife, Caroline. All dwellings had a parlour with oven and boiler, bedroom and pantry.

Preference was given to people who had worked in the mill and were known to Sir Titus or, after his death, to the trustees of the estate; but others of good character were also eligible. Tenancy conditions were strict. The houses were inspected regularly to make sure that they were kept tidy and that the occupants were themselves clean and sober. Occupants lived rent-free, and married couples received a dole of 10s per week and single persons 7s 6d. A chapel was provided for the pensioners in the north-west corner to save them having to walk far to worship, especially in winter. The building is, however no longer used as a place of worship, having been recently converted into another dwelling. Adjacent to the almshouses, on the east side of the square, Salt provided a small hospital with three wards of nine beds each, one for men, one for women and one for children. It had its own dispensary and surgery where accidents could be dealt with urgently. The hospital was not solely for the almspeople, although it is likely that they made the most use of its facilities.

Not far away, across the city of Bradford, at Lilly Croft in Heaton Road, another group of almshouses was being erected at about the same time as Saltaire. The Bradford Tradesmens' Homes charity was set up in 1856, its purpose being to provide retirement accommodation for the tradesmen of Bradford and their dependents who had fallen on hard times and were no longer able to support themselves. The foundation stone was actually laid by Sir Titus Salt, who donated two thousand guineas, a magnificent sum at the time. With this and other donations, the first three blocks, comprising thirty dwellings, were completed at a cost of some £15,000. Later, in 1878, a fourth block of thirteen dwellings was erected by Mrs Elizabeth Wright in memory of her husband at a cost of £5,200. The present estate comprises forty-three almshouses, a master's house and a chapel, all of which are classed as Grade II listed buildings. The rectilinear plan encloses an area containing lawns and flowerbeds with sitting-out areas for the occupants. The chapel is situated in the centre of the northern block and can accommodate some three hundred people. Beautiful stained-glass windows were subsequently donated in memory of local worthies, notably Sir Titus Salt, and a clock was donated in 1897 in memory of Mr James Drummond. The whole comprises one of the most peaceful and picturesque almshouse groups in the north of England.

Moving a little further south, to Halifax, two further monumental groups were provided by the brothers Sir Francis and Joseph Crossley, whose carpet mill at Dean Clough was at the time the largest in the world. Sir Francis had, in 1850, commissioned the building of a mansion in the French Renaissance style, Belle View in Hopwood Lane, for his own occupation. In 1855, he built on adjoining land a group of almshouses in a similar style, ostensibly to house his aging workforce, but in reality to act as an embellishment to his mansion. The two-storey, stone dwelling-houses front onto Margaret Street behind a low boundary wall with neat gardens.

Two hundred yards to the south, across Joseph Paxton's People's Park in Arden Road, his brother Joseph built, eight years later in 1863, another group set in landscaped gardens, this time around an open square facing due east. Of dark millstone grit under a Yorkshire slate roof, the design of the group was reminiscent of the Tudor period with Gothic window details and a crenellated tower over the chapel.

Perhaps the most imposing Victorian almshouse in Yorkshire is situated at Aberford on the outskirts of Leeds, where the Gascoigne sisters, daughters of the local squire, erected a group as a monument to their father's memory. The building, in white limestone, was commenced in 1844 and consisted of eight dwellings, four for men and four for women, separated by a lofty entrance hall with clock tower over, together with chapel at one end and dining-room at the other, the whole design in Victorian high Gothic. The almsfolk were looked after by a matron who had her own cottage in the extensive grounds, and the whole charity was administered by trustees drawn from the local clergy. As with many almshouses built with motives other than strictly the provision of good housing, the Gascoigne Almshouses are no longer in use for their original purpose, having been converted firstly into museum workshops and more recently into family living accommodation. New almshouses were provided during recent years with more up-to-date accommodation nearer to Aberford.

At Whitby on Yorkshire's east coast, in 1842 Sir George Gilbert Scott (1811-78), that most prolific of Victorian architects, designed the Seamen's Houses in the Jacobean style, whilst Pugin, his contemporary, in 1847 designed St Anne's Bedehouse at Lincoln for Richard Waldo Sibthorpe. Breaking away from mock-Tudor, the almshouses were of single-storey in brick with stone dressings with a chapel and warden's house. Sir George Gilbert Scott was active throughout the whole country. In 1865, he built the Sudely Almshouses at Winchcome in Gloucestershire and, appropriately, at Godstone in Surrey he designed the St Mary's Homes in asymmetrical half-timbered style.

As might be imagined, London, which was at the time the wealthiest capital in the world, produced some of the most magnificent almshouse groups. Four stand out particularly.

Following the success of the Licensed Victuallers' Benevolent Institution, founded in 1827, the Metropolitan Beer and Wine Trades Society built an asylum in 1852 on land adjoining Nunhead Green, in Southwark. Again a mock Tudor design was chosen, of brick with stone dressings, heavily buttressed with five centred arches to all entrances and tall chimneys built on the skew. The Free Watermen and Lightermen's Asylum in High Road, Penge, were built between 1840 and 1841. Of grey brick with again a Tudoresque crenellated gatehouse, the almshouses occupy three sides of a landscaped quadrangle with trestled walkways across the garden and eccentric statues. Not far away in St Johns Road, again in Penge, is situated the King William IV Naval Asylum, built by Queen Adelaide in 1847 as a memorial to King William, whose brief reign spanned the years 1830-37. Much more truly Tudoresque than the previous group, the building has five centred arches to windows and door surrounds, tall octagonal chimney stacks and chequered brickwork to gable ends. Sadly, the building is no longer used as an almshouse, although it is used for council housing.

Finally, Sir William Powell's foundation adjoining Fulham's parish church, was endowed in 1680 and was rebuilt on its present site in 1869. L-shaped, around a leafy courtyard, the almshouses catch the full sunlight which throws into high relief the high Gothic details of the loggia and dormer windows. At the entrance, a heavily ornamented campanile houses figures of Faith, Hope and Charity in deep niches, with the inscription 'God's Providence, Our Inheritance'.

## THE PRESENT DAY

With the coming of the twentieth century the provision of almshouses gradually diminished. Now, hardly any new ones are being built. The reasons for this are many and various.

The principal reason has been a change in the status of working class people generally and old people in particular. From Edwardian times onwards, and especially since the First World War, the dependence of the workforce on the patronage of the landed gentry and industrial employers has reduced. Home ownership is now over 60 per cent. Government has assumed greater responsibility for social welfare, and with increasing regular earnings and mobility people are able to make their own provision for old age, either through personal pension arrangements or, at the very least, by qualifying for the state old-age pension.

The incidence of charitable giving has also changed markedly in recent years. In late Victorian times, certain industrial philanthropists, generally Quakers, began social inquiries and experimentation which had far-reaching effects on the housing conditions of the working classes. As we have seen, Engels and others documented the plight of the urban poor, and in 1879 the Cadbury brothers, George and Richard, began to build a model village at Bournville on the outskirts of Birmingham which was to become an example for all public sector housing for over half a century. The Cadburys had in turn derived inspiration from the co-operative endeavours of Robert Owen at New Lanark and industrial reformers such as Sir Titus Salt, who, as mentioned previously, had built the first English model village of any consequence at Saltaire. Benjamin Disraeli (1804-81) contributed indirectly to the housing reform movement also; his best-selling novel, *Sybil*, extolled the virtues of philanthropy through the provision of good housing to rent.

In 1902 Joseph Rowntree, a chocolate manufacturer living in York, observed the damage to family life which was being brought about by bad housing conditions there. Overcrowding and a lack of personal outdoor living space drove the breadwinner into the ale-house, where his meagre earnings were dissipated, to the detriment of his family. Rowntree reasoned that if working-class families could be given decent houses with gardens where the menfolk could be usefully and profitably employed, family life might be enriched and, as a by-product, industrial output might be improved. Accordingly, he caused a model village to be built, New Earswick, close to his chocolate factory on the outskirts of York. The village was laid out with spacious rows of modern houses and gardens, interspersed with allotments and open public spaces. Shops and schools were provided, as well as special dwellings, bungalows, for those who had grown too old

New Earswick, York, North Yorkshire (1904).

to work. These were not almshouses in the strict sense of the word since the Rowntree Trust was a registered charity in its own right, but they served the same purpose. About this time too, in the London area, other philanthropists were making a slightly different but significant contribution to housing the poor.

Thomas Sutton, Edward Cecil Guinness and George Peabody set up charitable trusts whose objects were to provide housing to rent for the working classes. These of course tended to be tenement dwellings for families in the more densely populated areas of the metropolis, but again, the aged were not forgotten.

Housing Associations, as we now know them, also emerged at this time. The first, the Society for Improvement of the Conditions of the Labouring Classes, was set up in 1830, and was quickly followed by a plethora of others, spreading to all the main cities in the country.

In 1892 the first municipal housing authority, the London County Council, was formed, whose example was again copied nationwide. Responsibility for housing was passing from private philanthropic hands into the public domain. The main thrust of the new housing movement was still to provide family accommodation; but as heads of households grew older, they needed special, generally smaller, dwellings to also be provided. Regularly, throughout the early years of the last century, Acts of Parliament were being passed which made provision both for improving existing housing and the building of new ones. At the peak in 1965, 400,000 homes a year were being built by local authorities, with a generous proportion of them intended for elderly people.

But other, equally significant social changes have also had an effect on charitable relief. During the early years of the century, many new outlets for charitable giving emerged. Charities were set up for such diverse needs as sick animals, sick and abused children, blind people, deaf people, those suffering from all sorts of diseases and illnesses, to name a few of the new causes. And in the late 1950s, charitable giving expanded overseas with the formation of Oxfam, Save the Children and other similar bodies, who saw the plight of the starving millions of the Third World as greater than that at home. There are many charities still catering solely for the aged and infirm; Help the Aged, Age Concern, Sue Ryder, to mention but three. But the general pattern is of resources being spread across the whole spectrum of society, with the elderly now receiving only a small proportion of the available relief. The introduction of the twice-weekly National Lottery, together with the plethora of scratch cards, has also had the effect of reducing charitable income significantly.

Until the turn of the twentieth century, almshouses were very much parochial institutions providing accommodation in small groups, located specifically to satisfy local needs. However, with the urbanisation of the Industrial Revolution came a new form of the institution; what might be called corporate almshouses. These were charities providing housing for the needy elderly over large areas.

Durham Aged Mineworkers' Cottage Homes.

Among the first such corporate almshouses was the Durham Aged Mineworkers' Homes Association, founded in the City of Durham in 1898, with the aim of providing retirement bungalows for mineworkers throughout the Durham coalfield. The brainchild of Joseph Hopper, once a mineworker himself, the homes were seen by Hopper as a logical extension of the superannuation scheme which had been set up by the National Union of Mineworkers, and which at the time paid 4s a week to each retired mineworker. Out of this he had to provide food, clothing, heating and shelter for himself and his wife (if he had one). But housing was in any case very hard to find and much sought-after by working mineworkers and their families. Mine-owners who provided groups of cottages close to their mines preferred to have workers as tenants rather than pensioners. At first Hopper's idea of the subvention of 6d a week per mineworker to pay for the building of the homes was ridiculed by most influential people, but he persisted with his vision and in 1899, just one year after the association's formation, the first bungalows were completed in the village of Haswell. Joseph Hopper died in 1909, but he had every reason to be proud of the achievements of the Homes Association; small groups of bungalows were springing up throughout the whole of County Durham, and by 1925 they numbered over 1,000. The association is still going strong today, with well over 1,200 homes in management. It has recently completed the modernisation of all the bungalows originally built by levies from miners. It has also built several new developments, both in the form of bungalows and sheltered dwellings with full warden care.

Joseph Hopper's example was followed on the opposite bank of the River Tyne when the Northumberland Mineworkers' Aged Homes Association was formed in 1900. It too has over five hundred bungalows in management, whose tenants' rents are subsidised by subventions from working mineworkers' pay.

After the First World War, the perceived need to house veterans spawned many local war memorial homes, as well as another corporate almshouse charity, the North East Railway Cottage Homes and Benefit Fund. The Fund was founded in 1919 to provide accommodation for the elderly, infirm and injured railwaymen returning home from the war as part of the 'Homes Fit for Heroes' movement. It all started with a bequest from a Mrs Ellen Granger of £10,000 in memory of her brother, Tempest Anderson. A further sum of £1,000 was contributed by the railwaymen themselves, together with a pledge of up to £20,000 during the first three years of the fund's existence by the North East Railway Company.

As constituted in 1921, the fund had a dual purpose. Firstly, and it must be said, primarily, it was to pay sickness benefit to railwaymen and their dependents during their working lives. This was accomplished, as was usual, by a system of contributions deducted from the men's wages. The other purpose, of no less importance to the contributors, was the provision of cottage homes for their retirement, and to this end some four hundred and forty dwellings were built over the years throughout the North East, in thirty-seven different locations from Leeds to Berwick-upon-Tweed. Originally, the men paid 1$d$ per week each into the fund. The aims of the organisation have changed slightly over the years, and although it has retained its charitable status it has ceased to be an almshouse in the strict sense of the word and is no longer affiliated to the National Association.

The Cottage Homes movement, which had its origins in Edwardian times as an extension of the Garden City movement, promoted many groups of almshouses, two large groups of which are of national importance.

The Linen and Woollen Drapers' Homes at Mill Hill in north-west London was founded in 1900 by James Marshall, a London store magnate – he owned Marshall & Snellgrove's – and provided one- and two-storey cottages, generally of brick, although some were half-timbered, very much the vogue at the time. The almshouses were set in gardens with a central facility, clubhouse and offices, again in a mock-Elizabethan style. Although not all that unusual in itself, the Mill Hill scheme provided the model for one of the largest almshouse complexes built to date, that at Whiteley Village in Surrey.

Whiteley Village was built as a memorial to William Whiteley – the 'Universal Provider' and owner of the well-known Bayswater store – and as a consequence of a legacy of his. In 1911 the trustees of the Whiteley estate bought 230 acres of land in Surrey and initiated a design competition which was won by Frank Atkinson, the architect of the Mill Hill scheme.

Housing for 350 pensioners was provided. Each cottage consisted of a living room with sleeping lobby; the traditional almshouse accommodation. The village was completed by a village hall, store, library, church, both Nonconformist and Roman Catholic chapels, a public hall, club and restaurant. Since its inception, a special home for the frail elderly has been added, Whiteley House, housing thirty-eight single residents and five couples, together with a cottage hospital with thirty-five beds, which provides acute medical, post-surgical and permanent nursing care. The village runs its own bus service every weekday, ferrying residents to and from Walton-on-Thames. Each cottage has now been modernised and the estate is administered by the trustees, who keep the grounds immaculate, and each tenant is expected to cultivate his or her garden. All the almsfolk emanate from either commercial or agricultural occupations.

A remarkable modern-day example of philanthropy can be found at South Chailey, Haywards Heath, East Sussex. The Grantham Trust had been established in Chailey since 1951, founded under the will of Mrs Sybil Grantham to provide homes for elderly gentlewomen in distressed circumstances. In 1965 the local GP, Dr Jack Palmer, formed an old folks' welfare committee with the aim of co-ordinating activities for the elderly people of the village. Following a survey of all the elderly residents, it became clear that their greatest anxiety was that as they became frail and infirm they would no longer be able to cope with their current accommodation and may have to move away. What was needed was sheltered housing; that is, easily managed small flats or bungalows where they could live out their days independently, yet under the watchful eye of a warden.

A housing association was formed with the objective of building such sheltered accommodation and, during its search for a suitable site, the committee made contact with the Grantham Trust who owned, among other assets, a field called Hoggs Mead in the south-east corner of the village.

During negotiations for the purchase of the land, it was clear that the two organisations had similar objects and with the agreement of the Charity Commision, the association took over the management of the trust, changing the wording of the trust deed from 'distressed gentlewomen' to 'poor women over 50'.

Thirty-four flats were planned at Hoggs Mead, originally in five blocks. When the first block was completed in 1979, and named Palmer Court in memory of Dr Jack Palmer, the trust ran out of money and, being a private trust, was not eligible for building grants or loans. However, three individuals eventually came forward with offers to finance the completion of the development.

Mrs Christine Reckitt of Chailey Moat offered to fund the second block of six flats, provided that they would house poor men as well as women. This was agreed to by the Charity Commissioners. The block was named Reed House, the middle name of her late husband.

Mrs Jean Follett Holt was then introduced to the trust by David Scott, the director of the Almshouse Association, who was aware that she wished to provide some almshouses in memory of her late husband, Colonel Frank Follett Holt. Having visited the site and seen the first two blocks, Mrs Follett Holt readily agreed to provide finance for the third block of seven flats, which on completion in 1984 was named Follett Holt House. Following an appeal through the local parish magazine, an anonymous donor funded the fourth block containing a further six flats, which was named Meadow Court. The whole development was constructed in the local 'oasthouse' style of architecture and is one of the most striking almshouse developments built in recent years.

## THE ALMSHOUSE ASSOCIATION

In February 1946, in the Chapter House of Southwark Cathedral in England, a meeting was held of the representatives of London's almshouses with a view to forming a committee to safeguard the interests of almshouse buildings and the welfare of almsfolk. Its actual terms of reference were 'to safeguard the interests of almshouses and to promote the welfare of beneficiaries in view of the proposed changes of legislation'.

Concern was expressed that these changes in legislation, culminating in the National Assistance Act 1948, which heralded the arrival of the welfare state, would adversely affect charitable institutions generally and almshouses in particular, since it was feared that statutory provision would supplant voluntary effort. After six long years of war, many of London's 138 historic almshouses were in a poor state of repair. Many were empty and had suffered bomb damage. The London Almshouse Committee, as it was called, felt that almshouses were 'of great potential benefit to aged people in keeping the spirit of voluntary service alive, whatever may be the bounty or pension assured by the State'.

Pending details of the new legislation, a review of London's almshouses was undertaken and later a constitution was adopted. The Committee was renamed the Association of London Almshouses, and, with a grant of £1,000 from the National Corporation for the Care of Old People, a full-time member of staff was appointed, firstly as an appeals organiser and then as General Secretary. His name was Leonard Hackett. Supported by Miss R.G.M. McAuliffe, the Hon. Secretary of the Association and incidentally, the convenor of the original meeting at Southwark, Hackett began a vigorous campaign to modernise substandard almshouses and, despite an acute problem with funding, made sufficient progress to encourage the committee to extend its remit to the whole country. In 1950 the Association became The National Association of Almshouses with the following aims:

> To advise members on any matters concerning almshouses and the welfare of the elderly.
> To promote improvements in almshouses.
> To promote study and research into all matters affecting almshouses.
> To keep under review existing and proposed legislation affecting almshouses and where necessary take action.
> To make grants and loans to members.
> To encourage the provision of almshouses.

With the increasingly complex legislation surrounding the improvement and day-to-day running of almshouses, trustees down the years have had reason to be grateful for the advice provided by the National Association, recently renamed The Almshouse Association. Now it represents the interests of over 1,730 charities owning some 26,000 dwellings throughout the whole country.

*Hotel-Dieu*, Beaune, Burgundy, France (1443).

## HOSPITALS AND ALMSHOUSES IN OTHER COUNTRIES

Before the Reformation, Europe was, from Iceland in the north-west to Sicily in the south-east, largely dominated by Rome. As a consequence, and as might be expected, organised charitable provision was more or less uniform throughout. Italy will be covered briefly in Part Two.

In France, the system of charitable establishments was similar to that in England. Apart from the monasteries, most of which had their mother houses in France, there were basically four types of provision: leproseries or 'maladreries' as they later became known; hostels for wayfarers; hospitals providing residential care for the poor, the sick and the elderly; and almshouses providing out-relief, principally for people who had fallen on hard times. As in England, the first three were originally administered by the church, the fourth usually by local village and city worthies. Again as in England, endowments were provided by the local aristocracy and landowners, on the understanding that the inmates said prayers daily for the souls of their benefactors and their descendants.

One of the reasons for the Reformation, and the principal criticism levelled at the church by Luther, was the decadence of the clergy, their affluent lifestyle and neglect of their duties. The criticism was also directed at the administrators of maladreries, hostels, hospitals and almshouses – it being alleged that much of the revenue from the endowments was being diverted to other uses, and went particularly into the pockets of those who were charged with its distribution to the deserving poor.

But in the mid-sixteenth century, this state of affairs changed radically. There were two reasons for this. Firstly, with growing urbanisation, many people were moving from the countryside into the towns where they hoped to find work. Often they failed, and increasingly the migrants became reliant on charitable handouts from the four types of charitable organisation, which became lumped together under the generic name of 'hospital'.

The government, under pressure from the large towns which were experiencing great pressure on their charity, decided upon a system very similar to that of England under the old Poor Laws,

*Left:* Neukoop Hospital, The Hague, Holland (1608).

*Right:* Meulenaer Almshouses, Bruges, Belgium (1613).

but one which went much further and, in fact, anticipated the Victorian Poor Laws in severity. What was proposed was that, effectively, the old system should be dismantled and in its place should be built two types of hospital: *Hotels-Dieu*, which would provide for the sick and the aged, and *Hopitaux-Generaux*, which would provide for the poor, but the vulnerable poor only. The sturdy beggar, as in England, would not be entertained.

The second element of change was instigated by King Louis XIV, the founder of Les Invalides, who was under great pressure to provide pensions for the retired officers and men in his armies who had rendered such valuable service to France during the preceding decades. The king, like Henry VIII of England, saw hospitals with their great endowment wealth as being ideal *milch* cows to provide the money he so desperately needed. Accordingly, he decreed that all moribund hospitals should be closed down and their revenues diverted to a new Order which he had founded especially for the purpose, the Order of Notre Dame of St Carmel and St Lazare. The Order was to rigorously examine the accounts of all the thousands of hospitals in the country and, with the revenues which were to be sequestered from those found to be not doing their job, pay out pensions to retired and wounded soldiers. The king saw this as a charitable cause which was just as valid as ministering to the general poor and needy. The *Hotels-Dieu* and *Hopitaux-Generaux* were indeed provided in many cities, but the king's plans were thwarted and many small hospitals continue to this day.

Perhaps the most photographed hospital in France is the *Hotel-Dieu* in Beaune, Burgandy. The hospital was founded in 1443 by Nicolas Rolin, Chancellor of Burgandy, together with his wife Guigone de Salins, in response to the extreme poverty being experienced by many of the inhabitants of Beaune. The hospital, situated in one of the most famous wine-growing regions where agricultural wages were very low, is a marvel of Bergundian/Flemish art; a complex of buildings around a central courtyard with ambulatories on both the ground and first floor, together with gabled dormers and turrets. Its most significant feature, which attracts the photographers, is its steep roof covered with multi-coloured tiles laid in jazzy geometric patterns. In its heyday, as well as providing residential care for the poor and aged, the hospital provided medical and surgical services not only to the occupants of the Chambre de Pauvrers, but to residents of the surrounding area. It ceased to function as a hospital in 1948, and is now a museum and hotel.

In Holland and Belgium – originally the Spanish and Austrian Netherlands respectively – and to a certain extent in Germany, the hospital system followed roughly the same course as in

France. There were several hospitals of major importance, perhaps the most famous being St John's in Bruges, founded in 1188. But there were also many smaller groups of almshouses similar to those in England, providing much the same type of care, principally for the aged. Many of these almshouses continue to this day.

In Spain, a staunchly Catholic country to this day, many famous hospitals were established, at Toledo, Grenada and Santiago de Compostela, to name but three of the most famous.

In Ireland, as might be expected, and to a lesser extent in Scotland, the care of the sick, poor and feeble was for a long time entrusted to the monastic orders, each monastery taking an example from its sister house on the Continent. Town and village names such as Hospital, Spital, and Spiddel can still be found throughout the Republic. A hospital was known in Gaelic as *forus tuarthe*, or the house of the territory, indicating that each hospital served a particular area. The Brehon Laws provided that the hospital 'shall be free from debt, shall have four doors and should have a stream of water running through the middle of the floor', and that 'Dogs, fools and female scolds must be kept away from the inmates, lest they be worried'.

The Knights of St John – the Knights Hospitallers – had a number of hospitals in Ireland, the most important being at Kilmainham near Dublin, which was founded in approximately 1174 by Richard Strongbow. Other preceptories, as the hospitals were sometimes known, were Kirkhill Hospital near Emly in Co. Limerick, Kilsaran in Co. Louth and that at Wexford. Towards the end of the twelfth century, the Crutched Friars established several hospitals throughout Ireland. Hospitals of St John the Baptist were founded at Kells in 1189, at Ardee in 1207, and at Neuagh, Co. Tipperary, known as *Teach Eoin*, in 1200.

Apart from that at Kilmainham mentioned above, several hospitals were established in Dublin and its environs. At Steyal, near the west gate, the Priory of St John in 1220 founded a hospital dedicated to God and St James, and in the city proper a hospital for the sick was provided, appropriately enough, by Alfred de Palmer. A 'Palmer' was a pilgrim wearing two crossed palm leaves as a sign that he had visited the Holy Land.

There were a number of leper hospitals in Ireland, but it is not easy to distinguish them from mainstream establishments for the poor and the sick. St Stephen's Hospital in Dublin, founded in 1344, was certainly provided for 'the poor lepers of the city', and lepers were the occupiers of hospitals in Kilbixy in Co. Down, at Cloyne and at least one of the four hospitals in or near Cork.

In Scotland at least seventy hospitals were founded before the Reformation; four in Aberdeen, five in Edinburgh and others elsewhere. King David founded a hospital dedicated to St Mary Magdalene at Roxburgh in about 1135, and King Malcolm IV founded the Holy Trinity Hospital at Soltre in approximately 1155. James I founded St Mary Magdalene's hospital at Linlithgow in 1430.

As might be expected, the Pilgrim Fathers took the European system of charitable relief with them when they emigrated to America. But such charity was tempered with the Puritan ethic, under which only the destitute could benefit. The sturdy beggar should, as in England, be made to earn his keep.

The first almshouses or 'poorhouses', as they came to be called, were established on the east coast, in the states of Massachusetts, Illinois and Maryland, although in time they spread throughout all the states. The first recorded was the Massachusetts Poorhouse, built in Boston in 1662. Many more were built during the period immediately following the Revolutionary War, and during the trade embargo of 1807, when poverty was widespread throughout the young United States. But they were all, without exception, provided by local authorities, particularly the overseers of the poor for each county.

From the start they were designed to be minimalist and self-supporting, often designated as poor farms in rural areas. However, they supported a wider range of needs than in Europe, including people with chronic physical illnesses, mental illnesses, and single mothers, as well as the more usual elderly. The Cook County Almshouse, built in 1835, was originally located in

*Almshouses: A Social and Architectural History*

Cook County Almshouse, Chicago, USA (1835).

Tewksbury Almshouse, Tewksbury, Massachusetts USA (1852).

downtown Chicago, but in 1841 it was transferred to a 160-acre rural site where it was envisaged – optimistically, as it turned out – that the inmates would pay their way. It has been described by historians as: 'Infamous for its corruption, mismanagement, deplorable living conditions and maltreatment of inmates, the almshouse was regarded as a refuge of last resort.'

A new building was erected in 1908 and the institution's name was changed to the Cook County Poor House. The number of residents ranged from seventy-five in 1854 to a peak of 4,300 in January 1932, of whom 10 per cent were children. The attached asylum for the insane housed a further 500 to 1,000 people!

Many American almshouses specialised more in medical needs than geriatric care, and over the years have, like some o the London almshouses, become general hospitals, although still keeping the appellation 'Almshouse'.

Tewksbury Almshouse in Massachusetts is a good example. It was originally established in 1852 as an almshouse to cater for the unprecedented influx of immigrants from Europe, with a capacity for 500 inmates, and by 1854 it was catering for some 2,200 paupers. It became a State Hospital in 1900, catering for patients with chronic and infectious diseases. It is, however, very proud of its origins and retains its name of the Tewksbury Almshouse.

# PART TWO
# ARCHITECTURAL CONTEXT

Almshouses have always been built in the local vernacular style and, despite many shortcomings in the actual accommodation, they usually were constructed of durable materials with architectural detailing which reflected both fashion and the resources of their patron, be he commoner or king. As a result of this attention to detail, as many as 4,000 individual groups of almshouses remain for posterity, although with modern living standards, most have proved to be too small even for a single person, and many have been combined to make larger units or converted to other uses. It is now estimated that there are some 2,000 separate groups, comprising approximately 20,000 to 25,000 units, still in residential use.

The first medieval hospitals took as their model the farmery, or infirmary – that part of the monastery which housed the aged or infirm monks. Each farmery had a hall with bedspaces along the inside walls, a kitchen where nourishing meals could be prepared, and a chapel usually, but not always, at the end of the hall, so that the brethren could see the altar from their beds. Perhaps the best preserved record of a medieval farmery is that at Fountains Abbey, near to Ripon in North Yorkshire, undoubtedly the best-preserved Cistercian house in the whole country.

Although the walls of the farmery and its associated buildings have long since disappeared, enough has survived to enable scholars to speculate how it would have looked. Fig.1 shows a plan view of the farmery as it would have been around 1240. The Great Hall, measuring some 180ft long by 78ft wide, was one of the largest in medieval Britain. It originally had bed spaces around the walls, and, because of its size, fireplaces in both the north and south gables. To the east is thought to have been the quarters reserved for sick or retired abbots, together with the chapel and kitchen with its associated rooms.

It is difficult to appreciate just what a prodigious amount of building took place during the early Middle Ages, when the population of the entire country was less than five million people. This was the period that built castles, manor houses, monasteries, cathedrals and the majority of the country's 12,000 parish churches, as well as all the usual domestic and agricultural buildings. Moreover, during the pre-Reformation period alone, between the twelfth and sixteenth centuries, something of the order of 800 hospitals were erected. Such studies of hospital buildings that have been carried out by antiquarians, notably the Victorian architect, F.T. Dolman, cite four distinct building types, each one a development of its predecessor, and all of them owing their lineage to monastic or educational prototypes. They were, in chronological order:

1. Great Hall with chapel attached.
2. Great Hall with chapel detached.
3. Cruciform layout.
4. Courtyard.

We shall examine each of these phases in turn.

## GREAT HALL WITH CHAPEL ATTACHED

This was the most direct descendant of the monastic farmery. It was single-storey in its earliest form, and its basic design was epitomised by St Mary's Hospital, Chichester, which was founded in about 1229 on the site of a defunct nunnery. Fig.2 shows the typical ground plan of this hospital with the

*Almshouses: A Social and Architectural History*

A model of the Farmery, Fountains Abbey, North Yorkshire (1240).

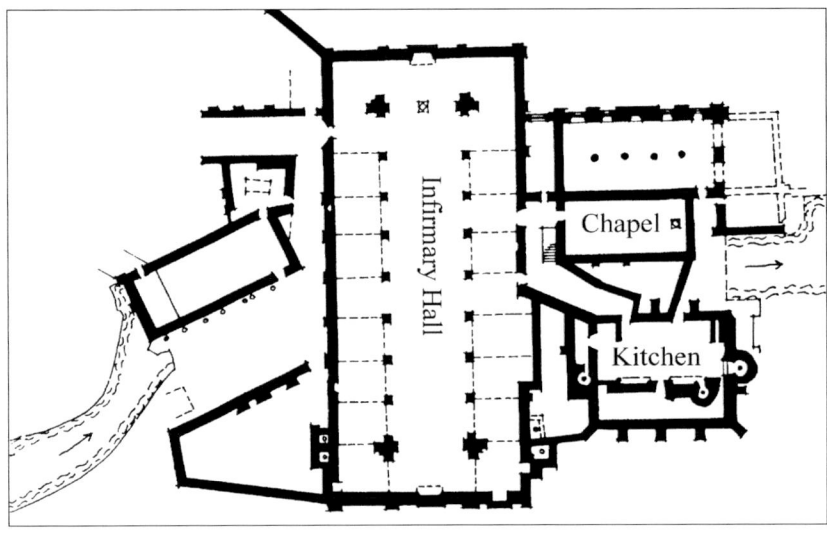

Fig.1 The Farmery, Fountains Abbey, North Yorkshire (1240).

chapel built as an extension to the hall, although in this particular case it is thought that the chapel preceded the hall. The great hall – originally of six bays, but truncated to four sometime in the early sixteenth century – is covered with a massive trussed rafter roof, some 42ft to the ridge, which sweeps down almost to ground level over the side aisles, which form the individual cubicles for the eight inmates. Fig.3 shows a section through the building, after Dolman.

The plan of the Hospital of St Nicholas, Salisbury (Fig.4) is a variation on the basic design. This time it is a double hospital with both the hall and the chapel at the eastern end divided longitudinally into two by arcading. This hospital, thought to have been the model for Hiram's Hospital in Trollope's novel *The Warden*, was founded as early as 1214.

A further variation on the theme of a double hospital is that of St John the Baptist, Winchester (Fig.5) where the chapel was built in 1290 as an extension of the southern infirmary hall.

Yet another variation on the basic design, although a more conventional one, is Bishop Bubwith's Hospital of St Saviour, Wells (Fig.6). Founded in 1424, it is again a double house for twelve men and twelve women. The chapel is built as usual at the eastern end, whilst the city's guildhall – now also used as almshouses – was situated at the other extremity.

*Architectural Context*

St Nicholas' Hospital, Salisbury, Wiltshire (1214).

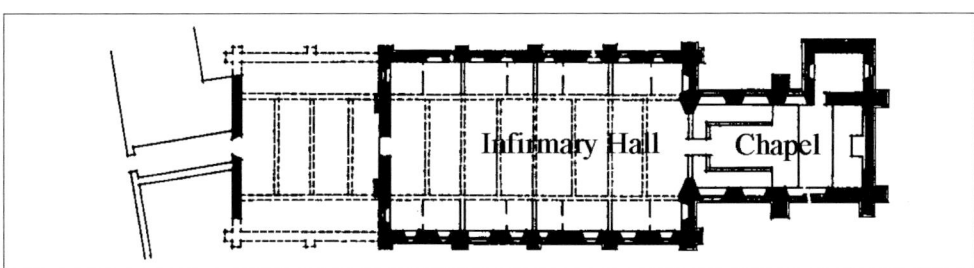

Fig.2 Hospital of St Mary, Chichester, West Sussex (1229).

Founded in 1423 by Henry Chichele, Archbishop of Canterbury – one year earlier than Wells – the Bedehouse at Higham Ferrers, Northamptonshire, is generally thought to have replaced an earlier hospital dedicated to St James, since fragments of that building have been incorporated into the fabric of the current building. Archbishop Chichele endowed three institutions in his native town: a college, a school and the Bedehouse, though only the last two mentioned institutions survive. The Bedehouse, occupied by bedesmen who tolled their rosary beads in prayer, follows the conventional plan of a Hall with chapel opening from it at the eastern end (see Fig.7). Its striking features are the alternate courses of red and cream stone from which the walls are constructed, together with a central fireplace with five-centred arch, around which the twelve male inmates and their nurse would likely have gathered on chilly evenings. The building fell into disrepair in the late Middle Ages, the bedesmen having become out-pensioners, but it was restored in the 1850s and is now used as a Sunday School.

Finally, we have an example of a hospital which has been converted into self-contained almshouses, that of St Mary Magdalene, Glastonbury – another institution founded in the thirteenth century. From this plan (Fig.8), the original hospital form can be seen, with the chapel in the usual place at the eastern end. However, instead of the usual cubicles, the hall has been

*Almshouses: A Social and Architectural History*

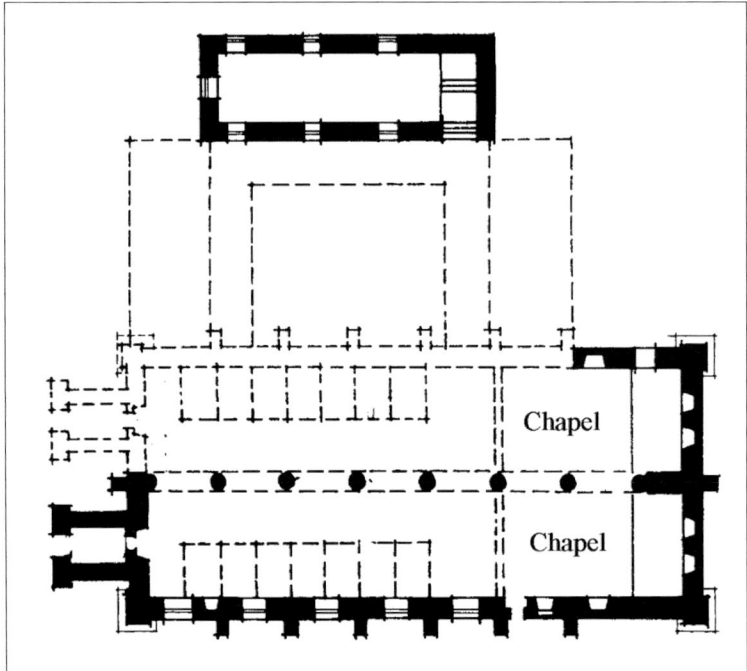

*Above:* Fig.3 Hospital of St Mary, Chichester, West Sussex, section (1229).

*Left:* Fig.4 Hospital of St Nicholas, Salisbury, Wiltshire (1214).

*Architectural Context*

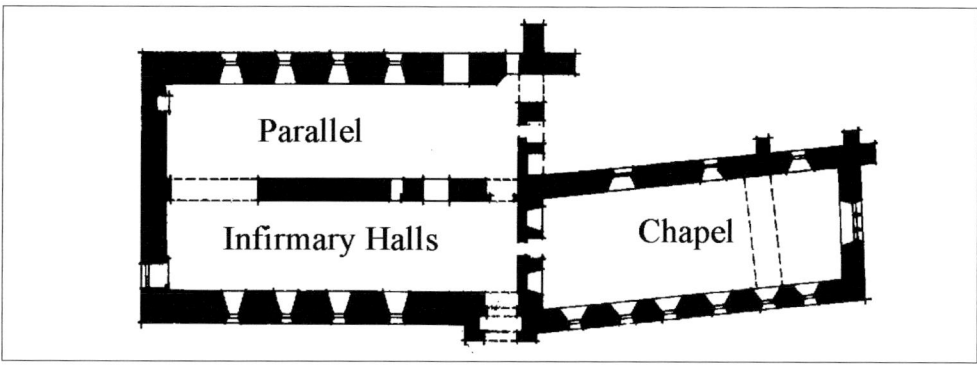

Fig.5 Hospital of St John the Baptist, Winchester, Hampshire (1290).

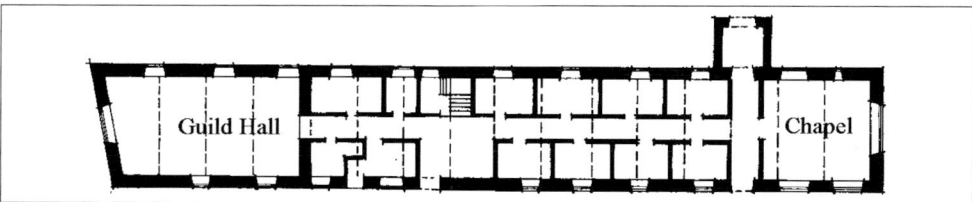

Fig.6 Hospital of St Saviour, Wells, Somerset (1424).

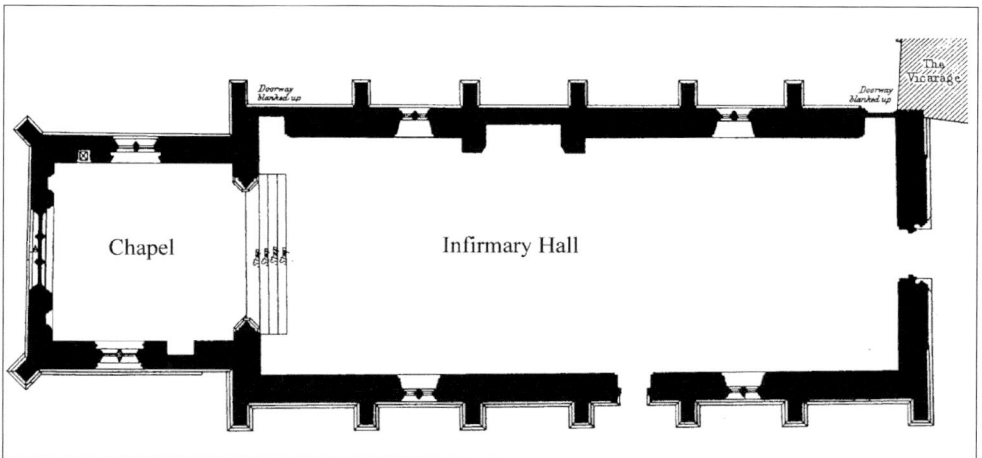

Fig.7 The Bedehouse, Higham Ferrers, Northamptonshire (1423).

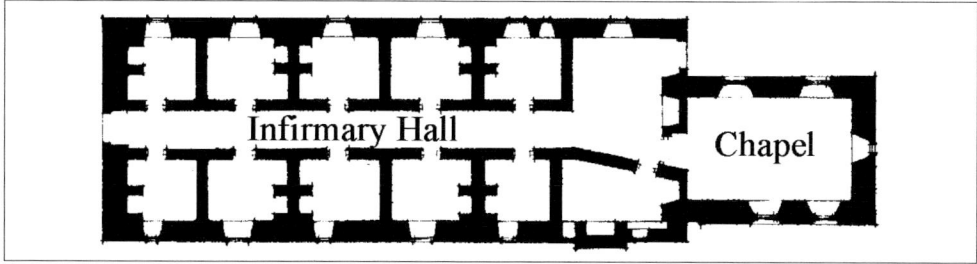

Fig.8 Hospital of St Mary Magdalene, Glastonbury, Somerset (thirteenth century).

*Almshouses: A Social and Architectural History*

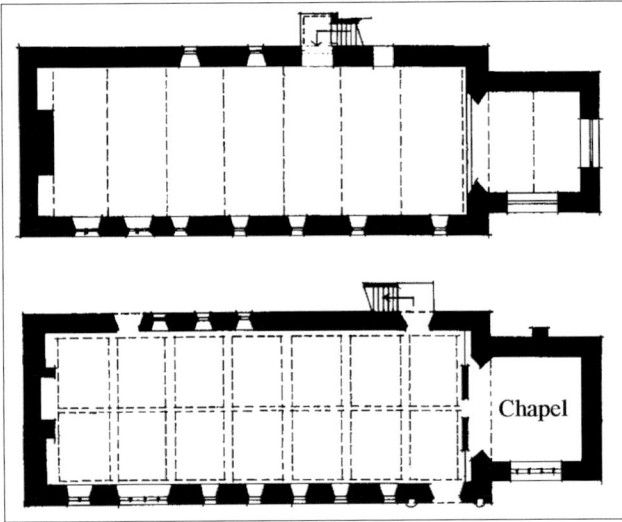

*Above:* Sint Jan's Hospitaal, Bruges, Belgium (1188).

*Left:* Fig.9 Hospital of St John the Baptist and John the Evangelist, Sherborne, Dorset (1437).

divided into eleven self-contained, two-storey dwellings with access from the central corridor. Unfortunately, only one half of this important almshouse remains.

Some hospital buildings like St Mary Magdalene, Glastonbury were converted to two or more storeys sometime after they had been built, and the Newarke – or Trinity – Hospital in Leicester had a further floor added during the seventeenth century. There are others which were constructed with two storeys from the very beginning, which were generally founded towards the end of the pre-Reformation period during the fifteenth and very early sixteenth centuries. The most conventional, bearing the greatest similarity to the original design, was the hospital of St John the Baptist and St John the Evangelist at Sherborne, Dorset (Fig.9). Founded in 1437 by the townspeople of Sherborne after a quarrel with Sherborne Abbey deprived them of the

*Architectural Context*

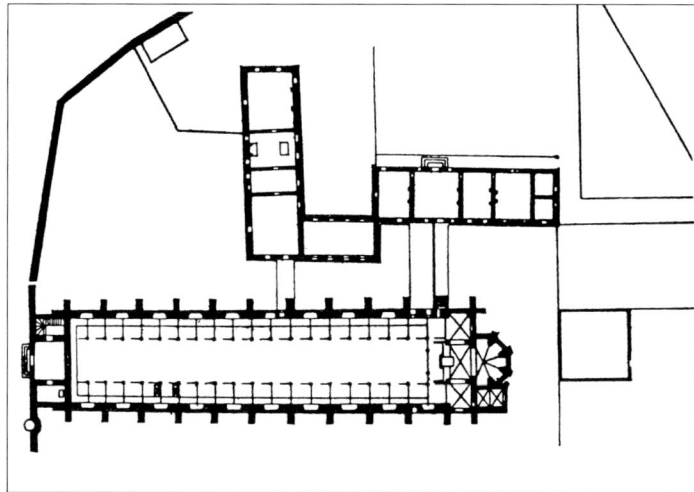

Fig.10 Tonnerre Hospital, France (1300).

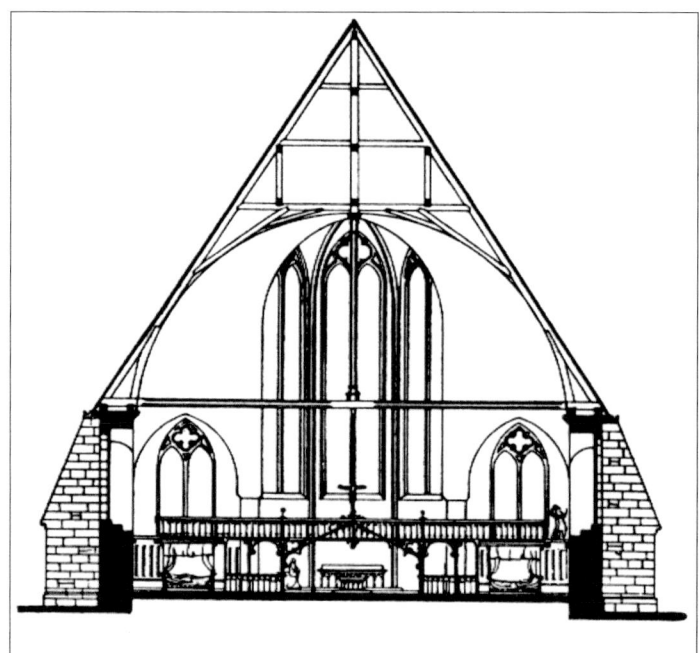

Fig.11 Tonnerre Hospial, France, section (1300).

use of the monastic hospital, the hospital housed six men on the ground floor and six women on the upper, the latter being reached via an external stair with both sexes having access to the diminutive chapel at the altar rail situated at the eastern end of each floor.

On the continent the Great Hall with chapel attached was also used extensively. Sint Jan's Hospitaal, Bruges, Belgium is a classic example. Commenced in 1188, the hospital was built to provide accommodation for pilgrims and wayfarers, but was expanded in the thirteenth century to cater for the sick and infirm.

France had, and still has, perhaps the finest range of medieval hospitals; those at Angiers, founded in 1153, and Tonnerre, from 1293 (Figs.10 and 11) being exceptional. But the most famous – or infamous – hospital in the whole of France was the *Hotel Dieu* in Paris, founded in 829 and situated

83

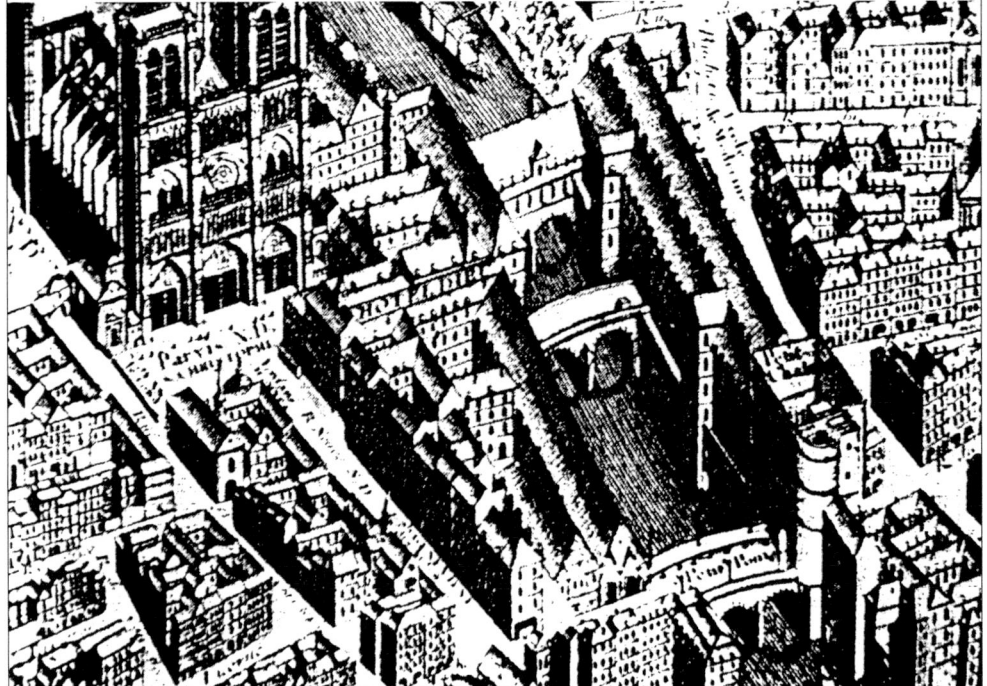

Fig.12 *Hotel Dieu*, Paris, France, woodcut (1260).

opposite the west front of Notre Dame Cathedral (Fig.12). The institution grew prodigiously from its foundation and by the seventeenth century had spread across the Seine on to the south bank. Nothing of the original buildings have survived, but we know from accounts and contemporary drawings that it had four long wards; three in a row, and the other one at right angles. The estimated number of beds at the end of the Middle Ages was 450, and the the estimated number of inmates was 1,280 – which makes three to each bed, without discrimination as to condition or illness. Its mortality figures were horrendous; 2,057 died in 1416, with 5,311 in 1418 and 5,729 in 1525.

The *Hotel Dieu* at Beaune in Burgundy, referred to briefly in Part One, was built between 1443 and 1452 and is unusual for its striking roof tiling.

## GREAT HALL WITH CHAPEL DETACHED

Lanfranc, in building his pre-1089 Hospital of St John at Canterbury, designed it for inmates of both sexes; thirty men and thirty women in a double hospital with a long hall, 150ft by 28ft wide, divided into two halves (Fig.13). At right angles to this hall, again divided into two but this time longitudinally, was the chapel. Each half had a separate altar in order that men and women could worship separately. Very little is left of the building other than its famous timber gatehouse, but from what remains it would appear that the chapel was accessed directly from the hall.

Founded in 1158, St Mary Magdalene, Winchester – again with detached chapel but this time separated from the hospital proper by the master's dwelling – provides perhaps the most complete plan of a lazer-house which has come down to us. The buildings remained until 1788, the plan being recorded in *Vetusta Monumenta* (Fig.14), showing a row of cells on the east–west axis, with the chapel on the south-eastern end. The side opposite to the church is thought to have been occupied by a common hall, although no details exist. The whole building was destroyed in

*Architectural Context*

*Right:* Gateway of St John's Hospital, Canterbury, Kent (1089).

*Below:* Fig.13 Hospital of St John, Canterbury, Kent (1089).

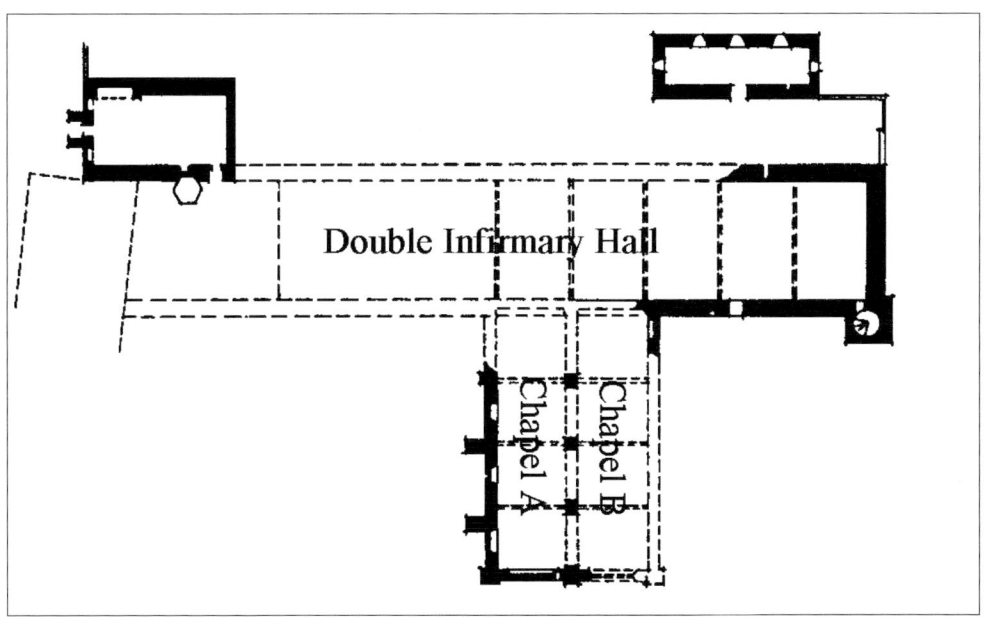

85

*Above:* Hospital of St John the Baptist, Northampton, Northamptonshire (1327).

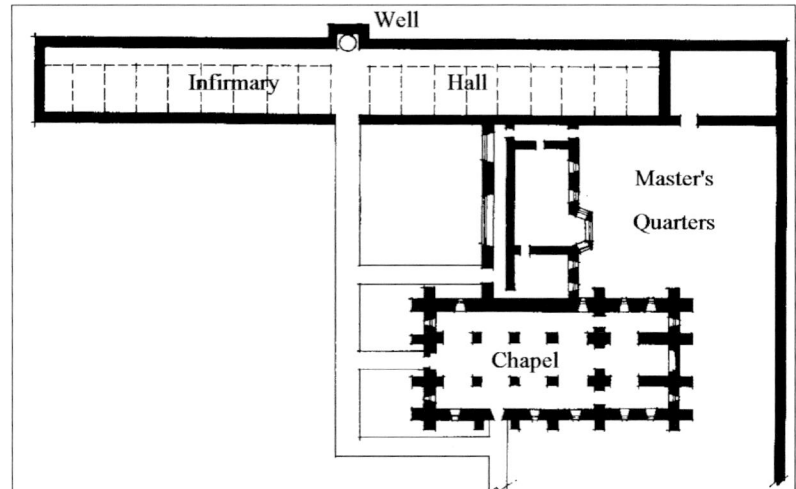

Fig.14 Hospital of St Mary Magdalene, Winchester, Hampshire (1158).

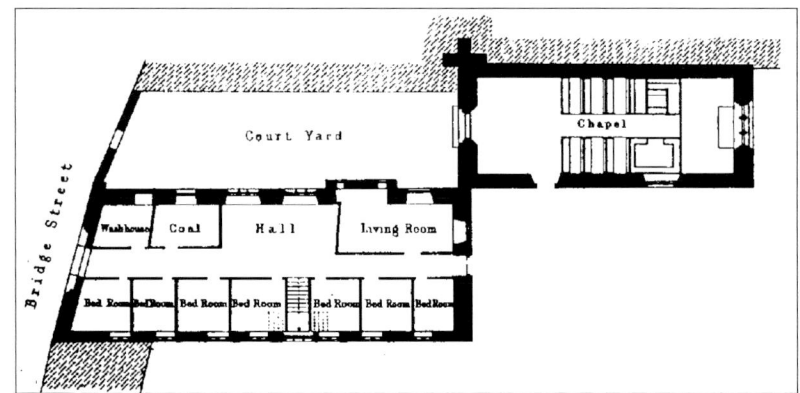

Fig.15 Hospital of St John the Baptist, Northampton, Northamptonshire (1327).

*Architectural Context*

Fig.16 Hospital of St John the Baptist, Northampton, Northamptonshire, elevation (1327).

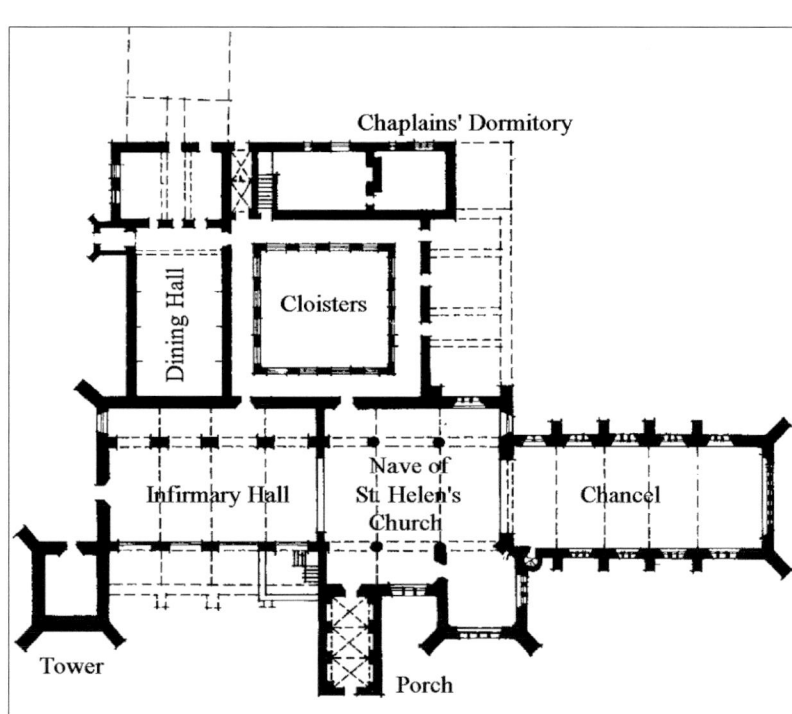

Fig.17 The Great Hospital, Norwich, Norfolk (1249).

the early nineteenth century, although the Norman doorway was moved to a building in Peter Street.

Finally, perhaps the most complete example of this type of hospital in existance is that dedicated to St John the Baptist in Northampton (Figs 15 and 16). However, there is some confusion as to the origins of this building. According to the historian Leland, the hospital was founded by William Sancte Clere, Archdeacon of Northampton, in 1327, although there is documentary evidence pointing to its existence 189 years earlier, as having been built by Archdeacon Walter to receive the infirm poor. The hospital had endowments throughout Northamptonshire and elsewhere, amounting in 1555 to £51 19s 6d, although nine years later, at the time of the suppression of chantries and hospitals, it was valued only at £25 6s 2d.

From the disposition of the hall relative to the chapel, it would seem that this was not the first such building. Rather, it appears that as is usual with early hospitals, the original hall was situated to the west of the chapel. However, as time passed, the old idea of a general hospital – accessible to all for short periods – gave way to permanent housing for almspeople, and in the fourteenth century the original hall was removed and replaced by a residential hall on adjoining land. Because of this, direct access was curtailed, and the pensioners thereafter had to use a side door.

The hospital was administered by a master who, unusually, did not necessarily have to be a clergyman, assisted by two co-brothers or chaplains. The master appointed the co-brothers, he himself being appointed by the Bishop of Lincoln. The two chaplains lived on the premises, in rooms above the first floor of the hospital building, whilst the master lived in a house nearby.

The gradual change in the purpose of hospitals from general care of the sick and infirm to permanent accommodation for the elderly was accelerated by the dissolution of religious houses under Henry VIII and Edward VI. As a result, many newly formed institutions had to use the local parish church for worship, as they now lacked their own chapels.

Before considering the transition from the medieval hospital to the almshouse, we must consider one further hospital which, although founded in the late Norman period, went through many vicissitudes during the ensuing 800 years. It now exhibits most, if not all, of the features discussed so far.

The Great Hospital of St Giles, Norwich was founded by Walter de Suffield, Bishop of Norwich in 1249 for a master, four chaplains, a deacon, sub-deacon and four sisters to minister to thirteen poor people and seven poor scholars. The original plan (Fig.17), different from any described so far, was monastic in concept, the main buildings surrounding a cloister-garth, some 50ft square. Unlike most monasteries, the conventual buildings were situated on the northern, rather than the southern side of the church. The infirmary hall, now only four bays long with aisles (although the southern one is missing), lies to the south of the cloisters and to the west of the diminutive parish church of St Helen, which was included in the precincts because the founding bishop demolished the original church building when the hospital was erected. The chancel to the east of St Helen's, although designated as the hospital chapel, was in fact used by the chaplains, whose dormitory lay to the north of the cloisters adjoining the master's lodgings. Both these buildings have since been replaced with almshouse dwellings. The in-pensioners' hall lies to the west of the cloisters, whilst the eastern side was occupied by the chapter house, long since gone except for its western wall.

The original hospital was dissolved by Henry VIII, but following a petition by the townspeople of Norwich, it was refounded in 1553 by Edward VI (1547-53) when its character was altered and further wards inserted at first floor level in the hall and the chancel, which were reached by external staircases. The residential accommodation was at this time separated from the parish church by solid walls, so access for worship had to be via the cloisters or through a long vaulted porch from the road. Since its second foundation, several groups of cottages have been added and the hospital now supports over 200 almspeople, both in- and out-pensioners.

## CRUCIFORM LAYOUT

England is by no means the only country where the erection of hospitals and almshouses has been undertaken.

As mentioned in Part One, the main impetus for the building of British monastic institutions came after the Norman Conquest. For centuries before that, many conventual establishments, both large and small, had been founded abroad; firstly throughout Eastern Europe following the beginnings of monasticism in the more remote corners of the Holy Land, and later spreading to Western Europe, where particularly the Rules of the Augustinian and Cistercian Orders were codified.

*Architectural Context*

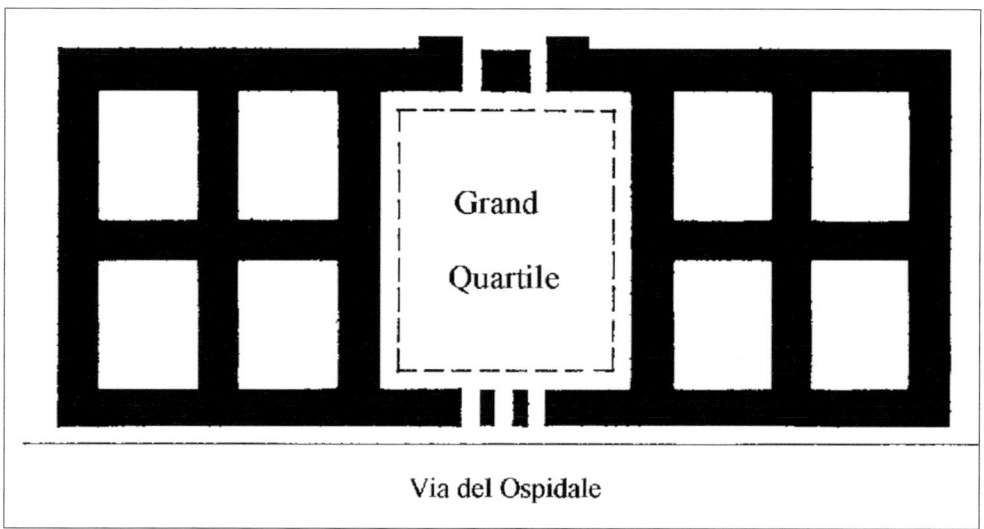

*Above:* Fig. 18
*Ospidale Maggiore*, Milan, Italy (1546).

*Right:* Fig. 19
Hospital of Santa Cruz, Toledo, Spain (1540).

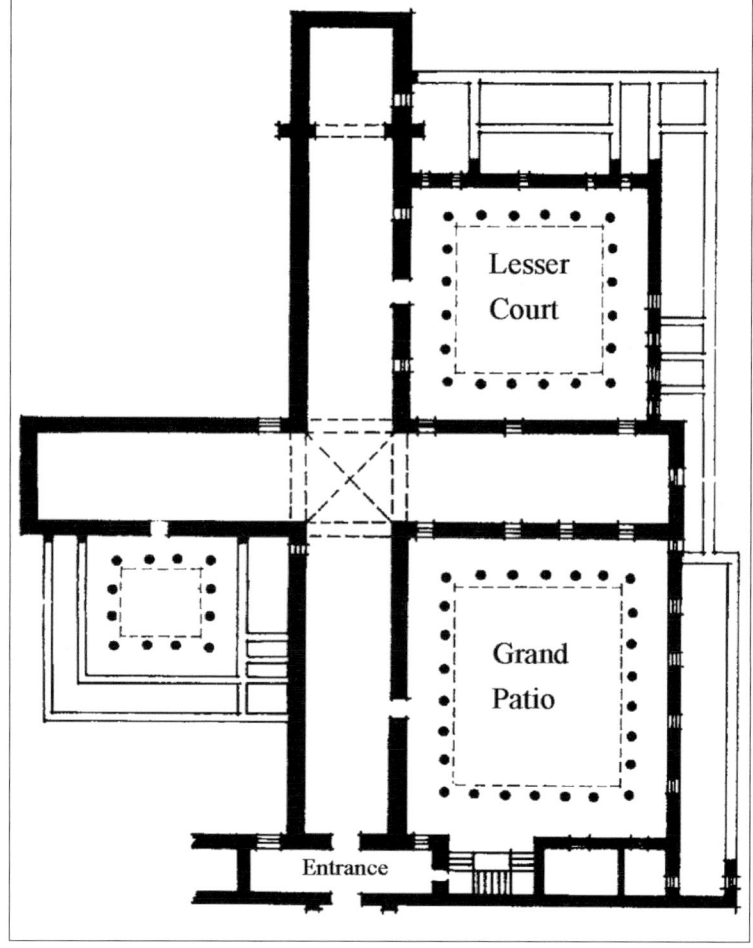

*Almshouses: A Social and Architectural History*

Hospital Royale, Grenada, Spain (1504).

The Savoy Hospital, London (1519).

As in England, the designs of the earliest hospitals on the Continent were based upon monastic models, but in Italy particularly, with its dominance by the Papal See, the increasing sizes of these establishments in the sixteenth centuries forced a review of administrative practices and a complete rethink of their designs. From this emerged the Cruciform and later the Courtyard layout.

Before the sixteenth century, the two most important Italian hospitals were situated in Florence and Sienna. In 1546 the architect Filarate, in addition to being the sculptor responsible for the bronze gates of St Peter's in Rome, was asked to design a hospital to bring together under one roof the numerous charities which existed at the time in Milan. He studied all the contemporary buildings of the type, and his *Ospidale Maggiore* successfully resolved the differing secular and religious needs of charitable institutions by providing a range of buildings around a series of interconnected courtyards (Fig.18).

Architectural Context

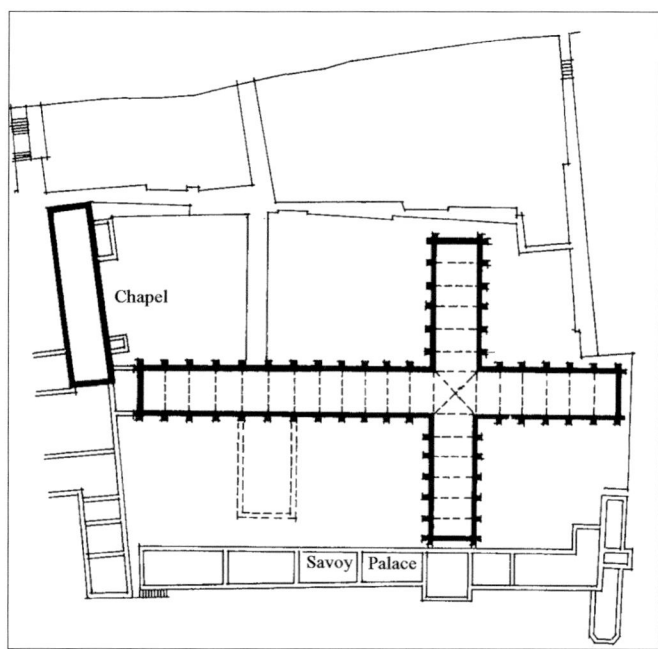

Fig.20 The Savoy Hospital, London (1519).

This design was widely used throughout Italy and Spain; at the Hospital of Santo Spirito in Sassio in Rome, and at Santiago de Compostela (1499), Granada (1504), Tavera, Toledo (1540) and Santa Cruz, Toledo (1501) in Spain. The plan of the Hospital of Santa Cruz at Toledo, designed by Enrique Egan and reproduced in Fig.19, is typical of the smaller-than-average hospital based upon the cruciform plan, a derivation of the original infirmary hall. This plan form allowed four large wards to be conjoined at the crossing where the altar, visible to all, was provided, generally under a tower. Originally four cloister courts were planned – one at each corner, with conjoined wards forming two of the four sides of each – but in the event only two were built.

Only one hospital of this type is known to have been erected in England; that endowed by Henry VII (1485-1509) in 1503, on the north bank of the Thames at The Savoy (Fig.20). The original building on the site was the Savoy Palace, which had been totally destroyed by a rampaging mob in 1381. Before commissioning the building of this hospital, the king made extensive enquiries into contemporary practices concerning the design and running of hospitals abroad, as can be ascertained from a remarkable document in the Bodleian Library at Oxford, which gives a long and detailed account – specially commissioned by the king – of the hospital in Florence by its master, Francis Portinary. The king superintended the building's design:

> We have begoune to erecte, buylde and establisshe a commune Hospital ... and the same we intend with Godd's grace to finish, after the maner, fourme and fashion of a plat which is devised for the same, and signed with our hande.

The Savoy Hospital was completed in 1519 when a master and four chaplains were appointed and beds for one hundred poor people were provided. Apparently no cloisters as such were built, although a cemetery was provided to the north-west, between the hospital buildings and the church of St Mary le Savoy, which still exists. The hospital was suppressed by Henry's son Edward VI in 1537, only to be reinstated by Queen Mary, although by the time of her death the mastership had become a sinecure. The hospital was demolished in 1558, but the chapel remains in Savoy Street off the Strand.

Bond/Bablake Hospital, Coventry, West Midlands (1507).

## THE COURTYARD DESIGN

The true cruciform hospital was large and extravagant in the use of land, with each of the four cloisters having buildings on two adjacent sides only, and the other two open to view. It did not take long, however, for someone to realise that by moving the four bays around one cloister garth, much less land was needed. The building was architecturally more satisfying, there was much more privacy for the occupants, and the whole undertaking was easier to manage. As a result, the courtyard form was adopted as the most common type of design for almshouses during the next 500 years or so, with generally two variations on the theme; some were totally enclosed with pedestrian access only, and others open on one side, with a screen wall with gate and railings to restrict vehicular access. The courtyard design also became popular in many kinds of religious and educational establishments, notably at the colleges of Oxford and Cambridge, and, just as the infirmary hall plan had dominated the early medieval period, so the courtyard design dominated the post-Reformation years and continued to do so, with modifications, until Victorian times.

All manner of charities can trace their origins back to early monasticism; many educational establishments, schools, colleges and universities, and of course almshouse charities themselves. However, the sixteenth century was a particularly fruitful period for such foundations. It was during this time, when the medieval craft guilds were at their most influential, that many hospitals were founded, most of them for the care of the aged, but increasingly, as the century bore on, also as charity schools for the education of the children of the poor. Some of these have survived as the great public schools of today.

To start with, many of these newly formed hospitals provided for both the young and the old; in many cases the hospitals were founded by wealthy guild masters to provide, on the one hand, for members in their declining years, and on the other for the sons and daughters of less fortunate guildsmen, feeding, clothing, housing them and educating them for a life similar to that of their parents. But the establishments became more specialised in later centuries, either by taking on the whole function of an almshouse and dropping the educational role or vice versa.

A classic example of the latter is Christ's Hospital, London, which was originally founded during the reign of Edward VI by Bishop Ridley, to provide not just education, but complete

*Architectural Context*

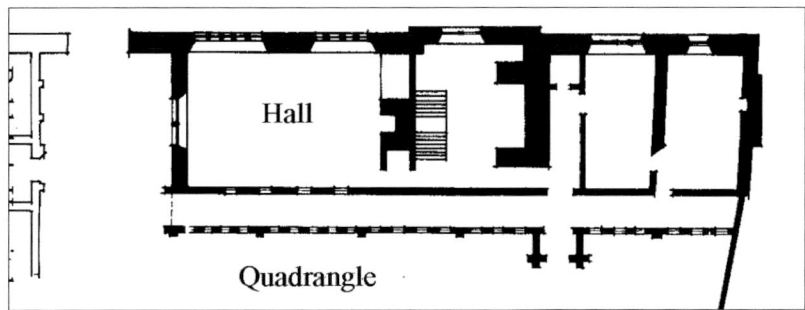

Fig.21 Bond's Hospital, Coventry, West Midlands (1507).

maintenance for destitute children and infants, as well as out-relief for the aged. The hospital was supported entirely by the citizens of London and by a royal grant. Edward actually signed its charter on his death bed in 1552. However, very early on in its history it ceased to cater for the elderly altogether, concentrating instead on education, and went on to become one of the most prestigious schools in the country.

Another, less well-known example is Bond's or Bablake's Hospital in Coventry, founded in 1507 by Thomas Bond, sometime Mayor of Coventry, for the care and maintenance of ten poor men of the Trinity and Corpus Christi Guilds. Some fifty years later, another institution was founded alongside by the Corporation for the maintenance and instruction of poor boys. The two charities lived happily side by side into the twentieth century, the old hospital being known as Bablake's and the new one as Bond's. The two hospital buildings form the north and east sides of a small quadrangle (Fig.21). The west side is occupied by a later master's house, and the south by the churchyard of the original guild's church, now the parish church of St John. Incidentally, this was where, in 1647, several hundred prisoners from the defeated Scottish army of the Duke of Hamilton were billeted. The citizens of the town boycotted the prisoners, and it is from this episode that the expression 'sent to Coventry' is supposed to have originated.

Many of these new institutions adopted the new collegiate or courtyard form of development. Buildings were erected on all four sides of a rectangular open space, with access for pedestrians only through archways at ground floor level. These were usually in the centre of each range, although very occasionally they were provided at the corners.

The open space varied in size from extremely; small courts around which between eight and twelve dwellings were situated, to large imposing compositions of up to a hundred or more almshouses with master's lodgings, church or chapel, communal hall and sometimes an audit or committee room where the trustees conducted the formal business of the charity. Perhaps the best example of a small-to-medium-sized almshouse of this type is that at Ewelme, a few miles to the south-west of Oxford.

William de la Pole, sometime Earl of Suffolk, together with his wife Alice – a granddaughter, incidentally, of Geoffrey Chaucer – founded this hospital together with the adjoining free school in 1437. King Henry VI (1421-71) granted the couple a charter for the purpose:

> ... that they or either of them should found an hospital at their manor at Ewelme, in the county of Oxford and settle a sufficient endowment not exceeding two hundred marks for the maintenance of two chaplains and thirteen poor men to be incorporated and to have a common seal.

And further:

> ... that the above number of persons should be ever maintained in it one of the chaplains of the Almshouse, who shall govern it and shall administer the affairs thereof.

93

Almshouses: A Social and Architectural History

Ewelme Hospital, Ewelme, Oxfordshire (1437).

William de la Pole, who by this time had been elevated to a dukedom, made final provision for the endowment of the charity in his will dated 1448. This was only just in time, however, since he fell out of favour with the king and was beheaded one year later. Alice continued to build the almshouses under the terms of her husband's will, and lived to a great age. She died in 1475 and was buried in the parish church which adjoins and connects with her almshouses.

Upon the attainder of the Earl of Lincoln, one of William's descendants, during the reign of Henry VIII, the Suffolk estates were forfeit to the Crown, and the manor of Ewelme became a royal manor. Early in the reign of James I (1603-1625), the rectory and the canonry of Christ Church was vested in the Professorship of Divinity at Oxford, and in 1617 the mastership of the hospital went to the Regius Professorship of Physic at the same university. Both appointments continue to this day.

Fig.22 shows a plan of the entire complex – church, almshouses and school. The church is situated upon the higher ground with its tower dominating the village. Further down the slope, to the west end of the church and connected to it by a passage and a short flight of steps, lie the homes of the almsfolk, occupying four sides of a quadrangle, approximately 50ft square, each dwelling consisting of a sitting-room on the ground floor with a bedroom above. A covered ambulatory or cloister extends all round the quadrangle in front of the dwellings. The steeply pitched shingle roof, which was once thatched, sweeps down over the cloisters, with small dormer windows obtruding into the roofscape, providing illumination to the tiny bedrooms. In the centre of each side of the ambulatory, a clerestoried and gabled entrance gives access to the cloister-garth, in the centre of which stands an ancient pump, from which the almsfolk formerly drew their water. The external walls of the dwellings are of stone to match the church, although the frontages to the courtyard are of brick, thought by some historians to be one of the first uses of this material for domestic buildings in the country. The oak uprights and herringbone brick spandrels are a distinctive and characteristic feature of this type of construction in Oxfordshire. Over the west side of the courtyard and, owing to the rapid fall of the land down from west to east, almost at the same level as the church, are the audit and muniment rooms and a suite of accommodation originally provided for the schoolmaster. These were used in times gone by for the administration of the hospital's affairs, but have since been converted for the use of the almsfolk. At the bottom of the slope is situated the free grammar school, separated from the hospital by the under-schoolmaster's house and an entrance porch, a picturesque brick-built structure of great charm.

Architectural Context

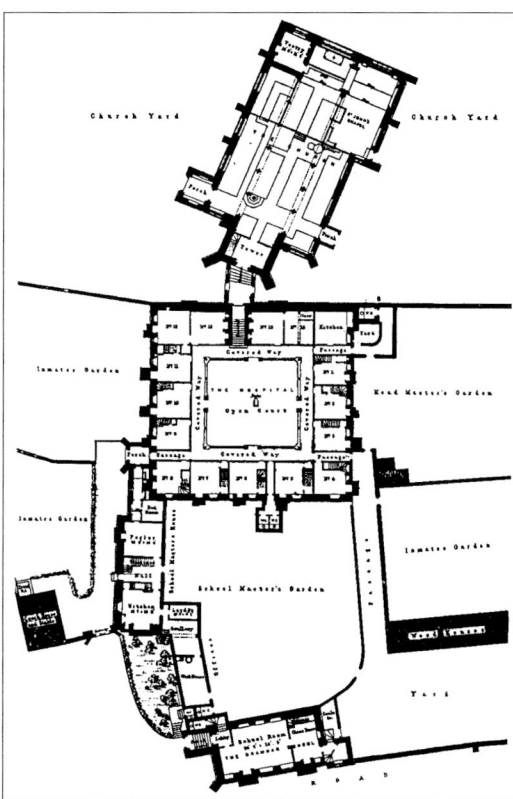

Fig.22  Ewelme Hospital, Ewelme, Oxfordshire (1437).

The whole composition forms a most interesting example of medieval domestic architecture, combining as it does provision for the public offices and ministrations of the church, the comfort of a home for the aged and needy, and a place of instruction for the village children.

Another, much larger collegiate-type almshouse, St Cross Hospital, alluded to earlier, was established in 1136 near Winchester by Henry de Blois, Bishop of Winchester and brother to King Stephen. In those days its plan form would have been that of the conventional infirmary block, with presumably the usual chapel attached.

Thirteen 'impotent poor men' were to be maintained permanently in the hospital and provided with lodging, suitable raiment and sufficient food. This was stipulated to be a daily allowance of a loaf of bread 3lb 4oz in weight, a gallon and a half of small beer, together with a pottage composed of milk and bread called mortrel and wastel, and a dish of flesh or fish according to the day of the week and the season, with further supplies for supper.

In addition to the thirteen occupants, provision was made for a hundred other poor men 'of good conduct of the more indigent classes', to be maintained as out-pensioners, each receiving daily a loaf of bread and three quarts of small beer. A special building was erected for this purpose in the outer curia, called the 'hundred mennes hall', much of which remains to this day.

There was in addition a foundation for a master, a steward, four chaplains, thirteen clerks, seven choristers, who were to be educated in the hospital, and sundry servants. The comptrollers or administrators of the charity, appointed by Henry de Blois, were the Hospitallers of St John of Jerusalem, the Knights Hospitallers, who had a Preceptory at Baddesly near Lymington in Hampshire. The appointment of the prior or master was vested in the Bishop of Winchester and the rents and other endowments, among which were several parish churches in Hampshire and elsewhere, were to be enjoyed by the hospital forever.

*Almshouses: A Social and Architectural History*

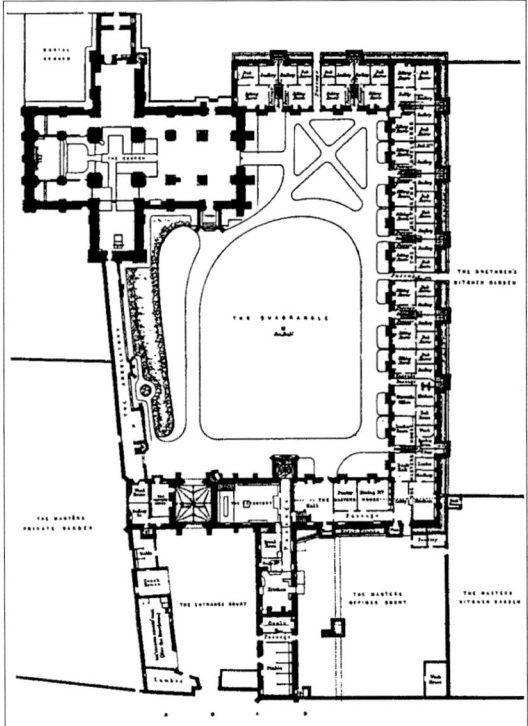

Fig.23 St Cross Hospital, Winchester, Hampshire (1136).

After Henry de Blois had died, a series of disputes concerning the administration of the hospital broke out between his successor as Bishop of Winchester, Richard de Toclyve, and the Knights Hospitaller, which resulted in the intervention of King Henry II (1154-89), who finally decreed that the hospital should be under the total control of the bishop and his successors. In 1185 Bishop Toclyve added a further hundred out-pensioners, but the income was insufficient to provide all the necessary alms and there followed a century where funds were perverted from their original purposes and various appointments were misapplied. In 1372 the government of the charity fell into the hands of William of Wykeham, that prolific founder of educational establishments who, with great difficulty, recovered many of the institution's possessions, repaired the buildings and restored the system to its original order. He installed John de Campden as master, whose brass still exists in the floor of the church.

William Wykeham's immediate successor was Cardinal Beaufort, younger brother of Henry IV (1399-1413), who was responsible for the rebuilding and enlarging of the hospital and for the endowment of a second charity within its precincts, the House of Noble Poverty, an almshouse for elderly gentlemen. This second institution consisted of two priests, thirty-five brethren and three sisters, all under the master of the hospital and his successors. Cardinal Beaufort unfortunately died before all his plans could be fully commissioned and it was left to his successor, William of Wayneflete, to procure the new charter from King Henry VI and complete the works. Later, during the Wars of the Roses, the endowment of the second charity was much reduced, so much so that the number of inmates had to be reduced to one chaplain and two brethren only.

The hospital was fortunate to escape the depredations of Henry VIII, but by the late seventeenth century the regulations for its government had been lost and the establishment was administered by custom only. Under the mastership of Revd Dr Abraham Markland a new code was drawn up called the *Consuetudinarium*, which, with some modifications, continues to this day to be the governing instrument. Under its provisions, in addition to the inmates – then consisting of the master, one chaplain, one steward and thirteen brethren, twenty-eight women and twelve men – all

*1* St Nicholas' Hospital chapel, Harbledown, Kent, 1084.

*2* Hospital of St Mary B.V., Canterbury, Kent, 1225.

3   *Above:* Merchant Venturers' Hospital, York, North Yorkshire, 1280.

4   *Opposite:* St Edmund's Hospital chapel, Gateshead, Tyne and Wear, 1247.

5   Trinity Hospital (the Newark), Leicester, Leicestershire, 1351.

6   The Bedehouse, Higham Ferrers, Leicestershire, 1423.

7   Hospital of St John the Baptist and St John the Evangelist, Sherborne, Dorset, 1437.

8  St Leonard's Hospital, Tickhill, South Yorkshire, 1470.

9  Forde's Hospital, Coventry, West Midlands, 1529.

10   *Above:* Long Alley Almshouses, Abingdon, Oxfordshire, 1553.

11   *Left:* Lord Leycester's Hospital, Warwick, Warwickshire, 1571.

12  Lord Leycester's Hospital, Warwick, Warwickshire, 1571.

13    Beamsley Hospital, Craven, North Yorkshire, 1593.

14    *Opposite above:* Browne's Hospital interior, Stamford, Lincolnshire, 1610.

15    *Opposite below:* Moretonhampstead Almshouses, Moretonhampstead, Devon, 1639.

16  Sir William Turner's Hospital, Kirkleatham, Cleveland, 1676.

17  Holy Jesus Hospital, Newcastle-on-Tyne, Tyne and Wear, 1682.

18 *Left:* Shireburn Almshouses, Stydd-under-Langridge, Lancashire, 1728.

19 *Below:* Shireburn Hospital, Hurst Green, Lancashire, 1706.

20  *Above:* Tyne Master Mariners' Asylum, Tynemouth, Tyne and Wear, 1836.

21  *Below:* Aberford Almshouses, Aberford, West Yorkshire, 1844.

22  *Left:* Sir Francis Crossley's Almshouses, Halifax, West Yorkshire, 1855.

23  *Below:* Roebuck Memorial Homes, Huddersfield, West Yorkshire, 1928.

out-pensioners were to occupy the 'hundred mennes hall'. There were in addition two other brethren termed 'reversioners', who were to succeed on a death or vacancy. The master was to have authority over all persons belonging to the hospital and was empowered to receive all revenues, from which he was to defray expenses and keep the buildings, including the church, in good repair. He was to keep the common seal of the hospital, which was to be used on all leases and conveyances; he would appoint the steward and chaplain; and in the event of any death or vacancy among the brethren or any in the 'hundred mennes hall', he would appoint a replacement. Further, on the occurrence of any misdemeanour he was to have power to punish or even expel the offender. The brethren were, on their admission, to take an oath of obedience to the master and the ordinances of the hospital, and were required to be present at prayers twice each day. The steward was empowered to deputise for the master when he was away, and the chaplain was, in addition to his clerical duties in the hospital, required to visit the sick in the adjoining parish.

The forty out-pensioners were allotted meat or soup with bread and a small allowance of money weekly. An allowance of bread and beer was also made to give alms at the gate to such poor persons as may claim the dole. There were also to be special doles six times during the year: on Christmas Eve, Good Friday, 3 May (the anniversary of the foundation of the hospital), 10 August (the anniversary of the founder's death) and the Eve of All Saints. On these days, a distribution of small loaves was to be made to all applicants, a custom which still remains to this day. The *Consuetudinarium* was to be read publicly on 3 May every year. The general plan of the Hospital is shown in Fig.23.

Generally, the plan consists of two courtyards, connected by a monumental gatehouse. The smaller, entrance court, accessed from the road, is on the north side of the hospital. On the eastern side lies the 'hundred mennes hall', now converted to other uses, and some modern buildings; to the west lie the kitchen and domestic quarters. On the fourth, southern side, is the noble gatehouse erected by Cardinal Beaufort, with its four-centred moulded archway with a coat of arms in each spandrel; that of the Crown to the right and that of the founder to the left. In a niche over the doorway stands an effigy of Cardinal Beaufort himself. Adjoining the gatehouse, between it and the kitchen, the remainder of the fourth side of the court has two of the windows of the hall, arch-headed with tracery and transom. The ceiling of the gatehouse is groined, and on the left of the entrance lies the porter's lodge.

The larger, inner court is magnificent. On the northern side is the gatehouse, the octagonal stair turret of which breaks up its symmetry. Adjoining this lies the hall and the master's residence. The approach to the hall externally is via a flight of stairs and through a groined porch. On the eastern side lies a covered way connecting the gatehouse with the north entrance to the church. Over this is situated the hospital infirmary, with a window from which one can see the church altar.

The western side of the main court is occupied by the brethren's dwellings, and until 1789 these extended round the south side, abutting the church. Each dwelling consists of sitting-room, bedroom, scullery and a latrine for each inmate, which discharged into a sluice on the western side of the range from the gabled projection. On this western side also lies the brethren's garden.

The brethren's dwellings on the courtyard side are extremely simple in design, consisting only of square-headed two-light windows and low, four-centred arched doorways, together with a series of projecting chimney stacks, rather like those at Vicars' Close, Wells.

To quote an unknown visitor who, in the mid-nineteenth century, was describing the locale in which the hospital is situated:

> No one can pass its threshold without feeling himself landed, as it were, in another age. The ancient features of the building, the noble gateway, the quadrangle, the common refectory, the cloisters and, rising above all, the lofty and massive pile of the venerable church; the uniform garb and reverend mien of the aged brethren, the common provision for their declining years; the dole at the gatehouse, all lead back our thoughts to days when men gave their best to God's honour, and looked on what was done to his poor as done to Himself and were as lavish of architectural beauty on what modern

Spence's Hospital, Carleton-in Craven, North Yorkshire (1698).

habits might deem a receptacle for beggars, as on the noblest of royal palaces. It seems a place where no worldly thought, no pride or passion, or irreverence could enter; a spot where as a modern writer has beautifully expressed it, 'a good man, might he make his choice, would wish to die'.

The most comprehensive composite courtyard layout, however, is that of the Charterhouse in London, again referred to in Part One. This comprises three major courtyards: Washhouse Court, Master's Court and Chapel Court, all totally enclosed, together with the outer court which gives access onto Charterhouse Square (Fig.24).

In size as well as location, the tiny Spence's Hospital at Carleton-in-Craven, on the southern fringes of the Yorkshire Dales, contrasts sharply with that of St Cross. Founded in 1698 by Ferrand Spence, with additional endowment in 1872 by Agnes Vardill Niven, this almshouse must be among the smallest courtyard developments in the country, particularly for one with dwellings on two floors with balcony access.

Originally the hospital consisted of twelve single-room dwellings with a boardroom, built on three sides of a courtyard with an open access gallery to the first floor, reached by two flights of steps, one on each side of the entrance gateway. Each dwelling's front door opens on to the court or gallery, with the windows facing out to views of the north, east and south. The remaining western side of the court consists of a fine stone gateway with ball finials and wrought-iron gates (Fig.25). In 1898 it was proposed to pull the buildings down and rebuild it as six separate dwellings, but this proposal was abandoned, and a few years later four water closets were installed, accessible from the covered passage downstairs and from the gallery on the first floor. In 1958 considerable improvements were carried out. The timbers of the gallery were replaced, and new doors and windows and modern sinks were installed together with communal bathrooms, although the twelve separate rooms were retained.

Finally, in 1974 the whole hospital was refurbished to provide separate, self-contained dwellings consisting of a bed–sittingroom, kitchen and bathroom. The number of units was necessarily reduced to eight, although a warden's flat was provided by converting the boardroom. Apart from essential repairs, the exterior was hardly touched; each flat was provided with an extra window

*Architectural Context*

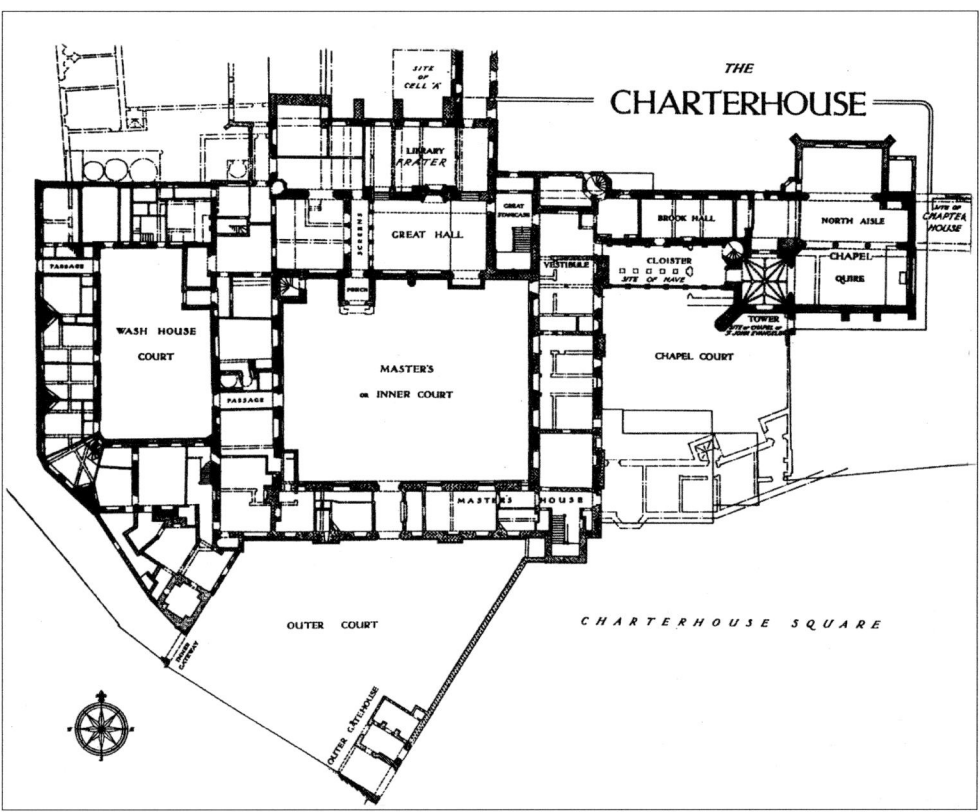

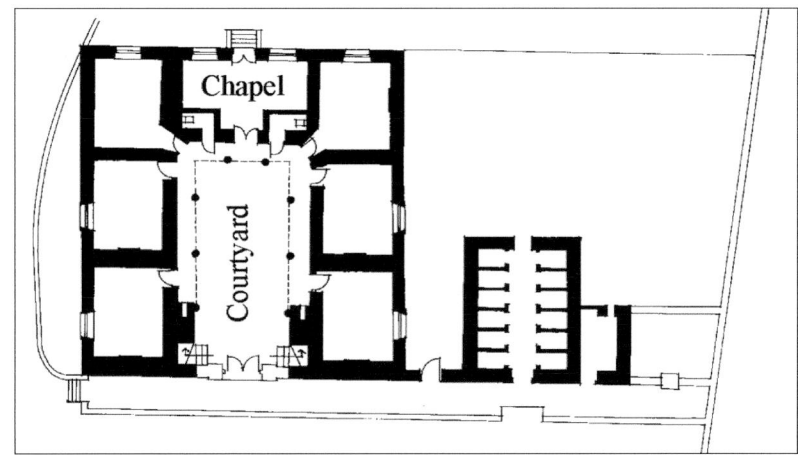

*Above:* Fig.24 The Charterhouse, London (1611).

*Right:* Fig.25 Spence's Hospital, Carleton-in-Craven, North Yorkshire (1698).

overlooking the courtyard to give interest value, and a small building to house the central heating boiler was tucked away in a corner. All the fine stone chimney-stacks were retained, although only two flues are actually used. As an historic almshouse, it is a little gem. It is a little unfortunate, however, that the trustees have decided to dispense with the name 'Hospital', a venerable appellation, and have renamed the building Spence's Court.

This section on courtyard design cannot be concluded without mention of two further almshouses of early foundation, both of national importance.

*Almshouses: A Social and Architectural History*

Browne's Hospital, Stamford, Lincolnshire (1493).

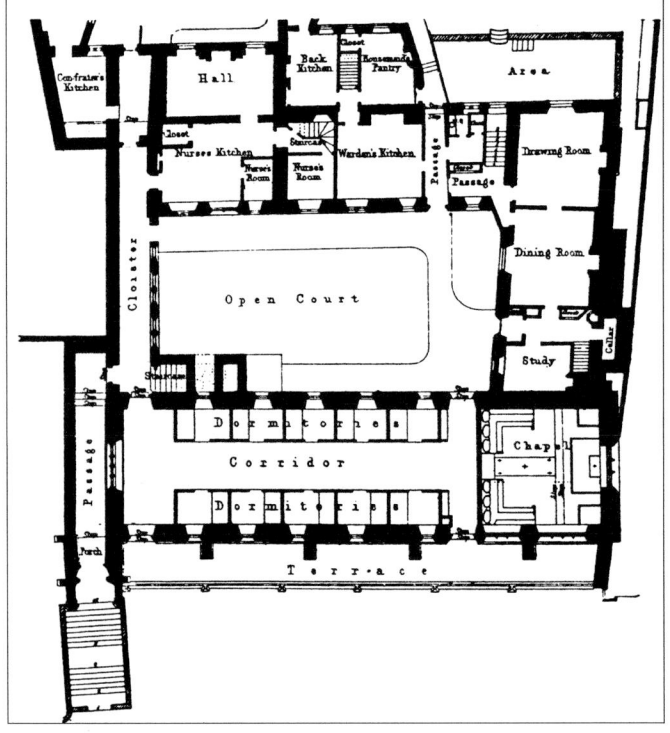

Fig. 26 Browne's Hospital, Stamford, Lincolnshire (1493).

*Architectural Context*

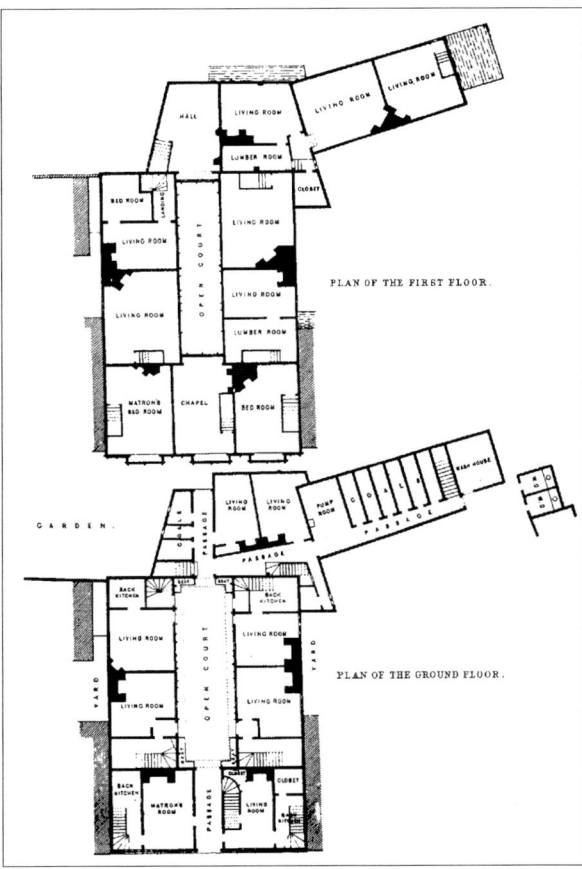

Fig.27 Forde's Hospital, Coventry, West Midlands (1529).

Browne's Hospital in Stamford, Lincolnshire, was founded in 1493, although it was refounded in 1610 when it consisted of a warden, confrater, ten poor men and two poor women 'advancing in age'. The hospital building proper, forming the south side of the courtyard, was of stone with handsome tower over, and of medieval style with cubicles against the outside walls and a chapel at the eastern end. The warden's accommodation and nurses' kitchen formed a further two sides to the court, with the western end being enclosed by cloisters (Fig.26). Sadly, the buildings on the northern side have been replaced with more modern dwellings and the symmetry of the courtyard has suffered somewhat. However, the main building remains, and is now used as a museum devoted to the history of almshouses.

Forde's delightful little hospital in the centre of Coventry was founded in 1529 and is one of the few half-timbered groups in the country. Originally, the foundation was for five poor men and one woman, the original inscription on the wall declaring:

> May the 4th anno 1529, Mr William Fourd of this city, Merchant of the Staple, founded this almes-house for five men and one woman, and gave to each of them fivepence a week for their maintenance; afterwards Mr William Pisford, his executor, gave other lands, and appointed six men and their wives to be placed therein, and each couple to have seven pence halfpenny a week, and the nurse the same. And in the room of the sixth poor man and his wife, there shall be one honest good woman of the said city taken into the Bedehouse, which shall be about the age of forty, or betwix forty and fifty, to be the keeper of the said five poor men and their wives as need shall require, to see them clean kept in their persons and houses and for dressing their meat, washing of them, and ministering all things necessary to them.

*Almshouses: A Social and Architectural History*

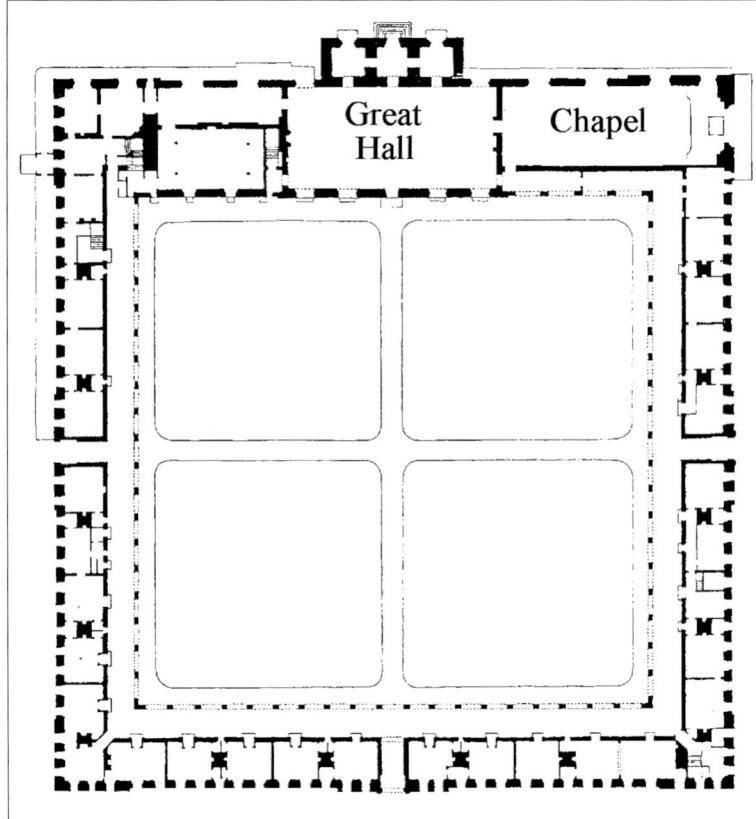

*Left:* Fig.28 Kilmainham Hospital, Dublin, Republic of Ireland (1680).

*Below:* Fig.29 Lord Leycester's Hospital, Warwick, Warwickshire (1571).

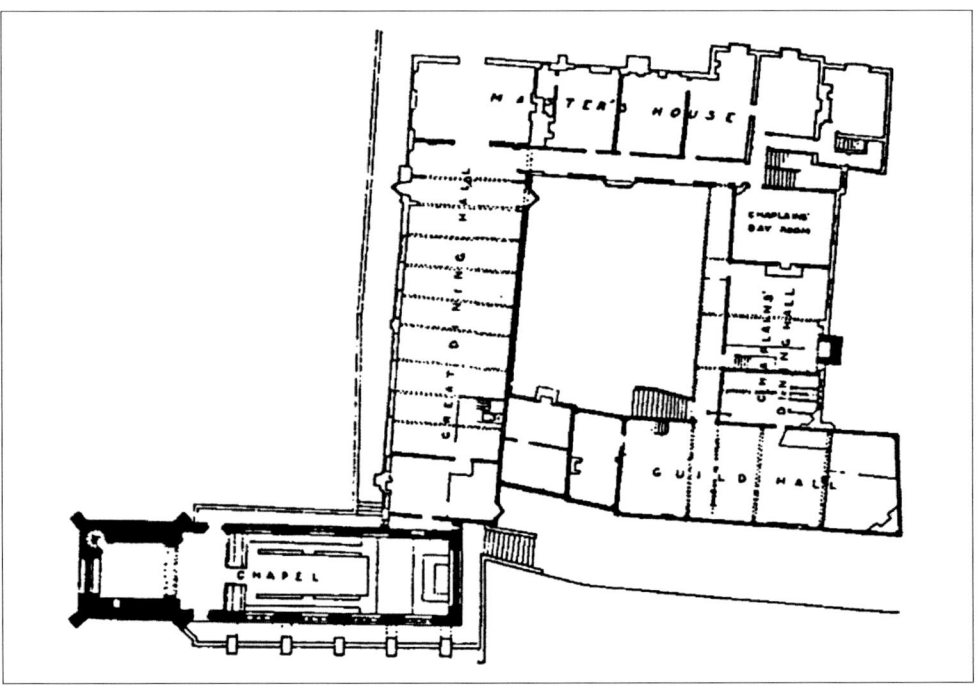

*Architectural Context*

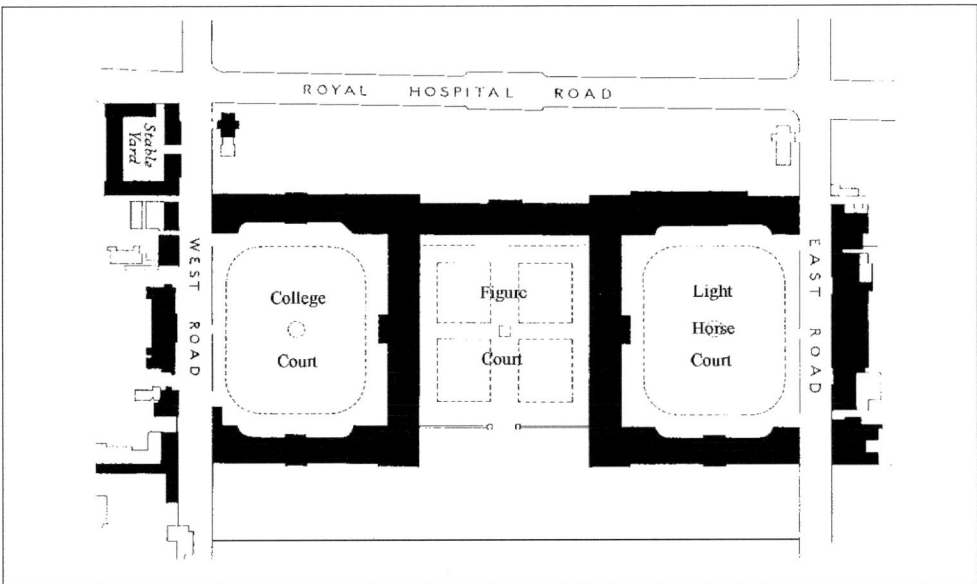

Fig.30 The Royal Hospital, Chelsea, London (1692).

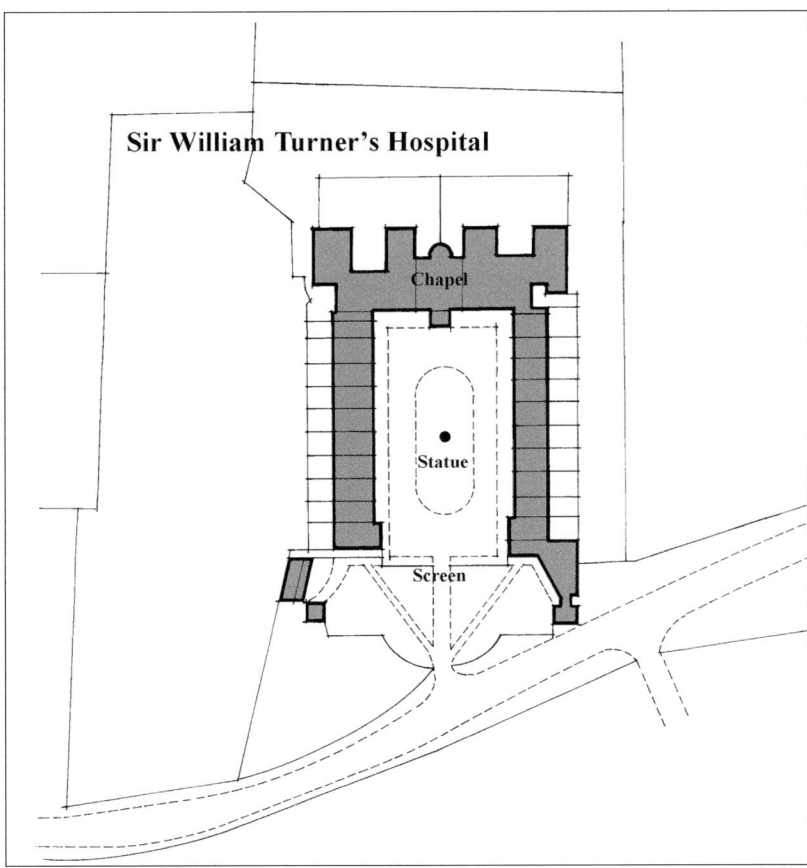

Fig.31
Sir William
Turner's Hospital,
Kirkleatham,
Cleveland (1676).

*Almshouses: A Social and Architectural History*

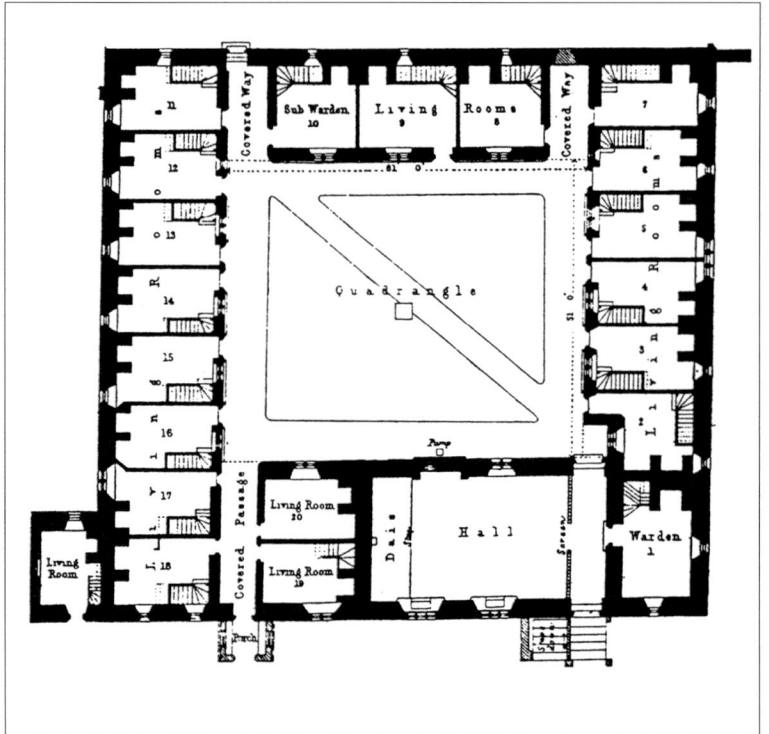

Fig.32
Cobham College,
Cobham, Kent (1598).

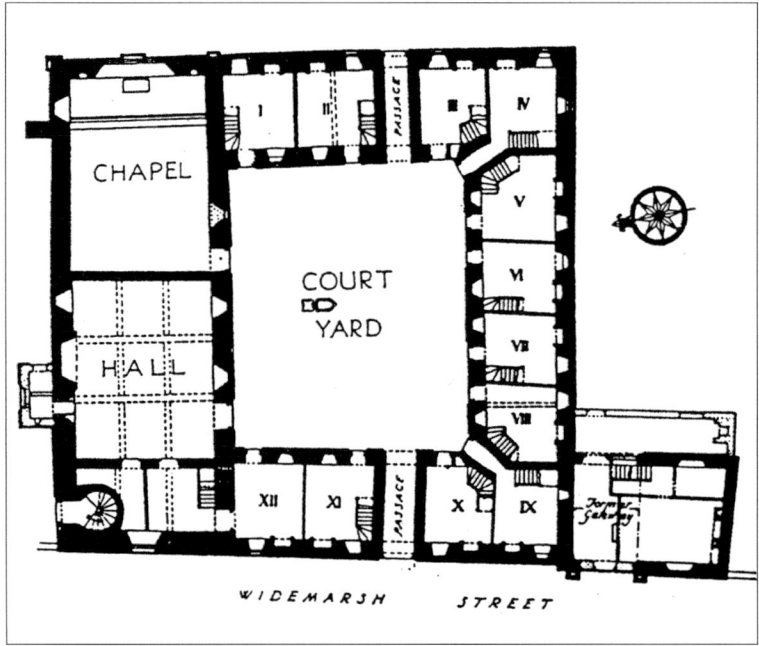

Fig.33
Coningsby Hospital,
Hereford, Hereford
and Worcester (1615).

*Architectural Context*

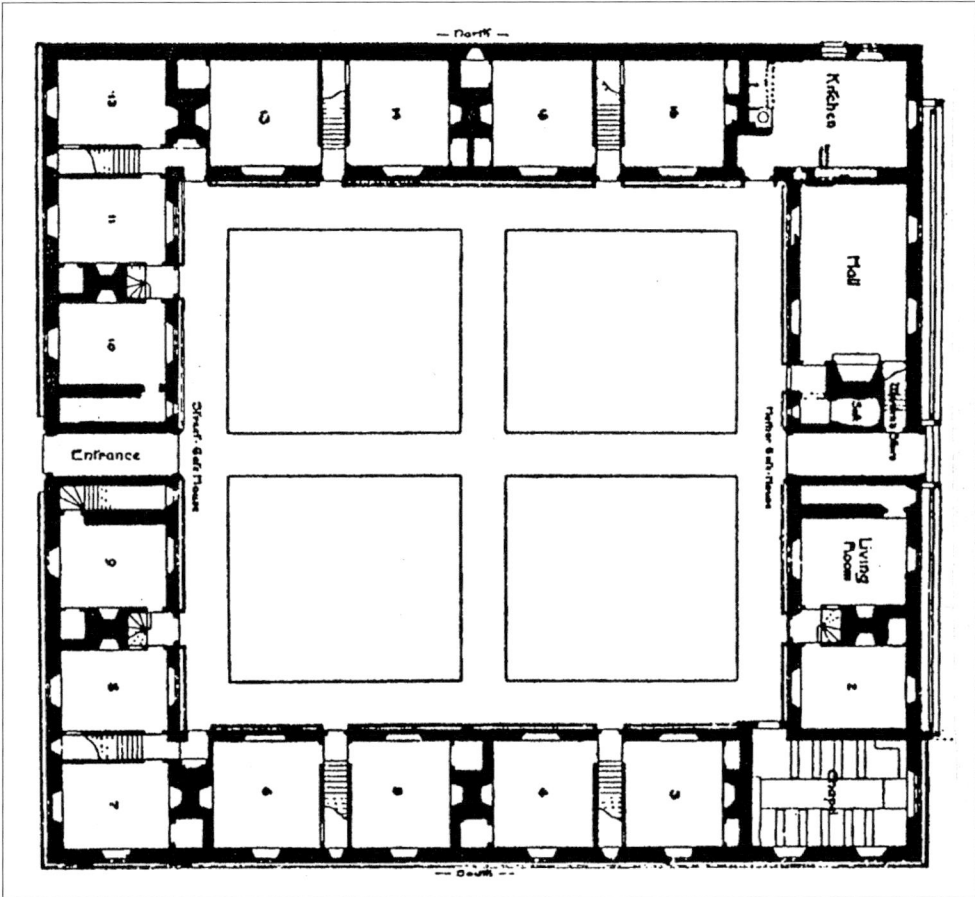

Fig.34 Whitgyft's Hospital, Croydon, London (1596).

The plan (Fig.27) consists of a narrow, open court, only some 40ft long by 12ft wide, entered at each end by a narrow doorway with a five-centred arch over. The first floor juts over, giving slightly more floor area to the upper dwellings compared with the ground floor, and leaves only some 8-9ft between opposite living-room windows. However, since the Second World War, when the hospital was extensively damaged by enemy bombing, the building has been modernised and rearranged internally to provide more comfortable and convenient accommodation for its occupants.

There are substantial numbers of almshouse groups built in the courtyard style throughout the country, but space permits only a representative sample to be illustrated here. Many were built during Victorian times, but as time passed and the great benefactors gave way to ordinary lay people, expenditure was reduced, resulting in smaller numbers of dwellings. From then onwards, the usual grouping was a simple terrace, sometimes as few as two or three dwellings, and it was these more humble residences which became the legacy of the later years of the nineteenth and early twentieth centuries.

Other significant courtyard layouts are: Kilmainham Hospital, Dublin (Fig.28) and Lord Leycester's Hospital, Warwick (Fig.29) (both totally enclosed), The Royal Hospital, Chelsea (Fig.30) (partially enclosed), Sir William Turner's Hospital, Kirkleatham, Cleveland (Fig.31) (with a narrow courtyard), all mentioned in Part One, together with Cobham College, Kent (Fig.32),

*Almshouses: A Social and Architectural History*

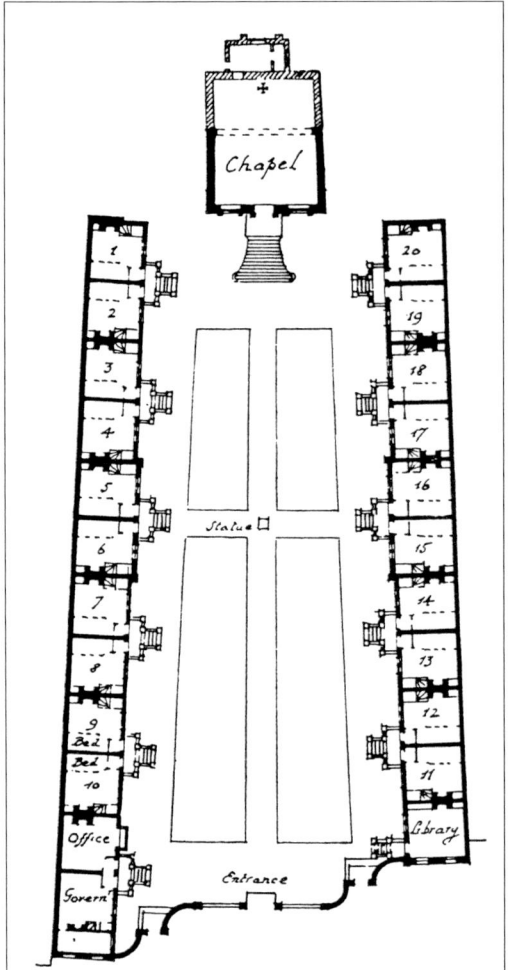

*Left:* Fig.35 Trinity Hospital, Mile End Road, London (1696).

*Below:* Frieston Hospital, Kirkthorpe, Wakefield, North Yorkshire (1595).

Coningsby's Hospital, Hereford (Fig.33) and Whitgift's Hospital, Croydon, London (Fig.34). Trinity Hospital, Mile End Road, London (Fig.35), attributed to Sir Christopher Wren, is most unusual in layout, in that the alignment of the two rows of bungalows facing each other across the green tapers, converging on the chapel, exaggerates the perspective and gives the illusion of a much larger composition than actually exists.

Before closing this section on the architectural features of our almshouse heritage, we must mention two groups which exist within a few miles of each other. Because of their unusual plan form, they are thought to have been built by the same builder, or at the very least to have been influenced one by the other.

Beamsley Hospital near Skipton in North Yorkshire is unusual because it is the only circular almshouse in the country; possibly it is unique (Fig.36). The charity was founded in 1593 by the Countess of Cumberland, although the almshouse group was not completed until 1650 by her daughter, Ann Clifford, Countess of Pembroke, who at the time occupied nearby Skipton Castle. The accommodation comprised seven one-room dwellings clustered around a small chapel which was lit by a turret or roof light, and where, twice each day, in the morning and the evening, the seven old lady occupants were called by the local vicar to say prayers for the founder.

As might be expected, one-room dwellings are no longer acceptable, and for some time now the buildings have been converted for use as a holiday let.

The other unusually shaped almshouse can be found not far from Skipton at Kirkthorpe, near Wakefield in West Yorkshire. Frieston Hospital was built in 1595, two years after Beamsley Hospital was started, and was very similar in concept to Beamsley except that it was built to a square instead of circular plan. Again, there were seven occupants, men this time, who were housed in the stone building. It had a central living hall instead of the chapel and seven small bed–sitting rooms opening off it on three sides (Fig.37). The need for a chapel on site was obviated by the proximity of Kirkthorpe parish church but, like at Beamsley, there was a clerestory or roof light illuminating the central hall from above. The actual windows were in four dormers, one to each side.

The almshouse was occupied until 1947 when it was closed and new dwellings provided nearby. The hospital building was sold and has since been converted to a private dwelling.

With, as mentioned previously, over two thousand separate groups of almshouses existing in the country, it has only been possible to properly discuss a representative sample. However, outline details of over 600 groups are covered in the Gazetteer.

In June 1986, a service of thanksgiving was held at Westminster Abbey in the presence of HM Queen Elizabeth the Queen Mother to celebrate 1,000 years of almshouses in England. With that it would seem that our story has come full circle, since it marked the anniversary of the founding in 986 of St Leonard's Hospital in York, mentioned at the beginning of Part One.

With the establishment of the welfare state and the range of new agencies, both voluntary and commercial, as well as local authorities who now care for the aged, both in purpose-built establishments and increasingly in their own homes, it may be imagined that the need for almshouse trusts has diminished. Nothing could be further from the truth. With the increasing longevity we now enjoy, there remains a growing and sustained need for all types of elderly people's accommodation. It is likely that the almshouse movement will be still going strong in another thousand years. Let us hope so.

*Almshouses: A Social and Architectural History*

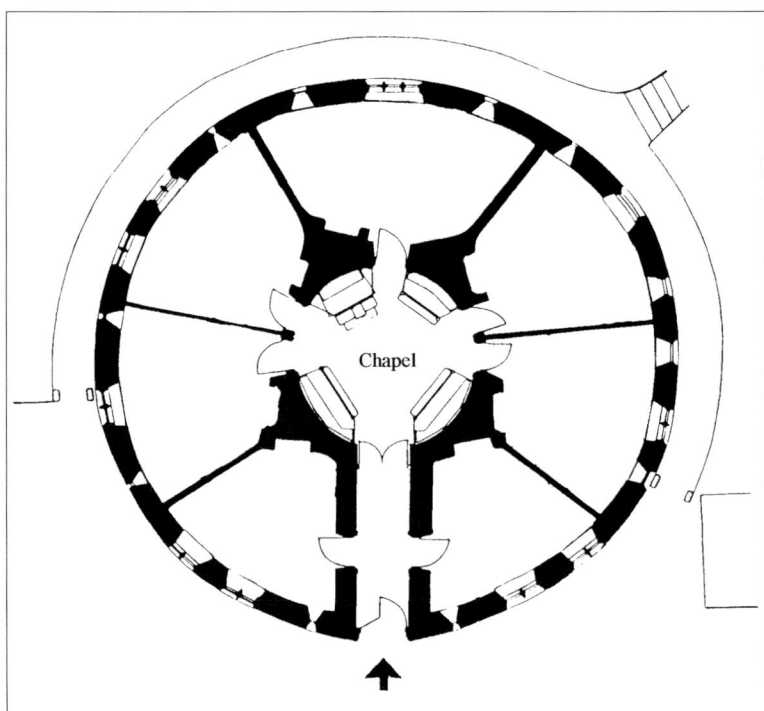

Fig. 36
Beamsley Hospital, Craven, North Yorkshire (1593).

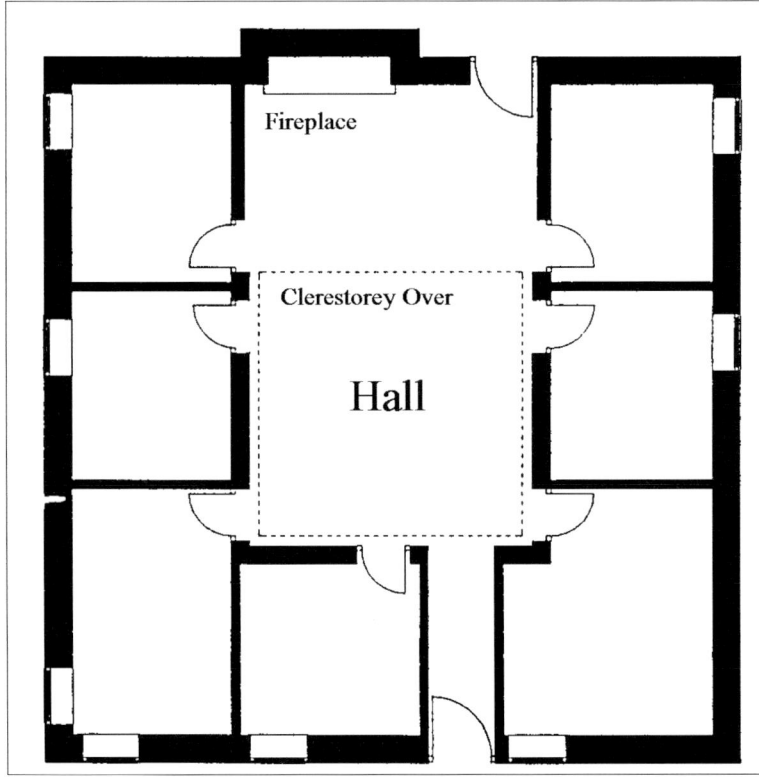

Fig. 37
Frieston Hospital, Kirkthorpe, Wakefield, West Yorkshire (1595).

# PART THREE
# GAZETTEER

It would be almost impossible to provide details of every single one of the 5,000 or so almshouse groups which are estimated to exist in England today; although some 2,500 almshouse trusts are registered with the Almshouse Association, it is thought that an equal number are not. Indeed, many have been converted to other uses over time. Moreover, as the limitations of space permit only a general study of the history of almshouses, the milestones down the years are illustrated by only a representative sample of building types. They are generally the great almshouses; those which are acknowledged to be masterpieces in their own right and have been singled out for special attention and preservation as some of the gems of our building heritage.

It is for this reason that the main geographic work of reference has been the forty-five volumes of Sir Nicholas Pevsner's *The Buildings of England*, supplemented by the current Yearbook of the Almshouse Association and, where necessary, by more detailed works of a more local nature. This is particularly so in the case of London and York where, as is to be expected, much more detailed research into historic buildings has been published over the years. The bibliography at the end of this volume gives further references concerning individual towns where important almshouse groups are located, and details of particular buildings, generally in the form of monographs, published both privately and by museums and other antiquarian bodies.

The Gazetteer is laid out alphabetically, both in county order and by towns within counties. By no means have all the almshouse groups mentioned been visited by the author; indeed it is possible that despite efforts to ascertain the position at the date of publication, some buildings may have disappeared or have been converted to other uses. The author would be pleased to receive details of changes in order to keep the record up to date.

## AVON

### Bristol

#### Bengough's Almshouses
Date founded: 1878
Date built: 1878
Location: Horfield Road.
OS ref. ST5872
Description: Three sides of courtyard; brick with stone dressings, cross windows and coved eves; pedimented entrance.

#### Colston's Almshouses
Date founded: 1691
Date built: 1691
Location: Lower Church Lane.
OS ref. ST5872
Description: Two-storey, with hipped roof; three sides of quadrangle with three-bay chapel.

#### Foster's Almshouses
Date founded: 1504
Date built: 1861
Location: Colston Street.
OS ref. ST5872
Description: Three wings with medieval chapel.

#### Fry's House of Mercy
Date founded: 1784
Date built: 1784
Location: Colston Parade.
OS ref. ST5872
Description: Three bays, two-storey; Y-traceried windows.

#### Merchant Taylors' Almshouses
Date founded: 1701
Date built: 1701
Location: Merchant Street.
OS ref. ST5872
Description: First brick buildings in Bristol. Centre of three bays. Two projecting wings each of three bays; two-storey; hipped roof.

#### Merchant Venturers Almshouses
Date founded: 1696
Date built: 1699
Location: King Street.
OS ref. ST5872
Description: Two-storey, quadrangular, rendered with gabled doorways.

#### St Bartholomews Hospital
Date founded: 1207

Date built: 1207
Location: Christmas Street.
OS ref. ST5872
Description: Medieval fragments of archway.

### St Nicholas' Almshouses
Date founded: 1652
Date built: 1652
Location: King Street.
OS ref. ST5872
Description: Low, two-storey, stone with eight gables.

### Stevens Almshouses
Date founded: 1679
Date built: 1679
Location: Old Market Street.
OS ref. ST5872
Description: Two gabled ranges at right angles to street; gables; upright oval windows.

### The College of St Raphael
Date founded: 1853
Date built: 1855
Location: Cumberland Road.
OS ref. ST5872
Description: Barge-boarded dormers and a timber verandah with pointed trefoiled arches.

### Trinity Hospital
Date founded: Fifteenth century
Date built: 1857
Location: Old Market Street.
OS ref. ST5872
Description: Tudor style; pretty open timber staircase with conical roof.

## Henbury

### Blaise Hamlet
Date founded: 1811
Date built: 1811
Location: In village.
OS ref. ST5678
Description: Nine picturesque cottages with nine different designs around village green.

## Marshfield

### Crisp's Almshouses
Date founded: 1619
Date built: 1619
Location: In village.
OS ref. SJ7773
Description: Eight cottages in Cotswold stone, four either side of a gabled chapel with tower and steeple.

## Wiston

### Portis College
Date founded: 1825
Date built: 1827
Location: Newgrige Hill.
OS ref. ST7266
Description: Late Georgian.

## Yatton

### Almshouses
Date founded: Nineteenth century
Date built: Nineteenth century
Location: In village.
OS ref. ST4365
Description: Modest.

# BEDFORDSHIRE

## Ampthill

### Feoffee Almshouses
Date founded: Sixteenth century
Date built: Sixteenth century
Location: Left of Brandreth House in Church Street.
OS ref. TL0337
Description: Timber-framed front with single-storey eighteenth-century wing at the rear.

### Oxford Hospital (for college servants)
Date founded: 1697
Location: Adjacent to Littlepark Farm, off Woburn Road.
OS ref. TL0337
Description: Stately almshouses founded by John Cross. Fine central bay with pediment.

## Bedford

### Almshouses
Date founded: 1801
Date built: 1806
Location: Dame Alice Street (north end of High Street).
OS ref. TL0549
Description: Dark-red brick with paired steep dormers.

### Hospital of St John
Date founded: 1216
Date built: 1840
Location: North of the church in Church Street.
OS ref. TL0549
Description: Tudor features, especially the roof timbers of the former hall, now hidden.

## Dustable

### Cart Almshouses
Date founded: 1723
Date built: 1723
Location: High Street.
OS ref. TL0221
Description: Plain two-storey, of blue and red brick.

*Marsh Almshouses*
Date founded: 1730
Date built: 1745
Location: High Street.
OS ref. TL0221
Description: Stucco facing with pediment with coat of arms.

## Leyton Linslade

*Wilkes Almshouses*
Date founded: 1857
Date built: 1873
Location: adjacent to Quaker Meeting Hall in North Street.
OS ref. SP9225
Description: Yellow brick with gables.

## Hungerford

*Somerset Hospital*
Date founded: 1686
Date built: 1686
Location: In village.
OS ref. SU3368
Description: Large composition. Enclosed courtyard with free-standing chapel.

## Woburn

*Almshouses*
Date founded: 1850
Date built: 1850
Location: High Street.
OS ref. SP9534
Description: Two ranges of yellow brick with thin Jacobean stepped gables.

# BERKSHIRE

## Bray

*Jesus Hospital*
Date founded: 1627
Date built: 1627
Location: South of village.
OS ref SU9079
Description: Large brick quadrangle with twenty-eight dwellings, generous dimensioned windows and dormers.

## Donnington

*Donnington Hospital*
Date founded: 1602
Date built: 1822
Location: In village.
OS ref. SU4669
Description: Red brick, single-storey, round courtyard with covered way on wooden posts. Central porch to street.

## Maidenhead

*Almshouses*
Date founded: 1895
Date built: 1895
Location: Bridge Road.
OS ref. SU8783
Description: Red brick; a number of pavilions.

*Smyth's Almshouses*
Date founded: 1659
Date built: 1659
Location: Bridge Road.
OS ref. SU8783
Description: Single-storey; gabled dormers; dark brick.

## Newbury

*Child's Almshouses*
Date founded: 1821
Date built: 1821
Location: Northbrook Street.
OS ref. SU4666
Description: Gothick; three bays.

*Hunt Almshouses*
Date founded: 1729
Date built: 1817
Location: West Mills.
OS ref. SU4666
Description: Plain; blank oval on front.

*St Bartholomew's Hospital*
Date founded: 1618
Date built: 1698
Location: Argyle Road.
OS ref. SU4666
Description: U-shaped; brick; two-storey, with hipped roof; cupola.

## Reading

*Vachel Almshouses*
Date founded: 1864
Date built: 1864
Location: Oxford Road.
OS ref. SU7272
Description: Two rows of cottages at right angles to street.

## Sonning

*Robert Palmer Cottages*
Date founded: 1850
Date built: 1850
Location: Thames Street.
OS ref. SU7575
Description: Plain, two-storey.

## Windsor

### Windsor Almshouses
Date founded: 1862
Date built: 1862
Location: Sheet Street.
OS ref. SU9676
Description: Yellow and red brick; Gothic with steep gables and dormers.

## Wokingham

### Lucas Hospital
Date founded: 1665
Date built: 1665
Location: Holme Green.
OS ref. SU8068
Description: Brick, long front with two projecting wings; two-storey, the windows mullioned; small cupola.

# BUCKINGHAMSHIRE

## Amersham

### Sir William Drake's Almshouses
Date founded: 1657
Date built: 1657
Location: High Street.
OS ref. SU9597
Description: Modest, single-storey, with two gables to street; windows mullioned with arched lights.

## Aylesbury

### Hickman's Almshouses
Date founded: 1871
Date built: 1871
Location: St Mary's Square.
OS ref. SP8213
Description: Nine bays; vitreous red brick.

## Brill

### Almshouses
Date founded: 1842
Date built: 1842
Location: The Green.
OS ref. SP6513
Description: Humble.

## Ellesborough

### Almshouses
Date founded: 1746
Date built: 1746
Location: South of church.
OS ref. SP8306
Description: Humble, single-storey.

## Eton

### Eton College
Date founded: 1440
Date built: 1440
Location: Slough Road.
OS ref. SU9678
Description: Founded as school and hospital, but school only since 1470.

## Great Linford

### Almshouses
Date founded: Seventeenth century.
Date built: Seventeenth century.
Location: Adjoining church.
OS ref. SP8542
Description: Single-storey with raised centre. Four end gables, all double curved with rounded tops.

## Hanslope

### Almshouses
Date founded: 1712
Date built: 1712
Location: Village Street.
OS ref. SP8046
Description: Plain, stone.

## High Wycombe

### Hospital of St John
Date founded: 1180
Date built: 1180
Location: Easton Street.
OS ref. SU8593
Description: Ruins; arcades of two bays; round piers, square abaci, moulded round arches.

### Queen Elizabeth's Almshouses
Date founded: 1856
Date built: 1856
Location: Easton Street.
OS ref. SU8593
Description: Tudoresque, white and red brick.

## Hughenden

### Almshouses
Date founded: Seventeenth century.
Date built: 1842
Location: South-west of church.
OS ref. SU8596
Description: Six gables; two brick, four timber framed; mullioned windows with hood moulds.

## Langley Marish

### Sir John Kederminster's Almshouses
Date founded: 1617

Date built: 1617
Location: South of church and north of church
OS ref. SU0079
Description: Humble, ground floor living room with bedroom upstairs in gable.

## Olney

### Almshouses
Date founded: 1819
Date built: 1819
Location: High Street.
OS ref. SP8851
Description: Two-storey, of chequered brick with central pediment.

## Quainton

### Winwood Almshouses
Date founded: 1687
Date built: 1687
Location: Near churchyard.
OS ref. SP7320
Description: Single-storey with dormers, two porches with Dutch gables.

## Ravenstone

### Ravenstone Almshouses
Date founded: Seventeenth century.
Date built: Seventeenth century.
Location: North of church.
OS ref. SP8540
Description: Two rows facing each other; single-storey with chequered brick.

## Shenley Church End

### Almshouses
Date founded: 1654
Date built: 1654
Location: In village.
OS ref. SP8336
Description: Plain, single-storey, of stone.

## Stoke Poges

### Stoke Poges Hospital
Date founded: 1765
Date built: 1765
Location: North of church.
OS ref. SU9983
Description: Composite group in red brick; dwellings at rear, master's house, chapel and clock-tower to front.

## Stoney Stratford

### Mr Fegan's Homes
Date founded: 1863
Date built: 1863
Location: High Street.
OS ref. SP7840
Description: Rock-faced stone with red brick dressings; chapel to front with rose window.

## Wing

### Dormer's Hospital
Date founded: 1569
Date built: Nineteenth century.
Location: South of church.
OS ref. SP8822
Description: Four doors and four dormer windows with brick frames.

## Worminghall

### Almshouses
Date founded: 1675
Date built: 1675
Location: In village.
OS ref. SP6308
Description: H-shaped, of brick with stone quoins and hipped roof; mullioned windows.

# CAMBRIDGESHIRE

## Babraham

### Bush and Bennett's Almshouses
Date founded: 1723
Date built: 1723
Location: Centre of village.
OS ref. TL5150
Description: Six one-storey brick houses to left and right of two-storey centre.

## Cambridge

### Chapel of Hospital of St Mary Magdalene
Date founded: Twelfth century.
Date built: Twelfth century.
Location: Newmarket Road.
OS ref. TL4658
Description: Chapel of original leper hospital; Norman flint rubble with shafted stone quoins.

### Royal Albert Almshouses
Date founded: 1859
Date built: 1859
Location: Brooklands Avenue
O.S.ref: TL4658
Description: Large composition in Gothic style with sharp gables; red and yellow brick.

## Duxford

### Chapel of St John's Hospital
Date founded: 1200

Date built: 1200
Location: West of Whittlesford Station.
OS ref. TL4745
Description: Plain, very fine thirteenth-century chapel; Kentish tracery; piscina and sedila.

## Ely

### St Mary's Almshouses
Date founded: 1844
Date built: 1844
Location: St Mary's Street.
OS ref. TL5380
Description: Single-storey, on three sides of courtyard; yellow brick in simple Tudor style.

## Gamlingay

### Almshouses
Date founded: 1665
Date built: 1665
Location: Church Street.
OS ref. TL2452
Description: Two-storey, brick; on second floor two large and two small windows alternate.

## Wisbech

### Mrs Mayer's Asylum
Date founded: 1815
Date built: 1815
Location: Churchill Road.
OS ref. TF4609
Description: Nice! Two-storey; grey brick.

# CHESHIRE

## Malpas

### Cholmondelly Almshouses
Date founded: Nineteenth century
Date built: Nineteenth century
Location: adjoining parish church.
OS ref. SJ4848
Description: Modest.

# CLEVELAND

## Greatham

### Hospital of God, St Mary and St Cuthbert
Date founded: 1272
Date built: 1803
Location: Adjoining parish church.
OS ref. NZ4928
Description: Rebuilt in 1803, a Regency design with clock tower and chapel.

### Parkhurst Hospital
Date founded: 1762
Date built: 1762
Location: At rear of Greatham Hospital.
OS ref. NZ4928
Description: Brick-built, for four women.

## Kirkleatham

### Turner's Hospital
Date founded: 1742
Date built: 1742
Location: Opposite museum, in village.
OS ref. NZ5922
Description: Large brick composition on three sides of square with chapel and spire. Chapel thought to be by Wren.

## Wolviston

### Londonderry Almshouses
Date founded: 1819
Date built: 1819
Location: The Green.
OS ref. NZ2545
Description: Simple, stone-built row, with arms of the founder, the Duchess of Londonderry, over main doorway.

# CORNWALL

## Paul

### Hutchens' Almshouses
Date founded: 1709
Date built: 1709
Location: Next to church.
OS ref. SW4627
Description: Two-storey; plain; two doors and six windows.

## St Germans

### Sir Walter Moyle's Almshouse
Date founded: Seventeenth century
Date built: Seventeenth century
Location: West of church.
OS ref. SX3557
Description: Six houses with six gables; ground floor and first floor flats with loggia/balconies in timber and whitewash.

## Tregony

### Almshouses
Date founded: 1696
Date built: 1895
Location: In village.
OS ref. SW9245
Description: Gallery of six short granite piers below, and wooden gallery over.

## Truro

### Almshouses
Date founded: 1631
Date built: 1631
Location: Pydar Street.
OS ref. SW8244
Description: Still have inscriptions but unrecognizable as almshouses.

# CUMBRIA

## Appleby

### St Anne's Hospital
Date founded: 1651
Date built: 1653
Location: Boroughgate.
OS ref. NY6921
Description: Seven bays, stone-built with internal courtyard and chapel.

# DERBYSHIRE

## Ashbourne

### Clergymen's Widows Almshouses
Date founded: 1768
Date built: 1753
Location: Church Street.
OS ref. SK1746
Description: Three storey; Georgian composition.

### Coopers Almshouses
Date founded: 1800
Date built: 1800
Location: Derby Road.
OS ref. SK1846
Description: Modest; associated with adjoining chapel.

### Owlfield Almshouses
Date founded: 1640
Date built: 1640
Location: Church Street.
OS ref. SK1746
Description: At right angles to Pegg's almshouses.

### Pegg's Almshouses
Date founded: 1669
Date built: 1669
Location: Church Street.
OS ref. SK1746
Description: At right angles to Owlfield's Almshouses.

### Spalden's Almshouses
Date founded: 1723
Date built: 1723
Location: South-east of church.
OS ref. SK1745
Description: Three sides of a square.

## Balborough

### Pole's Almshouses
Date founded: 1752
Date built: 1752
Location: Village Street.
OS ref. SK4070
Description: Mullioned windows.

## Derby

### Liversedge Almshouses
Date founded: 1836
Date built: 1836
Location: London Road.
O.S.ref: SK3636
Description: Gothic brick. Designs by John Mason.

## Duffield

### Patterell's Almshouses
Date founded: 1810
Date built: 1810
Location: Town Street, south-west of Baptist chapel.
OS ref. SK3443
Description: Plain, stone built

## Ewall

### Ewall Hospital
Date founded: 1550
Date built: 1681
Location: In village.
OS ref. SK2074
Description: Brick-built, three sides of a courtyard. Massive chimneys.

## Hopton

### Sir Philip Gell's Almshouse
Date founded: 1719
Date built: 1719
Location: In village.
OS ref. SK2553
Description: For two men and two women; single-storey, with gable.

## Mapleton

### Clergymen's Widows Almshouses
Date founded: 1727
Date built: 1727
Location: In village.
OS ref. SK1748
Description: Fine brick with stone dressings; five bays, two-storey, with central bay.

## Morley

### Sacheverell Almshouses
Date founded: 1656
Date built: 1656
Location: Morley Moor.
OS ref. SK3942
Description: Single-storey, stone, arms on central gable.

## Stanton-by-dale

### Almshouses
Date founded: 1711
Date built: 1735
Location: East of parish church.
OS ref. SK4638
Description: Plain brick; gables.

# DEVON

## Barnstaple

### Horwood's Almshouses
Date founded: 1674
Date built: 1674
Location: Church Street.
OS ref. SS5533
Description: Simple two-storey with wooden mullioned windows. Small court behind.

### Paige's Almshouses
Date founded: 1656
Date built: 1656
Location: Church Lane.
OS ref. SS5533
Description: Simple, two-storey with wooden mullioned windows.

### Penrose Almshouses
Date founded: 1627
Date built: 1627
Location: Lichdon Street.
OS ref. SS5533
Description: Symmetrical front with projecting centre and corners. Colonades of stone.

### Salem Almshouses
Date founded: 1834
Date built: 1834
Location: Trinity Street.
OS ref. SS5533
Description: Three ranges along three sides of court, open to street. Two-storey.

## Beere

### Lady Rolle Almshouses
Date founded: 1820
Date built: 1820
Location: In village.
OS ref. SS9801
Description: Pretty Gothic design with deep eves forming continuous porch. Pattern-tiled roof.

## Bishop Tawton

### Law Almshouses
Date founded: 1885
Date built: 1885
Location: Main Road.
OS ref. SS5630
Description: Three pairs of gables with Gothic entrances.

## Broadclyst

### Burrough's Almshouses
Date founded: 1605
Date built: 1883
Location: Church Lane.
OS ref. SX9897
Description: Victorian, modest.

## Cheriton Fitzpaine

### Almshouses
Date founded: 1594
Date built: 1594
Location: In village street.
OS ref. SS8706
Description: Plain with big chimneys towards the street.

## Combeinteignhead

### Bourchier Almshouses
Date founded: 1620
Date built: 1620
Location: In village.
OS ref. SX9071
Description: Red sandstone; Tudor; original timber window casements and four-centred doorway.

## Cullompton

### Almshouses
Date founded: 1522
Date built: 1522
Location: On edge of town.
OS ref. ST0107
Description: Much rebuilt; four-centred stone archway.

## Exeter

### Flaye's Almshouses
Date founded: 1880
Date built: 1880
Location: Grendon Road.
OS ref. SX9292
Description: Victorian Tudor.

### Attwill Palmer Almshouses
Date founded: 1839
Date built: 1839
Location: Beyond college.
OS ref. SX9292
Description: Two garden archways; groups of six dwellings; Tudor details; brick chimneys.

### Exeter Free Cottages
Date founded: 1862
Date built: 1862
Location: Mount Dinham.
OS ref. SX9292
Description: Four parallel rows in groupings of four. Tudor details.

### Licensed Victuallers' Almshouses
Date founded: 1872
Date built: 1872
Location: Devonshire Place.
OS ref. SX9292
Description: Tudor Gothic.

### Magdalen Road Almshouses
Date founded: 1863
Date built: 1863
Location: Magdalen Road.
OS ref. SX9292
Description: Victorian Tudor; brown volcanic stone.

### St Anne's and St Francis's Almshouses
Date founded: 1418
Date built: 1418
Location: Old Tiverton Road.
OS ref. SX9292
Description: L-shaped; much-restored Tudor; tiny chapel.

### St Catherine's Almshouses
Date founded: 1450
Date built: 1458
Location: Cathedral Close.
OS ref. SX9292
Description: Derelict enclosure with arched and straight headed windows. Ruins of free-standing chapel.

### The Livery Dole
Date founded: Eighteenth century.
Date built: Eighteenth century.
Location: Heavitree Hill.
OS ref. SX9292
Description: Founded for servants of a nearby estate, who were required to wear livery, hence the name.

### Wynard's Almshouses
Date founded: 1436
Date built: 1650
Location: Magdalen Street.
OS ref. SX9292
Description: Quadrangular, stone-built cottages with chapel.

## Great Torrington

### Rolle Almshouses
Date founded: 1843
Date built: 1843
Location: New Street.
OS ref. SS4919
Description: Symmetrical design with Gothic doorways.

## Honiton

### St Margaret's Hospital
Date founded: Twelfth century.
Date built: 1530
Location: New Street.
OS ref. ST1500
Description: Originally a lazer-house, now thatched cottages with Gothic glazing.

## Kenton

### Almshouses
Date founded: C19
Date built: C19
Location: South of church
OS ref. SX9583
Description: Red brick; symmetrical; gabled; fat chimneys.

## Moretonhampstead

### Moretonhampstead Almshouses
Date founded: 1639
Date built: 1639
Location: On edge of village.
OS ref. SX7585
Description: Picturesque with thatched roof and open gallery or cloisters, stone.

## Newton Abbot

### Hayman's Almshouses
Date founded: 1840
Date built: 1840
Location: East Street.
OS ref. SX8671
Description: Angular; Regency Gothic.

### Reynell's Almshouses
Date founded: 1845
Date built: 1845
Location: East Street.
OS ref. SX8671
Description: Granite; perpendicular windows and central archway.

## Pilton

### Almshouses
Date founded: 1860
Date built: 1860
Location: Pilton Street.
OS ref. SS5433
Description: At right angles to street.

## Poltimore

### Bampfylde Almshouses
Date founded: 1631
Date built: 1631
Location: North of church.
OS ref. SX9696
Description: Elaborate; little relief with medallions showing founder and Elizabeth I.

## Shirwell

### Almshouses
Date founded: Nineteenth century
Date built: Nineteenth century
Location: In village.
OS ref. SS5937
Description: Recessed porches and Gothic windows.

## Sidmouth

### Feoffees Almshouses
Date founded: 1802
Date built: 1802
Location: High Street.
OS ref. SY1287
Description: Tall, gaunt.

## Taddiport (Little Torrington)

### Hospital chapel
Date founded: 1344
Date built: 1344
Location: In village.
OS ref. SS 4916
Description: Chapel of leper hospital long gone. Narrow tower. Nave only 30ft long.

## Tiverton

### Greenways Almshouses
Date founded: 1517
Date built: 1517
Location: In Main Street.
OS ref. SS9512
Description: The gift of John Greenway, Clothier. Three floors, three rooms each; chapel.

### Slees Almshouses
Date founded: 1613
Date built: 1613
Location: On elevated walkway in Main Street.
OS ref. SS9512
Description: Half-timbered and stone with slate roof; for six poor widows.

### Tiverton Almshouse Charity
Date founded: 1968
Date built: 1968
Location: adj. Waldron's Almshouses in Wellbrook Street.
OS ref. SS9512
Description: Modern red brick with central Dutch gable.

### Waldron Almshouses
Date founded: 1579
Date built: 1579
Location: Weelbrook Road.
OS ref. SS9512
Description: For eight poor men; with open gallery, and attached chapel with porch.

## Trusham

### Stookes' Almshouses
Date founded: Seventeenth century
Date built: Seventeenth century
Location: Higher Town.
OS ref. SX8582
Description: Short wings with gabled ends.

# DORSET

## Beaminster

### Sir John Strode's Almshouses
Date founded: 1630
Date built: 1630
Location: Adjoining church yard.
OS ref. ST4799
Description: Single-storey for six poor persons. Simple with inscription 'God's House'.

## Blamford Forum

### George Ryves Almshouses
Date founded: 1685
Date built: 1685
Location: In town.
OS ref. ST8807
Description: Single-storey. Central pediment with cartouch.

## Dorchester

### Nappers Mite
Date founded: 1615
Date built: 1615
Location: South Street.

OS ref. SY6991
Description: Stone. Front block of quadrangle lengthened with storey over arcading.

## Milton Abbas

### Sir John Tregonwell's Almshouses
Date founded: 1674
Date built: 1780
Location: In village street opposite church.
OS ref. ST8102
Description: Rebuilt by Lord Milton as part of the re-siting of Milton Abbas. Thatched.

## Sherborne

### Hospital of St John the Evangelist and Baptist
Date founded: 1437
Date built: 1437
Location: In town.
OS ref. ST6417
Description: Stone. Men on ground floor and women on first floor, with common chapel.

## Wareham

### Streche's Almshouses
Date founded: 1741
Date built: 1741
Location: In village.
OS ref. SY9387
Description: Planned like a Georgian house.

## Wimborne Minster

### St Margaret's Hospital
Date founded: 1241
Date built: Seventeenth century
Location: Quarter of a mile north-west of Wimborne.
OS ref. SU0101
Description: Nine single-storey cottages with chapel attached. Founded by John of Gaunt.

## Wimborne-St-Giles

### Sir Anthony Ashley's Almshouses
Date founded: 1627
Date built: 1627
Location: Between the village school and the parish church.
OS ref. SU0312
Description: Ten brick-built cottages with central chapel.

# DURHAM

## Beamish

### Methold Houses
Date founded: 1863
Date built: 1863
Location: Adjoining Shepherd and Shepherdess Inn.
OS ref. NZ2254
Description: Stone-built with Dutch gables to short returns at ends of block.

## Durham City

### Bishop Cosin's Almshouses
Date founded: 1838
Date built: 1838
Location: Owengate.
OS ref. NZ2742
Description: Stone-built in the medieval manner with small enclosed courtyard.

### Bishop's Hospital
Date founded: 1666
Date built: 1666
Location: Palace Green East.
OS ref. NZ2742
Description: Single-storey, with central gable with arms over. Now used as tea room.

### Kepier Hopital Gatehouse
Date founded: 1341
Date built: 1341
Location: Kepier Lane, on south bank of River Wear.
OS ref. NZ2843
Description: Substantial remains of gatehouse to medieval hospital.

### Sherburn Hospital
Date founded: 1181
Date built: 1181-1760
Location: In Sherburn Village.
OS ref. NZ3142
Description: Substantial hospital buildings with medieval gatehouse.

### St Mary Magdalene Hospital chapel
Date founded: 1449
Date built: 1449
Location: Magdalene Lane.
OS ref. NZ2843
Description: Stone ruins of medieval hospital chapel.

## Houghton-le-Spring

### Davenport Almshouses
Date founded: 1668
Date built: 1668
Location: East of parish church.
OS ref. NZ3552
Description: Small, open courtyard, stone-built, with arms on plaques.

## Monkton

### Monkton Bedehouse
Date founded: Seventeenth century
Date built: Seventeenth century
Location: The Green.
OS ref. NZ3363
Description: Stone-built. Now a farmhouse.

## ESSEX

## Audley End

### College of St Mark
Date founded: Sixteenth century
Date built: Sixteenth century
Location: Village Street.
OS ref. TL5238
Description: Two courtyards with hall and chapel. Each courtyard has ten dwellings. All windows arched lights.

## Colchester

### Winsley's Almshouses
Date founded: 1630
Date built: 1728
Location: Old Heath Road.
OS ref. TM0025
Description: Two long wings with magnificent centre piece with pediment and Dutch gable.

## Felsted

### Almshouses
Date founded: 1878
Date built: 1878
Location: Next to Felsted School.
OS ref. TL6720
Description: Grouped round courtyard.

## Harlow

### Stafford Almshouses
Date founded: 1630
Date built: 1630
Location: Churchgate Street.
OS ref. TL4510
Description: Half-timbered.

## Ilford

### Ilford Hospital
Date founded: 1140
Date built: Fourteenth century
Location: High Road.
OS ref. TQ4007
Description: Chapel and two short projecting wings; single-storey with hipped roof each with end gable.

## Maldon

### St Giles' Hospital chapel
Date founded: Twelfth century
Date built: Twelfth century
Location: Near church.
OS ref. TL8506
Description: Ruins only.

## Stock

### Almshouses
Date founded: Twelfth century
Date built: Twelfth century
Location: Outside village, near church.
OS ref. TQ6998
Description: Single-storey, brick.

## Thaxted

### Almshouses
Date founded: Eighteenth century
Date built: Eighteenth century
Location: Adjoining church.
OS ref. TL6130
Description: Two rows, one thatched, the other with barge boards.

## GLOUCESTERSHIRE

## Chipping Camden

### Sir Baptist Hicks Almshouses
Date founded: 1612
Date built: 1612
Location: Opposite the parish church.
OS ref. SP1539
Description: Stone with Cotswold gables.

## Forthampton

### Yorke Almshouses
Date founded: 1863
Date built: 1865
Location: East of church.
OS ref. SO8532
Description: Stone with gables bearing Yorke coat of arms and their crest in the finials. Gothic windows.

## Gloucester

### St Mary Magdalene's Hospital
Date founded: Twelfth century.
Date built: Twelfth century.
Location: Wotton.
OS ref. SO8318
Description: Former hospital chapel; no nave; chancel enclosed in 1861; entrance through mid-twelfth century chancel arch; unused.

# HAMPSHIRE

## Alton

### Almshouses
Date founded: 1653
Date built: 1653
Location: Church Street.
OS ref. SU1546
Description: Block of four, brick, two-storey with mullioned windows.

## Amport

### Sheppard's Almshouses
Date founded: 1815
Date built: 1815
Location: West of gate piers to Amport House.
OS ref. SU2945
Description: Two-storey, eight bays with pediment.

## Laverstoke

### Portal Almshouses
Date founded: 1939
Date built: 1939
Location: South of church.
OS ref. SU4849
Description: Very extensive with thatched roofs and half-timbered gables.

## Southampton

### Hospital of St Julien (or God's House)
Date founded: 1185
Date built: 1861
Location: Winkle Street, left of High Street.
OS ref. SU3513
Description: Two simple brick blocks on two sides of a quadrangle; the third side, the warden's house, demolished in 1926; and the fourth, a chapel.

## Winchester

### Christies Hospital
Date founded: 1607
Date built: Nineteenth century
Location: Symonds Street.
OS ref. SU4830
Description: Brick, two-storey, with central gable.

### College of Matrons
Date founded: 1672
Date built: 1880
Location: The Square.
OS ref. SU4829
Description: Terrace of pseudo-Georgian houses.

### Hospital of St Cross
Date founded: 1136
Date built: 1136
Location: In village of St Cross.
OS ref. SU4728
Description: Large almshouse with courtyards, church hall and brethren's dwellings. Reputedly the oldest almshouse in the country still in use.

### St John's Hospital
Date founded: 1084
Date built: 1084-eighteenth century
Location: Eastern end of High Street.
OS ref. SU4928
Description: Medieval hall and chapel and Victorian dwelling-houses on both sides of the road.

# HEREFORD AND WORCESTER

## Hereford

### Conningsby Hospital
Date founded: 1614
Date built: 1614
Location: Widemarsh Street.
OS ref. SO5242
Description: Stone, two-storey, around courtyard and garden. Converted from a friary.

### Aubrey Hospital
Date founded: 1630
Date built: 1630
Location: Aubrey Street.
OS ref. SO5242
Description: Six half-timbered single-storey cottages.

## Worcester

### Berkleys Hospital
Date founded: 1702
Date built: 1702
Location: Foregate.
OS ref. SO0555
Description: Georgian coutyard dwellings with chapel.

### St Wulfston's Hospital (the Commandery)
Date founded: 1200
Date built: Sixteenth century
Location: Sidbury Gate.
OS ref. SO0652
Description: Black and white medieval hall, now a museum.

# HERTFORDSHIRE

## Baldock

### Wynne's Almshouses
Date founded: 1621
Date built: 1621
Location: High Street.
OS ref. TL2434

Description: Single-storey, brick with raised gateway in low brick front wall.

## Berkhamsted

### Sayer's Almshouses
Date founded: 1684
Date built: 1684
Location: High Street.
OS ref. SP9807
Description: Single-storey row of six brick houses with segmented pediments.

## Buntingford

### Ward's Hospital
Date founded: 1684
Date built: 1684
Location: North of church.
OS ref. TL3629
Description: Two-storey brick with stone dressings; three sides of a courtyard, open to street.

## Cheshunt

### Almshouses
Date founded: 1620
Date built: 1620
Location: Turner's Hill.
OS ref. TL3502
Description: Ten plain one-storey brick cottages.

## Chipping Barnet

### Garret's Almshouses
Date founded: 1731
Date built: 1731
Location: Wood Street.
OS ref. TL3532
Description: Very simple single-storey row of six cottages.

### Leathersellers' Almshouses
Date founded: 1544
Date built: Nineteenth century
Location: Union Street
OS ref. TL3532
Description: Three ranges round a courtyard; Tudor.

### Ravenscroft Almshouses
Date founded: 1679
Date built: 1679
Location: Wood Street.
OS ref. TL3532
Description: Only original central aarchway and gable.

## Cottered

### Almshouses
Date founded: Eighteenth century
Date built: Eighteenth century
Location: In village.
OS ref. TL3129
Description: Brick, single-storey with quoins and three dormers.

## Elstree

### Almshouses
Date founded: 1882
Date built: 1882
Location: Schopwick Place.
OS ref. TQ1795
Description: Half-timbered.

## Harpenden

### Almshouses
Date founded: 1870
Date built: 1870
Location: Southdown Road.
OS ref. Tl1314
Description: Red brick.

## Hertford

### Harrison Almshouses
Date founded: 1850
Date built: 1850
Location: East of church.
OS ref. TL3212
Description: Red brick; Tudor style.

## Hitchen

### Biggin Almshouses
Date founded: Seventeenth century
Date built: Seventeenth century
Location: St Mary's Square.
OS ref. TL1929
Description: Timber-framed; set around narrow irregular courtyard.

## Hunton Bridge

### Almshouses
Date founded: 1642
Date built: 1642
Location: In village.
OS ref. TL0800
Description: Red brick; altered.

## Sandridge

### Almshouses
Date founded: 1821
Date built: 1821
Location: Opposite church.
OS ref. TL1610
Description: Plain, red brick.

## St Albans

### Malbrough Almshouses
Date founded: 1736
Date built: 1736
Location: South-east of St Peter's church.
OS ref. TL1507
Description: Very large composition; open courtyard with buildings on three sides; wings; nine bays to central range.

### Pemberton's Almshouses
Date founded: 1627
Date built: 1627
Location: North of St Peter's church.
OS ref. TL1507
Description: Simple; single-storey, row of six.

## Standon

### Almshouses
Date founded: Nineteenth century.
Date built: Nineteenth century.
Location: In village.
OS ref. SU4226
Description: Brick and weather-boarding; thatched.

## Stanstead Abbots

### Baeshe Almshouses
Date founded: Seventeenth century
Date built: Seventeenth century
Location: Half a mile north-west of church.
OS ref. TL3811
Description: Brick, two-storey, with three gables.

## Watford

### Salter's Company Almshouses
Date founded: 1863
Date built: 1863
Location: Church Road.
OS ref. TQ1196
Description: Ideal example of charitable mid-Victorian architecture; red brick; Tudor style.

# KENT

## Aylesford

### Hospital of the Holy Trinity
Date founded: 1605
Date built: 1605
Location: In village.
OS ref. TQ7359
Description: Simple one-storey range of seven bays plus two added in 1892. Half-dormers in gables. Ragstone.

## Beckenham

### Rawlins Almshouses
Date founded: 1694
Date built: 1694
Location: Bromley Road.
OS ref. TQ3769
Description: Very humble. One-storey plus dormers.

## Belvedere

### Royal Alfred Home for Aged Seamen
Date founded: 1775
Date built: 1957
Location: Upper Park Road.
OS ref. TQ4978
Description: Modern four-storey replacement of original almshouses.

## Brasted

### Alms Row Cottages
Date founded: Eighteenth century
Date built: Eighteenth century
Location: West end of church
OS ref. TQ4654
Description: Various half-timbered houses now not used as almshouses.

## Bromley

### Bromley College
Date founded: 1666
Date built: 1670
Location: High Street.
OS ref. TQ4169
Description: Quadrangular, red-brick with raised bands. Hipped roof. Grand stone entrance with curved pediment.

### Sheppard's College
Date founded: 1840
Date built: 1840
Location: High Street.
OS ref. TQ4169
Description: Tudor style; for five spinsters.

## Canterbury

### Jesus Hospital
Date founded: 1595
Date built: 1595
Location: Northgate.
OS ref. TR1557
Description: U-shaped, two-storey block, with central gable and gabled ends.

### John Smith's Hospital
Date founded: 1657
Date built: 1657

Location: Barton Court.
OS ref. TR1557
Description: Single-storey with compass gables.

### Manwood's Hospital
Date founded: 1570
Date built: 1570
Location: St Stephen's Green.
OS ref. TR1557
Description: Red-brick diapered; long two-storey range with six doorways; stepped end gables.

### Poor Priests' Hospital
Date founded: 1373
Date built: 1373
Location: Stour Street.
OS ref. TR1557
Description: Large group of flint buildings including hall and two-storey master's quarters and chapel at right angles. Now a museum.

### St John's Hospital
Date founded: 1084
Date built: 1084
Location: In town centre.
OS ref. TR1557
Description: Most of the original buildings are gone with the exception of part of the chapel. Half-timbered gateway and Victorian cottages remain.

## Chatham

### Sir John Hawkin's Hospital
Date founded: 1592
Date built: 1790
Location: High Street.
OS ref. TQ7567
Description: Tiny quadrangle open to street; two-storey flanking council room; red brick; pump in centre of courtyard.

### St Bartholomew's Hospital chapel
Date founded: 1124
Date built: 1124
Location: High Street.
OS ref. TQ7567
Description: Stone nave and chancel with later north aisle and vestry.

## Cobham

### Cobham College
Date founded: 1362
Date built: 1598
Location: South of church.
OS ref. TQ6768
Description: Quadrangular, stone with hall and chapel.

## Dartford

### Lowfield Street Almshouses
Date founded: 1889
Date built: 1889
Location: Lowfield Street.
OS ref. TQ5474
Description: Decorative brickwork.

## Dover

### Maison Dieu
Date founded: 1221
Date built: 1221
Location: Biggin Street.
OS ref. TQ3141
Description: Part of large *maison-dieu* for travellers. Stone lancet windows; undercroft.

## Faversham

### Almshouses
Date founded: 1856
Date built: 1864
Location: South Road.
OS ref. TR0161
Description: Large group, of brick and Bath stone. Main range 470ft long with thin turrets at end.

## Gravesend

### Milton Hospital chapel
Date founded: 1322
Date built: 1322
Location: Fort Gardens.
OS ref. TQ6473
Description: Milton chantry was chapel of original hospital; flint, two-storey; now a museum.

## Harbledown

### St Nicholas' Hospital
Date founded: 1084
Date built: 1084
Location: London Road.
OS ref. TR1357
Description: Only the chapel remains of this, the first lazer-house, surrounded by cottages of a much later date.

## Maidstone

### Sir John Banks' Almshouses
Date founded: 1700
Date built: 1700
Location: St Faith Street.
OS ref. TQ7656
Description: Six two-storey; dusky red brick.

## The Boniface Hospital
Date founded: 1260
Date built: 1395
Location: Adjoining the River Medway.
OS ref. TQ7656
Description: Originally a hospital for poor travellers, only the gateway and the chapel remain; the former as a private residence, the latter as the parish church of St Peter.

## Margate

### Drapers' Almshouses
Date founded: 1708
Date built: 1708
Location: St Peter's Road.
OS ref. TR3670
Description: Single-storey with Dutch gables; knapped flint and brick.

## Mottingham

### Eltham College
Date founded: 1856
Date built: 1856
Location: Grove Park Road.
OS ref. TQ4272
Description: Nine bays, two-storey, with single-storey porches.

### Ironmongers' Almshouses
Date founded: 1710
Date built: 1912
Location: In village.
OS ref. TQ4272
Description: Moved from Shorediitch. Neo-Wren.

## New Romney

### Dering Almshouses
Date founded: 1770
Date built: 1770
Location: St John's Road.
OS ref. TR0624
Description: One-storey row of six.

### Southland's Almshouses
Date founded: 1734
Date built: 1734
Location: West Street.
OS ref. TR0624
Description: Quincunx windows.

## Pembury

### Almshouses
Date founded: 1716
Date built: 1716
Location: Facing church.
OS ref. TQ6240
Description: Two-storey range; rendered brick with pendulous bargeboards.

## Penge

### Free Watermen and Lightermen Almshouses
Date founded: 1840
Date built: 1840
Location: Beckenham Road.
OS ref. TQ3569
Description: Two-storey, three sides of a quadrangle. Tudor; battlemented turrets and ogee lead caps.

### King William Naval Asylum
Date founded: 1847
Date built: 1847
Location: St John's Road.
OS ref. TQ3569
Description: Tudor style, around an open-ended square. Red brick and stone with black diaper pattern.

## Rochester

### Foord Almshouses
Date founded: 1926
Date built: 1930
Location: Priestfields.
OS ref. TQ7467
Description: Large composition for sixty-three residents. Open-ended courtyard with two pumps.

### St Bartholomew's Hospital
Date founded: Thirteenth century
Date built: 1862
Location: New Road.
OS ref. TQ7467
Description: Now built over by modern hospital.

### Watts Almshouses
Date founded: 1858
Date built: 1858
Location: Maidstone Road.
OS ref. TQ7467
Description: Jacobean style; long symmetrical block for eighteen residents.

### Watts Charity
Date founded: 1579
Date built: 1771
Location: High Street.
OS ref. TQ7467
Description: Three even gables, small mullioned windows with classical mouldings.

## Sandwich

### St Bartholomew's Hospital
Date founded: 1217
Date built: Nineteenth century.
Location: Deal Road.

OS ref. TQ 8851
Description: Thirteenth-century chapel with Victorian almshouses.

### St Thomas's Hospital
Date founded: 1392
Date built: Nineteenth century
Location: Moat Sale.
OS ref. TQ 8851
Description: Thirteenth-century entrance arch with Victorian almshouses.

## Shorne

### St Katherine's Hospital chapel
Date founded: Fourteenth century
Date built: Fourteenth century
Location: North of village.
OS ref. TQ 6971
Description: Flint banded with stone; piscina.

## Sutton-at-Hone

### Almshouses
Date founded: 1597
Date built: 1597
Location: In village street.
OS ref. TQ 5570
Description: Red brick; two-storey.

# LANCASHIRE

## Goosnarg

### Goosnarg Hospital
Date founded: 1735
Date built: 1735
Location: Adjoining parish church.
OS ref. SD 5537
Description: Classical composition of three storeys in ashlar with parapets and urns.

## Hurst Green

### Sir Nicholas Shireburn's Almshouses
Date founded: 1700
Date built: 1700
Location: In village.
OS ref. SD 6838
Description: Stone-built Jacobean with raised terrace to front with steps and balustrading.

## Lancaster

### Gardiner's Almshouses
Date founded: 1485
Date built: 1792
Location: In town centre.
OS ref. SD 4862
Description: Modest.

## Manchester

### Chetham's Hospital
Date founded: 1651
Date built: 1651
Location: Next to cathedral
OS ref. SJ 8998
Description: Now a public school.

## Stydd-under-Langridge

### Shireburn Hospital
Date founded: 1727
Date built: 1727
Location: In fields half a mile north of Ribchester.
OS ref. SD 6535
Description: Five small units only; a curious, almost Baroque centrepiece, comprising an arcade on first floor, reached by steps with parapet.

## Waddington

### Waddington Hospital
Date founded: 1700
Date built: 1700
Location: In village.
OS ref. SD 7243
Description: Half-timbered bungalows on three sides of turfed quadrangle, with simple classical gateway.

# LEICESTERSHIRE

## Ashwell (Rutland)

### Almshouses
Date founded: Nineteenth century
Date built: Nineteenth century
Location: Cottesmore Road.
OS ref. SK 8613
Description: Whitewashed brick and timbering. L-shaped with individual houses off a court entered by roofed gateway.

## Barrow-on-Soar

### Old Men's Hospital
Date founded: 1686
Date built: 1694
Location: Opposite parish church.
OS ref. SK 5717
Description: Small, three ranges; stone below and brick above. Hipped roofs; large gateway in forecourt wall.

### Old Women's Hospital
Date founded: 1825
Date built: 1825
Location: Opposite parish church.
OS ref. SK 5717
Description: Pale brick, Tudoresque, symmetrical, small.

## Bottesford

### Earl of Rutland's Hospital
Date founded: 1590
Date built: 1590
Location: Opposite parish church gates.
OS ref. SK8138
Description: Founded by 4th Countess. Front range of rendered stone with two and three light mullioned windows.

### Flemmings Almshouses
Date founded: 1620
Date built: Eighteenth century
Location: Market Street.
OS ref. SK 8137
Description: Completely rebuilt like ordinary cottages in eighteenth century.

## Burton Lazars

### Remains of St Lazarus Hospital
Date founded: 1138
Date built: 1138
Location: 300 yards west of parish church.
OS ref. SK7616
Description: Remains of Leper hospital. Layout with moat and waterways traceable.

## Countesthorpe

### Cottage Homes
Date founded: 1884
Date built: 1884
Location: The Drive.
OS ref. SP 5898
Description: Ten well-designed Domestic Revival style houses built for pauper children, now used as almshouses.

## Frolsworth

### Frolsworth Hospital
Date founded: 1656
Date built: 1725
Location: In village.
OS ref. SP5090
Description: Brick cottages around three sides of a square, enclosed by wall with gabled gateway. Central chapel with clock.

## Leicester

### Trinity Hospital (The Newarke)
Date founded: 1331
Date built: 1331
Location: The Newarke.
OS ref. SK 0805
Description: Dedicated to The Annunciation of The B.V. in 1331, rededicated to The Trinity in 1614. Medieval Infirmary Hall with Jacobean-style wing of seventeen bays and a fourteenth century chapel.

## Lyddington (Rutland)

### Jesus Hospital
Date founded: 1480
Date built: 1514
Location: North of the parish church.
OS ref. SP8798
Description: Important building converted from bishop's palace by Lord Burleigh. Stone, buttressed with prominent chimneys and undercroft.

## Melton Mowbray

### Maison Dieu
Date founded: 1640
Date built: 1640
Location: Burton Street.
OS ref. SK 7518
Description: Symmetrical composition, stone-fronted, one-storey except for three gables. Doorway with four-centred arch.

## Osgathorpe

### The Residence (Almshouses)
Date founded: 1679
Date built: 1679
Location: Adjoining grammar school, opposite the church.
OS ref. SK4319
Description: Uncoursed Charnwood stone, mullioned windows, two sets of gate piers with ball finials.

## Ravenstone

### John Wilkins' Almshouses
Date founded: 1711
Date built: 1711
Location: West of parish church.
OS ref. SP8450
Description: Large, lavish group for thirteen women. Quadrangle with all doors facing outwards. Passages with Tuscan entrance. Two pavilions of 1784.

## Sapcote

### Almshouses
Date founded: 1847
Date built: 1847
Location: East of parish church.
OS ref. SK4090
Description: Gabled Tudoresque, symmetrical front.

## Stapleford

### Stapleford Bedehouse
Date founded: 1732

Date built: 1732
Location: In north-west corner of Stapleford Park.
OS ref. SK8018
Description: Thatched, picturesque.

## Sutton Cheney

### Almshouses (former)
Date founded: 1612
Date built: 1811
Location: East of parish church.
OS ref. SK4100
Description: Simple row of five cottages, stone below; dovecote in southern gable. Since converted to one dwelling.

## Whitwick

### Crapper Almshouses
Date founded: 1846
Date built: 1846
Location: South of Holy Cross RC church.
OS ref. SK4316
Description: Small, symmetrical, castellated.

# LINCOLNSHIRE

## Benington

### William Porril Almshouses
Date founded: 1728
Date built: 1728
Location: Next to churchyard.
OS ref. TF4045
Description: Georgian; modest.

## Denton

### Welby Almshouses
Date founded: 1654
Date built: 1653
Location: In Denton Manor Park.
OS ref. SK8632
Description: Ironstone and grey-stone dressings. Massive array of six chimney stacks between two roof ridges.

## Grantham

### Hurst Almshouses
Date founded: Nineteenth century
Date built: Nineteenth century
Location: In Swinegate.
OS ref. SK9135
Description: Modest.

## Lincoln

### St Anne's Bedehouse
Date founded: 1877
Date built: 1847
Location: adjoining city centre.
OS ref. SK9872
Description: Single-storey, brick with tall chimneys. Designed by Pugin.

## Market Deeping

### Almshouses
Date founded: 1877
Date built: 1877
Location: Church Street.
OS ref. TF1310
Description: Victorian; modest.

## Spalding

### Gamlyns' Almshouses
Date founded: 1843
Date built: 1843
Location: Church Street.
OS ref. TF2422
Description: Red brick, Tudoresque.

## Stamford

### Browne's Hospital
Date founded: 1485
Date built: 1485
Location: St Paul's Street.
OS ref. TF0207
Description: Stone-built, Gothic, originally two-storey hall and double chapel, but now converted to meeting hall and chapel with cottages.

### Hopkins' Hospital
Date founded: 1770
Date built: 1770
Location: St Peter's Street.
OS ref. TF0207
Description: Crenellations, pinnacles, windows with tracery.

### Lord Burleigh's Hospital
Date founded: 1597
Date built: 1597
Location: On the site of medieval hospital of St John the Baptist.
OS ref. TF0207
Description: Principal range facing the river. Detached west range has dormers and chimneys.

## Sleaford

### Carre's Hospital
Date founded: 1830
Date built: 1830
Location: South of the parish church.
OS ref. TF0645

Description: A nine-bay E range, seven-bay south range, castellations and porches. Chapel in centre of south range.

## Welby

### Bedehouses
Date founded: Eighteenth century.
Date built: Eighteenth century.
Location: In village.
OS ref. SK 9738
Description: One-storey with raised two-storey pedimented centre.

# LONDON

## Acton

### Goldsmiths' Almshouses
Date founded: Eighteenth century
Date built: Eighteenth century
Location: East Churchfield Road.
OS ref. TQ 2281
Description: Brick-built Georgian cottages with stucco pedimented central chapel.

## Camden

### Camden Town and Kentish Town Almshouses
Date founded: Nineteenth century
Date built: Nineteenth century
Location: Rousden Street, Camden Town.
OS ref. TQ 2985
Description: Brick-built with large gabled entrance porch.

### St Martins-in-the-Fields Almshouses
Date founded: 1817
Date built: 1817
Location: Balham Street, NW1.
OS ref. TQ2984
Description: Victorian cottages; chapel converted to almshouses.

### St Pancras Almshouses
Date founded: 1859
Date built: 1859
Location: Southampton Road, NW5.
OS ref. TQ2785
Description: Brick around three sides of square; picturesque porches.

## Dulwich

### Dulwich College
Date founded: 1619
Date built: 1619
Location: Gallery Road, Dulwich.
OS ref. TQ3273
Description: White stucco; Elizabethan; three sides of square.

## Fulham

### Sir W. Powell's Almshouses
Date founded: 1869
Date built: 1869
Location: Church Gate, Fulham.
OS ref. TQ2476
Description: Delightful Gothic around two sides of square with garden.

## Greenwich

### John Penn and Widow Smith's Almshouses
Date founded: 1884
Date built: 1866
Location: Greenwich South Street.
OS ref. TQ3877
Description: Red brick with white dressings.

### Mordon College
Date founded: 1695
Date built: 1695
Location: Kidbrooke Grove, Blackheath.
OS ref. TQ 4077
Description: Designed by Wren; brick with stone dressings; impressive.

### Queen Elizabeth College
Date founded: 1576
Date built: 1819
Location: Greenwich High Road.
OS ref. TQ 3877
Description: Three sides of a quadrangle.

### Royal Naval Hospital
Date founded: 1694
Date built: 1705
Location: Centre of Greenwich.
OS ref. TQ3978
Description: Most important group of classical Renaissance buildings in London. Four buildings by Wren, Vanbrugh and Hawksmoor.

### Trinity Hospital
Date founded: 1613
Date built: 1616
Location: Lovell's Wharf.
OS ref. TQ3979
Description: Two-storey, white, castellated, with clock tower.

## Hammersmith

### Sir Abraham Davies' Almshouses
Date founded: 1627
Date built: 1627
Location: Putney Bridge Road, SW18.

OS ref. TQ2576
Description: Extensively renovated.

## Harringay

### Wollaston and Pouncefort Almshouses
Date founded: 1722
Date built: 1722
Location: Southwood Lane, N6.
OS ref. TQ2988
Description: Brick, single-storey with central chapel.

## Islington

### Metropolitan Benefit Society's Asylum
Date founded: 1828
Date built: 1836
Location: Balls Pond Road.
OS ref. TQ3387
Description: Brick; three sides of large quadrangle.

## Kensington and Chelsea

### Royal Hospital
Date founded: 1682
Date built: 1692
Location: Chelsea Bridge Road.
OS ref. TQ2878
Description: Designed by Wren; massive brick-built structure with stone dressings and colonnade around three sides of a square.

### St Joseph's Almshouses
Date founded: Eighteenth century
Date built: Eighteenth century
Location: Cadogan Street, Chelsea.
OS ref. TQ1779
Description: Brick with stone dressings; Tudoresque.

## Lambeth

### Edward Edward's Almshouses
Date founded: 1717
Date built: Nineteenth century
Location: Clapham Road.
OS ref. TQ3077
Description: Modern rebuild.

### Gresham Almshouses
Date founded: 1884
Date built: 1884
Location: Ferndale Road, Brixham.
OS ref. TQ3075
Description: Modest.

### Kifford and Whicher's Almshouses
Date founded: 1855
Date built: 1855
Location: Stanley Close, Lambeth.
OS ref. TQ3175

Description: Victorian, modest.

### Noel Caron's Almshouses
Date founded: 1623
Date built: 1623
Location: Fentiman's Road, Lambeth.
OS ref. TQ3178
Description: Brick with stone dressings.

### Reform Almshouses
Date founded: 1884
Date built: 1884
Location: Ferndale Road, Brixton.
OS ref. TQ3075
Description: Two-storey walk-up flats, now used as council housing.

### Robert Rogers Almshouses
Date founded: 1884
Date built: 1884
Location: Ferndale Road, Brixton.
OS ref. TQ3075
Description: Gabled; brick with stone dressings.

### St Saviour's United College
Date founded: Nineteenth century
Date built: Nineteenth century
Location: Hamilton Road, Gypsy Hill, SE27.
OS ref. TQ3372
Description: Brick, around three sides of a courtyard with wrought-iron screen and gate.

### Trinity Homes
Date founded: 1822
Date built: 1822
Location: Acre Lane, SW2.
OS ref. TQ3074
Description: Brick with stone cornices, pediment and columns to main entrance.

## Lewisham

### Boone's Almshouses
Date founded: 1877
Date built: 1877
Location: Lee High Road, SE13.
OS ref. TQ3975
Description: Chapel designed by Wren; brick with stone dressings.

### J. Thackery's Almshouses
Date founded: 1840
Date built: 1840
Location: Felday Road, Lewisham High Street, SE13.
OS ref. TQ3775
Description: Six yellow brick cottages.

### Merchant Taylors' Almshouses
Date founded: 1683
Date built: 1855

Location: Lee High Road, SE13.
OS ref. TQ3975
Description: Large composition; brick, in landscaped gardens.

## Mile End

### Trinity House Almshouses
Date founded: 1695
Date built: 1695
Location: Mile End Road.
OS ref. TQ4083
Description: Classical design by Wren. Single-storey, brick with stone dressings; around two sides of courtyard with chapel at one end and screen wall at the other.

## Putney

### Dawes Cottages
Date founded: 1627
Date built: 1627
Location: Putney Bridge Street.
OS ref. TQ2575
Description: Extensively renovated.

## Southwark

### Beeston's Gift Almshouses
Date founded: 1834
Date built: 1834
Location: Scylla Road, Peckham.
OS ref. TQ3575
Description: Victorian, white stucco.

### Bethel Asylum
Date founded: 1838
Date built: 1838
Location: Havil Street, Peckham, SE5.
OS ref. TQ3378
Description: Georgian style, brick with stucco porches.

### George Palyn's Almshouses
Date founded: 1851
Date built: 1851
Location: Scylla Road, Peckham.
OS ref. TQ3575
Description: White stucco in landscaped gardens.

### Hopton's Charity
Date founded: 1730
Date built: 1730
Location: Hopton Street, off Southwark Street.
OS ref. TQ3480
Description: Modest; brick with sash windows.

### John Walters' Almshouses
Date founded: Twentieth century.
Date built: Twentieth century.
Location: Brandon Street, SE17.
OS ref. TQ3378
Description: Modern.

### Licensed Victuallers' Benevolent Institute
Date founded: 1827
Date built: 1828
Location: Asylum Road, Southwark.
OS ref. TQ3577
Description: Brick cottages around large courtyard with monumental stucco chapel with pediment and belfry.

### Metropolitan Beer and Wine Trades' Asylum
Date founded: 1852
Date built: 1852
Location: Nunhead Green, Peckham, SE15.
OS ref. TQ3576
Description: Pretty; brick with stone dressings.

### Richard Andrews' Almshouses
Date founded: Nineteenth century
Date built: Nineteenth century
Location: Scylla Road, Peckham.
OS ref. TQ3575
Description: White stucco.

### The Friendly Female Asylum
Date founded: 1821
Date built: 1821
Location: Neate Street, Camberwell.
OS ref. TQ3278
Description: Delightful; brick with lancet windows. Now derelict.

## Wandsworth

### Hibbert Almshouses
Date founded: 1859
Date built: 1859
Location: Wandsworth Road, SW11.
OS ref. TQ2976
Description: Modest.

### St Clement Dane's Holborn Estate Chantry
Date founded: 1552
Date built: 1849
Location: Garratt Lane, Tooting, SW18.
OS ref. TQ3772
Description: Brick; Tudoresque with tall chimneys.

### The Friendly Almshouses
Date founded: 1863
Date built: 1863
Location: Brixton Road, Clapham.
OS ref. TQ3176
Description: Surrounded by the huge Stockwell Park housing estate.

## Shoreditch

### Geffrye Museum (former Ironmongers Almshouses)
Date founded: 1620
Date built: 1620
Location: Kingsland Road.
OS ref. TQ3984
Description: large composition, two-storey, brick around landscaped court. Now used as a museum.

## Westminster

### Christian Union Almshouses
Date founded: 1868
Date built: 1868
Location: Crawford Place, Westminster.
OS ref. TQ2881
Description: Modest.

### Savoy Hospital Chapel
Date founded: 1519
Date built: 1519
Location: off the Strand.
OS ref. TQ3080
Description: All that is left of the Savoy Hospital. Stone with square tower.

### Westminster Almshouses
Date founded: 1881
Date built: 1881
Location: Rochester Row, SW1.
OS ref. TQ2979
Description: Three-storey, brick; imposing.

# NORFOLK

## Castle Rising

### Trinity Hospital
Date founded: 1614
Date built: 1614
Location: In village.
OS ref. TF6624
Description: Twelve dwellings together with governor's lodgings and chapel around small courtyard. Stone with steeply sloping roof. Twin towers to front.

## Great Yarmouth

### Fishermen's Hospital
Date founded: 1702
Date built: 1702
Location: Church Plain.
OS ref. TG5207
Description: Central courtyard surrounded by three ranges with return projections to fourth; brick-built; Dutch gables, dormers, lanterns.

## Horning

### St James Hospital chapel (former)
Date founded: Fourteenth century
Date built: Fourteenth century
Location: In village.
OS ref. TG3417
Description: Little left, now used as barn.

## Norwich

### Great Hospital
Date founded: 1249
Date built: 1249
Location: Bishopgate.
OS ref. TG2308
Description: Medieval with infirmary hall and cloisters. Parish church of St Helen incorporated.

### Lazer Houses
Date founded: Twelfth century
Date built: Twelfth century
Location: 219 Sprowston Road.
OS ref. TG2308
Description: Norman range preserved with two doorways, two round windows. Now used as branch library.

# NORTHAMPTONSHIRE

## Ayno

### Almshouses
Date founded: 1822
Date built: 1822
Location: In village north of grammar school.
OS ref. SP5233
Description: Grey and brown stone, two-storey, with tripartite windows and pedimented doorways.

## Barnwell

### Latham's Almshouses
Date founded: 1601
Date built: 1874
Location: South-east of parish church.
OS ref. TL0585
Description: Built in seventeenth-century style.

## Church Brampton

### Earl Spencer Almshouses
Date founded: 1858
Date built: 1858
Location: In village near to parish church.
OS ref. SP7266
Description: Neo-Tudor, built by John Wykes.

## Clipston

### Clipston Hospital
Date founded: 1667
Date built: 1673
Location: Adjoining parish church.
OS ref. SP7182
Description: Two-storey with a third in the gables. Originally the centre had the schoolmaster's lodgings in the ground floor with school room over, and a hospital for twelve men occupying the two wings.

## Cottesbrooke

### Langham's Hospital (and school)
Date founded: 1651
Date built: 1651
Location: On the road to Broxworth.
OS ref. SP7273
Description: Single-storey with three light mullioned windows.

## Deanshanger

### Carpenter's Charity Homes
Date founded: 1823
Date built: 1823
Location: Overlooking The Green.
OS ref. SP7540
Description: Eight bays in a two–four–two rhythm.

## East Carlton

### Almshouses
Date founded: 1866
Date built: 1866
Location: Near to church.
OS ref. SP8488
Description: Rebuilt in Tudor style.

### Finedon
Date founded: 1847
Date built: 1847
Location: Near to church.
OS ref. SP9373
Description: Modest.

## Higham Ferrers

### The Bede House
Date founded: 1428
Date built: 1428
Location: Within parish church precincts.
OS ref. SP9669
Description: Hospital building, now used as a Sunday School. Alternate bands of red and grey brick.

## Kettering

### Sawyers Almshouses
Date founded: 1688
Date built: 1688
Location: Opposite Civic Centre in Sheep Street.
OS ref. SP8878
Description: Very humble.

## King's Cliffe

### John Thorpe Almshouses
Date founded: 1668
Date built: 1668
Location: Bridge Street.
OS ref. TL0197
Description: Single-storey; mullioned windows with straight hoods.

### Spinsters' Almshouses
Date founded: 1754
Date built: 1754
Location: Bridge Street, west of girls' school.
OS ref. TL0197
Description: Georgian; modest.

### Widows' Almshouses
Date founded: 1749
Date built: 1749
Location: School Hill, adjoining Law's Library.
OS ref. TL0197
Description: Georgian; modest.

## Little Brinton

### Almshouses
Date founded: 1851
Date built: 1851
Location: In village.
OS ref. SP6763
Description: Designed by John Wilkes.

## Northampton

### Hospital of St John
Date founded: 1137
Date built: 1137
Location: Bridge Street.
OS ref. SP7560
Description: Hospital hall touching chapel at north-east corner is a rebuild. Now used as a RC church.

## Rothwell

### Jesus Hospital
Date founded: 1591
Date built: 1591
Location: South-east of church.

OS ref. SP8181
Description: Gateway, long south range with two L-shaped wings, originally for twenty-six men.

## Titchmarsh

### Pickeering's Almshouses
Date founded: 1756
Date built: 1756
Location: South of parish church and The Green.
OS ref. TL0299
Description: Single-storey with dormers, thatched.

## Weekley

### Montague Hospital
Date founded: 1611
Date built: 1611
Location: In village.
OS ref. SP8981
Description: Two-storey; widely spaced mullioned windows; centre with four-centred doorhead.

## West Haddon

### Almshouses
Date founded: Nineteenth century
Date built: Nineteenth century
Location: West end of village.
OS ref. SP6372
Description: Red and blue brick, with porches and cupola.

# NORTHUMBERLAND

## Alnwick

### Ruins of St Leonard's Hospital Chapel
Date founded: 1193
Date built: 1193
Location: Opposite Alnwick Castle.
OS ref. NV1814
Description: Ruins.

## Hexham

### Henry King Almshouses
Date founded: Nineteenth century
Date built: Nineteenth century
Location: Hallside Bank.
OS ref. NY9464
Description: Modest.

## Whittingham

### Whittingham Tower Almshouses
Date founded: 1845
Date built: 1845
Location: Whittingham village.
OS ref. NV0713
Description: Border tower dwelling converted to almshouses in Victorian times.

# NOTTINGHAMSHIRE

## Blyth

### Hospital of St John the Evangelist
Date founded: 1226
Date built: 1446
Location: Main Street; on The Green.
OS ref. SK6387
Description: Rectangular building with dog-tooth ornaments; segmental arch door.

## Bunny

### Bunny School and Almshouses
Date founded: 1700
Date built: 1700
Location: Between church and road.
OS ref. SK5829
Description: Schoolroom at one end, four almshouses at the other; brick with rusticated quoins and steep pitched dormers.

## Cossell

### Willoughby Almshouses
Date founded: 1685
Date built: 1685
Location: In village.
OS ref. SK4942
Description: Brick, the centre with saddleback roof with gables.

## Elston

### Ann Darwin Almshouses
Date founded: 1744
Date built: 1744
Location: Opposite church.
OS ref. SK7648
Description: Modest.

## Newark

### Bede House chapel
Date founded: 1556
Date built: 1556
Location: Bede House Lane.
OS ref. SK8154
Description: Stone-built chapel. The Bedehouse has been demolished.

## Nottingham

### Abel Collins Hospital
Date founded: 1709
Date built: 1709

Location: Friar Lane.
OS ref. SK5841
Description: Central arched entrance to quadrangle, around which are twenty two-storey houses of classical proportions.

# OXFORDSHIRE

## Abingdon

### Brick Alley Almshouses
Date founded: 1718
Date built: 1718
Location: Churchyard.
OS ref. SU4997
Description: Chequered brick and rubbed brick; seven bays, the centre solid and raised with pediment.

### Christ's Hospital (Long Alley Almshouses)
Date founded: 1446
Date built: 1605
Location: Churchyard.
OS ref. SU4997
Description: Wooden pentice with porch and lantern over. Cloister windows with arched lights.

### Twitty's Almshouses
Date founded: 1707
Date built: 1707
Location: Churchyard.
OS ref. SU4997
Description: Red brick; single-storey; hipped roof with gable and lantern.

## Broughton

### Elizabeth Bradford Wyatt Almshouses
Date founded: 1859
Date built: 1859
Location: Adjoining parish church to the east.
OS ref. SP4238
Description: A pair of two-storey houses linked by a low wall, gabled with trefoiled lancets.

## Burford

### Castle Almshouses
Date founded: 1726
Date built: 1726
Location: Church Lane.
OS ref. SP2512
Description: Four plain dwellings of no architectural interest.

### Great Almshouses
Date founded: 1457
Date built: 1828
Location: Church Lane.
OS ref. SP2512
Description: Founded by Richard, Earl of Warwick; rectangular, two-storey block with large central doorway and gothic details.

## Chipping Norton

### Henry Cornish Almshouses
Date founded: 1640
Date built: 1640
Location: Church Lane.
OS ref. SP3127
Description: A pair of eight gables and tall chimneystacks behind a low wall and gateway, with strapwork and crested finials.

## Deddington

### Almshouses
Date founded: 1818
Date built: 1818
Location: Church Street.
OS ref. SP4631
Description: Pointed doorways and windows with gothic glazing bars.

## Ewelme

### Ewelme Hospital
Date founded: 1437
Date built: 1437
Location: Adjoining parish church.
OS ref. SU6491
Description: Founded by William de la Pole. Courtyard development with adjoining school. Possibly one of the most important groups in the country.

## Glympton

### Almshouses
Date founded: 1949
Date built: 1949
Location: In village.
OS ref. SP4221
Description: Single-storey in traditional style with steeply pitched roof, central gable over a high entrance with coat of arms.

## Goring Heath

### Henry Alnut Almshouses
Date founded: 1724
Date built: 1724
Location: In village.
OS ref. SU6679
Description: Eight one-storey dwellings around three sides of a courtyard with screen and chapel, with clock.

## Little Tew

### Almshouses
Date founded: 1862

Date built: 1862
Location: In village, adjoining school teacher's house.
OS ref. SP2838
Description: Approached through a lych gate of red and blue brick with half-hipped gables. Picturesque.

## Mapledurham

### John Lister Almshouses
Date founded: 1613
Date built: 1613
Location: In village.
OS ref. SU6676
Description: Long one-storey range in chequer brick with stone dressings.

## Oxford

### Stone's Almshouses
Date founded: 1700
Date built: 1700
Location: St Clement's Street, to the east of Magdalene Bridge.
OS ref. SP5206
Description: Range of eleven bays, two-storey with hipped roof, doorway in centre, cross window and pediment.

## Spelsbury

### John Carry Almshouses
Date founded: 1688
Date built: 1688
Location: In village.
OS ref. SP3521
Description: Four single-storey buildings; gabled dormers with mullioned windows.

## Sutton Courtney

### Sutton Courtney Almshouses
Date founded: 1820
Date built: 1820
Location: North of church.
OS ref. SU5093
Description: One-storey, centre a little stressed.

## Thame

### Lord Williams Almshouses
Date founded: 1550
Date built: 1550
Location: Adjoining bandstand in Church Lane.
OS ref. SP7005
Description: Six dwellings half-timbered and brick with cross bracing, gable end facing High Street overhangs.

## Wallingford

### Angler's Almshouses
Date founded: 1681
Date built: 1681
Location: Reading Road
OS ref. SU6089
Description: Three gables, Gothic glazing bars to Tudor windows.

## Wantage

### Almshouses
Date founded: 1867
Date built: 1867
Location: Mill Street.
OS ref. SU4087
Description: Victorian Gothic.

## Witney

### Townsend's Almshouses
Date founded: 1821
Date built: 1821
Location: Oxford Road.
OS ref. SP3510
Description: A long rectangular block in a minimal Tudor style, for six aged unmarried women.

# SHROPSHIRE

## Barrow

### Barrow Almshouses
Date founded: 1621
Date built: 1816
Location: In village.
OS ref. SJ6600
Description: Plain brick with mullioned four light windows.

## Berwick

### Berwick Almshouses
Date founded: 1672
Date built: 1675
Location: In grounds of Berwick House.
OS ref. SJ4816
Description: Low, two-storey brick ranges on three sides of courtyard; fourth side encloses by wall with stone cut arch with semi-circular pediment.

## Bridgenorth

### Almshouses
Date founded: 1792
Date built: 1792
Location: Church Street.
OS ref. SO7293
Description: Red brick; low, seven wide bays with pedimented three-bay centre; pointed windows.

## Clun

### Trinity Hospital
Date founded: 1618
Date built: 1618
Location: Main Street.
OS ref. SO3081
Description: Single-storey, of stone round quadrangle; south façade; two end gables and three stepped central dormers.

## Ludford

### St Giles Hospital
Date founded: 1216
Date built: 1216
Location: North-east of church.
OS ref. SO5174
Description: Plain stone range of single-storey.

## Ludlow

### Fox's Almshouses
Date founded: 1593
Date built: 1593
Location: Corne Street.
OS ref. SO5175
Description: Low, two-storey stone front with four entrances.

### Hosyer's Almshouses
Date founded: 1486
Date built: 1758
Location: College Street.
OS ref. SO5175
Description: Red brick, two-storey with two projecting wings; seven-bay centre with three-bay pediment and cartouch.

### St John's Hospital
Date founded: Twelfth century
Date built: Twelfth century
Location: Low Bridge Street.
OS ref. SO5175
Description: Only tall pointed arch of chapel remains.

## Oswestry

### Morda Hospital
Date founded: 1791
Date built: 1791
Location: One-and-a-half miles south of Morda.
OS ref. SJ2929
Description: Red brick, regular composition with pedimented centre and projecting wings.

## Shrewsbury

### Drapers' Almshouses
Date founded: 1825
Date built: 1825
Location: St Mary's Street.
OS ref. SJ4912
Description: Red brick, Tudor style; symmetrical two-storey front with three straight gables; crenellated tower and cobbled court.

### Hospital of the Holy Cross
Date founded: 1853
Date built: 1853
Location: Princess Street.
OS ref. SJ4912
Description: Gothic brick.

### Millington's Hospital
Date founded: 1794
Date built: 1794
Location: Frankwell.
OS ref. SJ4912
Description: Ambitious composition; brick; two-storey with façade raised on large brick terrace; three-bay pediment with wooden cupola.

## St Martins

### St Martin's Almshouses
Date founded: 1698
Date built: 1810
Location: W of church
OS ref. SJ3336
Description: Single-storey range with central pediment and wooden cross windows.

## Tong

### Tong Charities' Almshouses
Date founded: Eighteenth century
Date built: Eighteenth century
Location: East of church.
OS ref. SJ7907
Description: Three sides of square, open to street; one-storey, brick; centre with arch and pediment over.

# SOMERSET

## Bishop Lydeard

### Bishop Lydeard Almshouses
Date founded: 1616
Date built: 1616
Location: In village.
OS ref. ST1629
Description: Doorways with cambered heads; mullioned windows.

## Broadway

### Every's Almshouses
Date founded: 1588
Date built: 1588

Location: In village.
OS ref. ST3115
Description: Mullioned windows and cambered heads.

## Bruton

### Sexey's Hospital
Date founded: 1619
Date built: 1619
Location: High Street.
OS ref. ST6634
Description: Quadrangular, with arches and balcony over giving access to the thirty almshouses, chapel and board room.

## Chard

### Harvey's Hospital
Date founded: 1841
Date built: 1841
Location: Fore Street.
OS ref. ST3208
Description: Neo-Tudor.

## Crewkerne

### Chubbs Almshouses
Date founded: 1644
Date built: 1644
Location: West Street.
OS ref. ST4409
Description: Modest.

### Davis's Almshouses
Date founded: 1707
Date built: 1707
Location: West Street.
OS ref. ST4409
Description: Single-storey with nine bays; three doorways; six flanking windows; central pediment of three bays.

## Donyatt

### Almshouses
Date founded: 1624
Date built: 1624
Location: In village.
OS ref. ST3313
Description: Range of six mullioned windows; four-centred door heads.

## East Coker

### Helyar Almshouses
Date founded: 1640
Date built: 1640
Location: In village next to church.
OS ref. ST5412
Description: Row with gabled dormers and mullioned windows.

## Evercreech

### Almshouses
Date founded: 1825
Date built: 1825
Location: In village square.
OS ref. ST6438
Description: Modest.

## Frome

### The Blue House
Date founded: 1726
Date built: 1726
Location: off Market Place.
OS ref. ST7542
Description: Adjoining Bluecoats School; Quoined arched windows and doorways.

### Steven's Asylum and Hospital
Date founded: 1803
Date built: 1803
Location: Keyford.
OS ref. ST7542
Description: Ten bays to front; three bays for poor children; the other for old men; cupola over.

## Glastonbury

### St Mary's Hospital
Date founded: Thirteenth century.
Date built: Thirteenth century.
Location: Magdalene Street.
OS ref. ST5039
Description: Two ranges facing each other; originally one medieval hospital hall.

### St Patrick's Almshouses
Date founded: 1517
Date built: 1517
Location: Magdalene Street.
OS ref. ST5039
Description: Much altered with gateway and chapel with bell cote.

## Shepton Mallet

### Strode's Almshouses
Date founded: 1699
Date built: 1699
Location: Market Street.
OS ref. ST6243
Description: Pre-classical; dormers and two-light windows.

## Somerton

### Hext Almshouses
Date founded: 1626
Date built: 1626
Location: Broad Street.
OS ref. ST422
Description: One-storey with curious windows.

## Taunton

### Almshouses
Date founded: Fourteenth century
Date built: Fourteenth century
Location: St James' Street.
OS ref. ST2225
Description: Timber framework of old almshouses now erected in park, adjoining council offices.

### Grey's Almshouses
Date founded: 1635
Date built: 1635
Location: East Street.
OS ref. ST2225
Description: Long row of brick Tudor almshouses with distinctive chimneys.

### Huish Almshouses
Date founded: 1615
Date built: 1615
Location: opp Corfield Hall, Hammet Street.
OS ref. ST2225
Description: Distinctive stone-built hospital building with lighter stone dressings and dormers.

## Wellington

### Sir John Fisher Almshouses
Date founded: 1833
Date built: 1833
Location: Mantle Street.
OS ref. ST1320
Description: Gothic; red brick with stone dressings.

## Wells

### Bishop Bubwith's Almshouses
Date founded: Fifteenth century
Date built: Fifteenth century
Location: Chamberlain Street.
OS ref. ST5445
Description: Originally a medieval hospital with chapel and guildhall – now all almshouses.

### Brick's Almshouses
Date founded:
Date built:
Location: Adjoining St Cuthbert's church.
OS ref. ST5445
Description: Stone-built with 'sedila' entrance.

### Harper's Almshouses
Date founded: Seventeenth century.
Date built: Seventeenth century.
Location: Chamberlain Street.
OS ref. ST5445
Description: Whitewashed cob.

### Llewellyn's Almshouses
Date founded: Nineteenth century
Date built: Nineteenth century
Location: Priest's Row.
OS ref. ST5445
Description: Two rows of brick-built almshouses facing each other with common footpaths and grounds.

### Still's Almshouses
Date founded: Eighteenth century
Date built: Eighteenth century
Location: Adjoining St Cuthbert's church.
OS ref. ST5445
Description: Stone-built, in 'close'.

## West Coker

### Manor House Almshouses
Date founded: 1718
Date built: 1718
Location: South-east of manor house.
OS ref. ST5113
Description: Doorways and windows arched with heavy square abaci and keystones.

# STAFFORDSHIRE

## Alton

### Hospital of St John
Date founded: 1840
Date built: 1840
Location: Next to Alton Castle.
OS ref. SK0742
Description: Three sides of a quadrangle, classical design by Pugin, comprising chapel, school and residences.

## Amblecote

### Corbett Hospital
Date founded: Eighteenth century
Date built: Eighteenth century
Location: In village.
OS ref. SO8985
Description: Brick, of nine bays, plain to front with Venetian windows at rear.

## Burton upon Trent

### Almshouses
Date founded: 1875
Date built: 1875
Location: Wellington Street.

OS ref. SK2423
Description: Gothic, brick, three ranges, one-storey with wooden porches. Two-storey centre with oriel.

## Lichfield

### Milley's Hospital
Date founded: Seventeenth century
Date built: Seventeenth century
Location: Beacon Street.
OS ref. SK1109
Description: Brick, with stone trim; middle porches and mullions.

### St John's Hospital
Date founded: 1140
Date built: 1495
Location: John Street.
OS ref. SK1109
Description: Chapel, hall and range of eight almshouses, with chimneybreasts.

## Madeley

### Almshouses
Date founded: 1645
Date built: 1645
Location: South-west of church.
OS ref. SJ7744
Description: Jacobean, brick with Victorian porches.

## Rolleston

### Almshouses
Date founded: 1712
Date built: 1712
Location: In village.
OS ref. SK2327
Description: Single-storey, range of brick with quoins and broken pediment.

# SUFFOLK

## Ampleton

### Almshouses
Date founded: 1693
Date built: 1693
Location: North of church.
OS ref. TL8671
Description: Modest.

## Boyton

### Mary Warner Charities' Almshouses
Date founded: 1736
Date built: 1828
Location: West of parish church.
OS ref. TM3747
Description: Three brick ranges of two storeys, the recessed middle range in the original; the other two additions.

## Bramfield

### Almshouses
Date founded: 1723
Date built: 1723
Location: In village.
OS ref. TM4073
Description: Red brick; modest.

## Brent Eleigh

### Colman's Almshouses
Date founded: 1731
Date built: 1731
Location: In village.
OS ref. TL9447
Description: Brick, two-storey with segmented headed windows.

## Bury St Edmunds

### Clopton Asylum
Date founded: 1744
Date built: 1744
Location: Angel Hill.
OS ref. TL8564
Description: Long two-storey front with two-bay projections. Ten bays deeply recessed; seven in centre; red brick with quoins.

## Elmswell

### Sir Robert Gardener Almshouses
Date founded: 1614
Date built: 1614
Location: In village.
OS ref. TL9964
Description: Red brick, one-storey with steep central gable.

## Hadleigh

### Pykenham Almshouses
Date founded: Fifteenth century
Date built: 1807
Location: George Street.
OS ref. TM0242
Description: Modest with timber-framed fifteenth-century chapel attached.

### Raven Almshouses
Date founded: 1636
Date built: 1636
Location: Benton Street.
OS ref. TM0242
Description: Modest.

## Hawstead

### Metcalfe Almshouses
Date founded: 1811
Date built: 1811
Location: In village.
OS ref. TL8559
Description: Grey bricks; two-storey, with eleven bays; castellated with pointed windows.

## Ipswich

### Tooley's Almshouses
Date founded: 1846
Date built: 1846
Location: Foundations Street.
OS ref. TM1744
Description: Big group of red brick with fancy timberwork, notably outer staircase in gable ends of projecting wings.

## Levington

### Sir Robert Hitcham Almshouses
Date founded: 1636
Date built: 1636
Location: North of church.
OS ref. TM2339
Description: Two small short ranges facing each other; red brick; one-storey.

## Long Melford

### Trinity Hospital
Date founded: 1573
Date built: 1847
Location: Westgate Street.
OS ref. YL8645
Description: Red brick; seven bays, central bay embattled with cupola; courtyard at rear towards church.

## Stowlangtoft

### Almshouses
Date founded: Eighteenth century
Date built: Eighteenth century
Location: In village.
OS ref. TL9568
Description: Red brick, one-storey with four doors and four windows of three lights; pediments, pitch roof and dormers.

## Ufford

### Wood Hospital
Date founded: 1690
Date built: 1690
Location: In village.
OS ref. TM2953
Description: Red brick with large simple gables; segmented headed windows; two-storey.

## Woodbridge

### Seckford Almshouses
Date founded: 1869
Date built: 1869
Location: Sechford Street.
OS ref. TM2749
Description: Brick with stone dressings.

# SURREY

## Cheretsey

### Thomas Willat's Almshouses
Date founded: 1837
Date built: 1837
Location: Alwyn's Lane.
OS ref. TQ0466
Description: Gothic cottages; yellow brick.

## Croydon

### Freemasons' Asylum
Date founded: 1852
Date built: 1852
Location: Freemasons' Road.
OS ref. TQ3365
Description: Red brick with stone trim. Central Dutch gable, the ends smaller. In between, three gabled porches.

### Whitgift Hospital
Date founded: 1596
Date built: 1599
Location: George Street.
OS ref. TQ3365
Description: Quadrangular, brick-built with stone dressings; rooms for forty men with hall and chapel.

## Farncombe

### Wyatt Almshouses
Date founded: 1622
Date built: 1622
Location: Guilford Road.
OS ref. SU9844
Description: Ten dwellings and a central gabled chapel; subdued Tudor.

## Guilford

### Abbot's Hospital
Date founded: 1619
Date built: 1622
Location: High Street
OS ref. TQ0049
Description: Quadrangular, Elizabethan in brick with

stone dressings. Monumental entrance with four turrets. Accommodation for nine men and nine women, plus hall and chapel.

### Onslow Almshouses
Date founded: 1879
Date built: 1879
Location: Farnham Road.
OS ref. TQ0049
Description: Single-storey, caryatid porches and large windows.

## Kingston upon Thames

### Cleave's Almshouses
Date founded: 1668
Date built: 1668
Location: London Road.
OS ref. TQ1869
Description: Range of six houses on each side of a gabled centre.

# SUSSEX (WEST)

## Chichester

### St Mary's Hospital
Date founded: 1229
Date built: 1229
Location: off St Martin's Street.
OS ref. SU8705
Description: Finest remaining example of Infirmary-type hospital.

## East Grinstead

### Sackville College
Date founded: 1609
Date built: 1619
Location: In town.
OS ref. TQ3938
Description: Built of sandstone, two-storey in courtyard form with kitchen with hall over and chapel opposite.

# TYNE AND WEAR

## Gateshead

### St Edmund's Hospital
Date founded: 1247
Date built: 1247
Location: In town
OS ref. NZ2663
Description: Now Holy Trinity parish church.

## Newcastle-upon-Tyne

### Holy Jesus Hospital
Date founded: 1683
Date built: 1683
Location: City Road.
OS ref. NZ2565
Description: Originally almshouses, now a museum.

### Hospital of St Mary B.V.
Date founded: 1189
Date built: 1189
Location: Big Market.
OS ref. NZ2564
Description: Now demolished. Only gate post survives.

### Keelman's Hospital
Date founded: 1701
Date built: 1701
Location: City Road.
OS ref. NZ2665
Description: Courtyard development high above the River Tyne.

### Trinity Almshouses
Date founded: 1787
Date built: 1787
Location: Broad Chare.
OS ref. NZ2664
Description: Almshouses, chapel and hall for Trinity Houses pensioners.

## Sunderland

### Aged Merchant Seamen's Homes
Date founded: 1819
Date built: 1840
Location: Off Crowtree Road.
OS ref. NZ4158
Description: Brick, two-storey, three sides of a square.

### Rectors' Almshouses
Date founded: 1721
Date built: 1860
Location: The Green, Bishopswearmouth.
OS ref. NZ3957
Description: Stone-built round courtyard.

## Tynemouth

### Tyne Master Mariners' Asylum
Date founded: 1837
Date built: 1837
Location: Tynemouth Road.
OS ref. NZ3668
Description: Stone-built with wings and central clock tower.

# WARWICKSHIRE

## Bedworth

### Chaimberlain Almshouses
Date founded: 1840
Date built: 1840
Location: To north of parish church.

OS ref. SP3587
Description: Tudoresque with cloister walks and chapel with turret, all on three sides of the lawn.

## Berkswell

### Almshouses
Date founded: 1853
Date built: 1853
Location: On village green.
OS ref. SP2478
Description: Modest.

## Ledmington Hastings

### Almshouses
Date founded: 1633
Date built: 1633
Location: Within the village.
OS ref. SP4468
Description: One range. The earlier mullions chamfered; the later ones round.

## Stoneleigh

### New Almshouses
Date founded: 1850
Date built: 1850
Location: East of Manor Farmhouse.
OS ref. SP3272
Description: Red sandstone with close-set gables.

### Old Almshouses
Date founded: 1594
Date built: 1594
Location: East of New Almshouses.
OS ref. SP3272
Description: Red sandstone; five very spacious houses with spacious gardens.

## Stratford upon Avon

### Almshouses
Date founded: 1269
Date built: 1427
Location: Adjoining the guildhall in Church Street.
OS ref. SP2055
Description: 150ft long; upper overhang with no gables; the walls with close studding.

## Temple Balsall

### Lady Katherine Leveson's Hospital
Date founded: 1677
Date built: 1677
Location: To the east of the parish church.
OS ref. SP2175
Description: A long oblong courtyard with wings sixteen bays long, with pediments without enrichment.

## Warwick

### Eiffler Almshouses
Date founded: 1696
Date built: 1696
Location: Castle Hill.
OS ref. SP2865
Description: Little of original features left.

### Lord Leycester's Hospital
Date founded: 1571
Date built: 1571
Location: Over and adjoining the west gate of the city.
OS ref. SP2765
Description: Converted from Guild premises. Medieval, half-timbered and stone, in courtyard configuration.

### Oken's Almshouses
Date founded: Seventeenth century
Date built: Seventeenth century
Location: Castle Hill.
OS ref. SP2765
Description: Little of original features left.

# WEST MIDLANDS

## Bournville

### Bournville Almshouses
Date founded: 1897
Date built: 1897
Location: Maryvale Road.
OS ref. SP0581
Description: By Ewan Harper, old tradition, single-storey set round spacious grassy quadrangle. Tudoresque.

## Coventry

### Bablake Hospital
Date founded: Sixteenth century
Date built: Sixteenth century
Location: Off Hill Street.
OS ref. SP3378
Description: Half-timbered with stone ground floor and open galleries to first and ground floor of west elevation.

### Bond's Hospital
Date founded: 1506
Date built: 1506
Location: off Hill Street.
OS ref. SP3378
Description: Half-timbered with stone entrance gates and details.

### Ford's Hospital
Date founded: 1529
Date built: 1529
Location: Greyfriar's Lane.

OS ref. SP3379
Description: Elizabethan, half-timbered, jettied with enclosed central courtyard.

### Hospital of St John (chapel)
Date founded: Twelfth century
Date built: Fourteenth century
Location: Hales Street.
OS ref. SP3379
Description: Red sandstone with tower nave of two bays; chancel of two bays, all under tunnel vault.

## WILTSHIRE

## Bradford on Avon

### Hall's Almshouses
Date founded: 1700
Date built: 1700
Location: Off High Road.
OS ref. ST8261
Description: Approached by a flight of steps, flanked by ball-topped pedestals, four cottages for almsmen and their wives. Crest with motto: *Deo et pauperibus*.

## Corsham

### The Hungerford Almshouses
Date founded: 1668
Date built: 1672
Location: High Street.
OS ref. ST8670
Description: Monumental, of brick, with oriel porch and bell turret. Accommodation for six old women.

## Farley

### Sir Stephen Fox's Almshouses (The Wardenry)
Date founded: 1681
Date Built: 1681
Location: In village.
OS ref. ST4274
Description: Long, low brick building, its centre in line with church yard gates. Centre of four bays and two-storey hipped roof with domes.

## Froxfield

### Somerset Hospital
Date founded: 1694
Date built: 1694
Location: In village.
OS ref. SU2968
Description: Thirty-seven bays long, to a street with long oblong courtyard; chapel in the middle.

## Heytesbury

### Hospital of St John and St Catherine
Date founded: Thirteenth century
Date built: 1769
Location: In village street.
OS ref. ST9242
Description: Three sides of a turfed square, the middle bay projects with pediment and lantern; hipped roof.

## Kington St Michael

### Lyte Almshouses
Date founded: 1675
Date built: 1675
Location: Main Street.
OS ref. ST9077
Description: Six houses, six gables, three light mullioned windows.

## Leigh Delamere

### Joseph Neeld Almshouses
Date founded: Eighteenth century
Date built: Eighteenth century
Location: East of the church.
OS ref. ST8879
Description: Low with five gables and projecting wings.

## Longbridge Deverill

### Thyne Almshouses
Date founded: 1840
Date built: 1840
Location: In village.
OS ref. ST8740
Description: Tudor; brick with stone trim.

## Salisbury

### Collegium Matrarum
Date founded: 1682
Date built: 1682
Location: Just within the cathedral close.
OS ref. SU1529
Description: Built for the widows of ten clergymen. Fine pediment and cupola projecting wings and elaborate cornice. Designed by Sir Christopher Wren.

### Edward Frowd's Almshouses
Date founded: 1750
Date built: 1750
Location: Off city centre.
OS ref. SU1529
Description: Planned like a Georgian house with fine entrance door and circular pediment with inscription.

### St Nicholas' Hospital
Date founded: 1214
Date built: 1214

Location: St Nicholas Road.
OS ref. SU1429
Description: Double hospital, two side by side with double chapel.

## Trinity Hospital

Date founded: 1702
Date built: 1702
Location: Trinity Street.
OS ref. SU1529
Description: Surrounding a miniature courtyard, entered through spacious loggia with three arches and columns with seats on each side. Chapel.

## West Lavington

### Almshouses

Date founded: 1543
Date built: 1831
Location: North-east of church.
OS ref. SU0053
Description: Humble brick.

## Wishford

### Grabham Almshouses

Date founded: 1628
Date built: 1628
Location: North-west of church
OS ref. SU0735
Description: Of stone, mullioned windows and hipped roof.

# YORKSHIRE (HUMBERSIDE)

## Beverley

### Ann Routh Hospital

Date founded: 1749
Date built: 1749
Location: Keldgate.
OS ref. TA0338
Description: Georgian 'block' with pediment.

### Bedehouses

Date founded: Eighteenth century
Date built: Eighteenth century
Location: Lairgate.
OS ref. TA0339
Description: Two-storey, brick with dormers.

### Chas. Wharton Hospital

Date founded: 1774
Date built: 1774
Location: Minstermoorgate.
OS ref. TA0338
Description: Row of brick almshouses.

### Elizabeth Westoby's Almshouses

Date founded: Nineteenth century
Date built: 1983
Location: New Walkergate.
OS ref. TA0340
Description: Modern replacement of almshouses recently demolished.

### Maison Dieu

Date founded: Thirteenth century
Date built: 1925
Location: Morton Lane.
OS ref. TA0341
Description: Replacement of historic almshouses in town, now demolished.

## Kingston-upon-Hull

### Chamberlain Almshouses

Date founded: 1804
Date built: 1804
Location: College Street, Sutton.
OS ref. TA3313
Description: Typically Victorian.

### Hull Charterhouse

Date founded: 1778
Date built: 1778
Location: George Street/Janet Street/Albion Street.
OS ref. TA1029
Description: Classical Georgian design with central pediment and cupola.

### Lees Rest Houses

Date founded: 1912
Date built: 1912
Location: Anlaby Road.
OS ref. TA0528
Description: Relatively modern.

### Pickering Almshouses

Date founded: 1909
Date built: 1909
Location: Beverley Road.
OS ref. TA0832
Description: Modern dwellings round a courtyard.

### Robinson Almshouses (former)

Date founded: 1822
Date built: 1822
Location: Princess Dock Street.
OS ref. TA1028
Description: Now used for commercial purposes.

### Trinity Almshouses (former)

Date founded: 1828
Date built: 1828
Location: Posterngate.
OS ref. TA0528
Description: Now moved to Anlaby Road.

### Trust Almshouses
Date founded: 1884
Date built: 1884
Location: Northumberland Avenue.
OS ref. TA0732
Description: Modest.

## Londesborough

### Londesborough Hospital
Date founded: 1680
Date built: 1680
Location: Next to parish church, in village.
OS ref. SE8745
Description: Stone-built.

## South Dalton

### Almshouses
Date founded: 1873
Date built: 1873
Location: Next to parish church.
OS ref. SE9645
Description: Modest.

# YORKSHIRE (NORTH)

## Beamsley (Skipton)

### Beamsley Hospital
Date founded: 1593
Date built: 1593
Location: On main Skipton/Harrogate road.
OS ref. SE0853
Description: The only known circular almshouse in existence. Now used as holiday accommodation.

## Burneston

### Robinson Almshouses
Date founded: 1680
Date built: 1680
Location: Opposite parish church.
OS ref. TA0193
Description: Three almshouses in brick with pan tile roof. Coat of arms and sundial on front wall.

## Carleton-in-Craven

### Spence's Hospital
Date founded: 1697
Date built: 1697
Location: On fringe of village.
OS ref. SD9850
Description: Stone-built courtyard composition with first floor gallery access to half of dwellings.

## Cowersby

### Almshouses
Date founded: Seventeenth century
Date built: Seventeenth century
Location: Village street.
OS ref. SE4690
Description: Plain stone-built row.

## Coxwold

### Fauconberg Hospital
Date founded: 1662
Date built: 1662
Location: In village street.
OS ref. SE5278
Description: Two-storey, stone-built almshouses under pan tile roof. Coat of arms over centre door.

## Easingwold

### Easingwold Almshouses
Date founded: Nineteenth century
Date built: Nineteenth century
Location: Spring Street.
OS ref. SE5270
Description: Single-storey, with attached hall.

## Firby

### Christ's Hospital
Date founded: 1608
Date built: 1608
Location: One mile south of Bedale in village street.
OS ref. SE2786
Description: Long stone-built row. Now a single-dwelling house.

## Harrogate

### Roger's Almshouses
Date founded: Nineteenth century
Date built: Nineteenth century
Location: Raglan Street.
OS ref. SE3055
Description: Stone-built Victorian two-storey cottages in open square, with central chapel with spire.

## Helperby

### Jonathan and Anne Coates Almshouses
Date founded: 1873
Date built: 1873
Location: Opposite Appletree Inn in village.
OS ref. SE4470
Description: Victorian composition of two-storey block with clock tower and bird's feet gables, and bungalows with heavily overhanging porches.

## Linton-in-Craven

### Fountaine's Hospital
Date founded: 1721
Date built: 1721
Location: Adjoining village green.
OS ref. SD9962
Description: Classically designed (by Vanbrugh). Six stone-built cottages of massive proportions, with central chapel with central tower.

## Longpreston

### Hospital of James Knowles
Date founded: Seventeenth century
Date built: Seventeenth century
Location: Near old railway on outskirts of village.
OS ref. SD8258
Description: Single-storey stone cottages with central chapel.

## Nunnington

### Almshouses
Date founded: Seventeenth century
Date built: Seventeenth century
Location: South of Hall.
OS ref. SE6779
Description: Modest.

## Ormesby

### Almshouses
Date founded: 1712
Date built: 1712
Location: On A-road.
OS ref. NZ5417
Description: Modest.

## New Earswick

### New Earswick Model Village
Date founded: 1904
Date built: 1904
Location: Haxby Road.
OS ref. SE6155
Description: Bungalows within the model village.

## Richmond

### Bowes Hospital
Date founded: 1607
Date built: 1607
Location: Darlington Road.
OS ref. NZ1802
Description: Stone-built, like small church. Now used as private house.

### Victoria Hospital
Date founded: Nineteenth century
Date built: Nineteenth century
Location: Quaker Lane.
OS ref. NZ1702
Description: Stone-built Victorian institution-like building.

## Ripley

### Ripley model village
Date founded: 1850
Date built: 1850
Location: Next to 'Hotel de Ville'.
OS ref. SE2861
Description: Almshouse-type dwellings.

## Ripon

### Hospital of St John the Baptist
Date founded: 1114
Date built: Nineteenth century
Location: On main Ripon-Harrogate road near bridge.
OS ref. SE3171
Description: Victorian almshouses surrounding church.

### Hospital of St Mary Magdalene
Date founded: 1139
Date built: 1139
Location: Stonebridgegate.
OS ref. SE3172
Description: Early leper hospital chapel with later almshouses and modern chapel nearby.

### St Anne's Hospital
Date founded: 1438
Date built: 1438
Location: High St, Agnesgate.
OS ref. SE3171
Description: Ruins of early hospital hall and chapel with Victorian almshouses nearby.

## Scarborough

### Weelhouse Dwellings
Date founded: 1865
Date built: 1865
Location: Dean Road.
OS ref. SE0388
Description: Modest.

### Wilson's Memorial Asylum
Date founded: 1836
Date built: 1836
Location: Castle Road.
OS ref. SE0489
Description: Victorian.

## Thornton Dale

### Lady Lumley's Almshouses
Date founded: 1657

Date built: 1657
Location: In village.
OS ref. SE8383
Description: Stone cottages with end chapel, now used as school.

## Well

### Well Hospital
Date founded: 1758
Date built: 1758
Location: Between church and Well Hall.
OS ref. SE2682
Description: Very plain. Windows two-light with mullions. Chapel with round arched doorway at end.

## Whitby

### Merchant Seamen's Hospital Houses
Date founded: 1675
Date built: 1675
Location: Church Street.
OS ref. NZ9111
Description: Nineteen stone-built dwellings with Victorian brick façade by Sir G.G. Scott (1880).

## York

### Ann Middleton Hospital
Date founded: 1829
Date built: 1829
Location: Skeldergate.
OS ref. SE6152
Description: Late-Georgian block with classical details and statue of founder in niche. Now used as a hotel.

### Dorothy Wilson's Almshouses
Date founded: 1812
Date built: 1812
Location: Walmgate.
OS ref. SE6153
Description: Georgian, three-storey plus dormers.

### Hospital, Merchant Adventurers' Hall
Date founded: 1411
Date built: 1411
Location: Fossgate.
OS ref. SE6151
Description: Stone undercroft under half-timbered guild hall.

### Hospital, St Anthony's Hall
Date founded: 1446
Date built: 1446
Location: Peaseholme Green.
OS ref. SE6153
Description: Stone undercroft beneath stone guild hall.

### Ingram Hospital
Date founded: 1635
Date built: 1635
Location: Bootham.
OS ref. SE5933
Description: Long row of brick almshouses with square, battlemented tower/gatehouse.

### Lady Hewley's Almshouses
Date founded: 1840
Date built: 1840
Location: St Saviourgate.
OS ref. SE6152
Description: Terrace of twelve almshouses plus chapel.

### St Leonard's Hospital
Date founded: 986
Date built: Thirteenth century
Location: Grounds of Yorkshire Museum.
OS ref. SE6052
Description: Ruins of large hospital with vaulted undercroft.

### St Mary's Abbey Hospitum
Date founded: Fourteenth century
Date built: Fourteenth century
Location: Grounds of Yorkshire Museum.
OS ref. SE6052
Description: Half-timbered stone undercroft.

### Terry Memorial Homes
Date founded: 1899
Date built: 1899
Location: Skeldergate.
OS ref. SE6051
Description: Single-storey pair of almshouses, now used as a brass rubbing centre.

### Wandesford Hospital
Date founded: 1739
Date built: 1739
Location: Bootham.
OS ref. SE6053
Description: Georgian; brick-built, three-storey with pediment and statue of founder.

# YORKSHIRE (SOUTH)

## Arksey (Doncaster)

### Sir Bryan Cooke's Almshouses
Date founded: 1660
Date built: 1660
Location: Opposite parish church.
OS ref. SE5807
Description: Single-storey around courtyard. Mullioned end-windows under hood-moulding.

## Bawtry (Doncaster)

### Hospital chapel of St Mary Magdalene
Date founded: 1280
Date built: 1839
Location: North-west of Crown Hotel.
OS ref. SK6593
Description: Victorian. Now used as chapel for local hospital.

## Hemsworth

### Holgate's Hospital
Date founded: 1546
Date built: 1546
Location: Half mile WSW of town centre in Robin Lane.
OS ref. SE4313
Description: Red brick with blue brick and stone trim. Sharply-gabled with many chimneys. Gateway and chapel.

## Tickhill (Doncaster)

### St Leonard's Hospital
Date founded: 1470
Date built: 1470
Location: Northgate.
OS ref. SK5993
Description: Fine timber-framed facade of 1470, restored 1851. Ground floor of ten bays. Oversailing upper floors. Now a private dwelling.

## Wentworth

### Wentworth Hospital
Date founded: 1697
Date built: 1697
Location: In village at Barrow.
OS ref. SK3999
Description: Brick; one and one-and-a-half-storey. Five-bay front with gabled centre bay with timber turret.

# YORKSHIRE (WEST)

## Aberford

### Gascoigne Almshouses
Date founded: 1844
Date built: 1844
Location: South of village, in open fields.
OS ref. SE4236
Description: Monumental stone-built Gothic with high central tower to chapel. Now used as a private residence.

## Ackworth

### Mary Lowther Hospital
Date founded: 1741
Date built: 1741
Location: Adjoining village green.
OS ref. SE4517
Description: Single-storey, with raised three-bay centre.

## Birkby (Huddersfield)

### Holroyd's Almshouses
Date founded: 1830
Date built: 1830
Location: Birkby Fold.
OS ref. SE1418
Description: Stone-built terrace of four almshouses.

## Bradford

### Bradford Tradesmen's Homes
Date founded: 1856
Date built: 1856
Location: Lillycroft
OS ref. SE1435
Description: Stone-built with blue slate roofs.

## Brighouse

### Brooke's Almshouses
Date founded: 1890
Date built: 1890
Location: North of town centre, in Halifax Road.
OS ref. SE1423
Description: Stone-built bungalows with verandahs.

## Farnley (Leeds)

### Farnley Almshouses
Date founded: 1896
Date built: 1896
Location: In village.
OS ref. SE2632
Description: Modest.

## Halifax

### Sir Francis Crossley's Almshouses
Date founded: 1855
Date built: 1855
Location: Margaret Street.
OS.ref. SE0826
Description: Sandstone, to match adjoining Bell Vue.

### Joseph Crossley's Almshouses
Date founded: 1863
Date built: 1863
Location: Arden Road off King Cross Road.
OS ref. SE0826
Description: Large composition of black mill-stone grit with extensive grounds.

### Abbot's Ladies' Homes
Date founded: 1870

Date built: 1870
Location: Skircoat Green Road.
OS ref. SE0825
Description: Twelve houses and a porter's lodge.

### The John Mackintosh Memorial Homes
Date founded: 1925
Date built: 1925
Location: Savile Park.
OS ref. SE0726
Description: Twelve almshouses in a terrace within large garden.

### Waterhouse Almshouses
Date founded: 1642
Date built: 1960
Location: Harrison Road.
OS ref. SE0825
Description: Modern stone-built bungalows.

### Elizabeth Wadsworth Charity
Date founded: 1832
Date built: 1832
Location: Popples, Holdsworth.
OS ref. SE0827
Description: Modest stone-built terrace.

## Huddersfield

### Roebuck's Memorial Almshouses
Date founded: 1932
Date built: 1932
Location: Huddersfield-Wakefield Road.
OS ref. SE1617
Description: Monumental, stone-built cottages with formal gardens to front.

## Kirkthorpe (Wakefield)

### Frieston's Hospital
Date founded: 1595
Date built: 1595
Location: West of parish church.
OS ref. SE3620
Description: Stone-built with slate roof; mullioned windows. Seven single-storey rooms surrounding central top-lit chapel. Now used as private dwelling.

## Leathley (near Poole)

### Almshouses
Date founded: 1769
Date built: 1759
Location: East of parish church.
OS ref. SE2347
Description: Handsome row with one-storey wings and two-storey central block.

## Ledsham (near Leeds)

### St John's Hospital
Date founded: 1670
Date built: 1670
Location: Near parish church.
OS ref. SE4630
Description: Long row of eleven two-storey almshouses. Two-light mullioned windows.

## Leeds

### Harrison and Potter Homes
Date founded: Nineteenth century
Date built: Nineteenth century
Location: Raglen Road.
OS ref. SE2935
Description: Brick-built with stone dressings.

## Saltaire

### Almshouses
Date founded: 1855
Date built: 1855
Location: In model village.
OS ref. SE1535
Description: Stone-built; monumental.

## Wakefield

### Dr Caleb Crowther's Almshouses
Date founded: 1840
Date built: 1840
Location: Adjoining city-centre shopping mall.
OS ref. SE3321
Description: Stone-built; Victorian.

# Bibliography

## BOOKS

Bailey, Brian, *Almshouses*, (Robert Hale, 1988)
Bean, David, *Tyneside, a Biography*, (Macmillan, 1971)
Berridge, Clive, *The Almshouses of London*, (Ashford, 1987)
Best, G., *Mid-Victorian Britain*, (Fontana, 1971)
Briggs, Asa, *Victorian Cities*, (Penguin, 1963)
Briggs, Asa, *Victorian People*, (Penguin, 1954)
Burn W.L., *The Age of Equipoise*, (Allan and Unwin, 1964)
Clay, Rotha Mary, *The Medieval Hospitals of England*, (Frank Cass and Co., 1909)
Costello et al., *An Introduction to the Royal Hospital, Kilmainham*, (Costello et al., 1987)
Darley, Gillian, *Villages of Vision*, (Architectural Press, 1975)
Davis, Terence, *The Architecture of John Nash*, (Studio Press, 1960)
Dickens, A.G., *The English Reformation*, (Fontana, 1967)
Dolman, F.T., *Ancient Domestic Architecture*, (1858)
Doubleday, H.A., *Victoria County History of Yorkshire*, (Inst. of Historical Research, 1907)
Elton, G.R., *England under the Tudors*, (Methuen, 1958)
Godfrey, W.H., *The English Almshouse*, (Faber, 1950)
Granshaw, L., ed., *The Hospital in History*, (Routledge, 1989)
Hallett, Anna, *Almshouses*, (Shire, 2004)
Hanson, Michael, *2,000 Years of London*, (Country Life, 1967)
Harrison, J.F.C., *Early Victorian Britain*, (Fontana, 1979)
Harrison, J.F.C., *Late Victorian Britain*, (Fontana, 1990)
Heath, Sidney, *Old English Houses of Alms*, (Griffiths, 1910)
Helm, P.J., *Exploring Tudor England*, (Robert Hale, 1981)
Hickey, D, *Local hospitals in the Ancient Regime, Paris*, (McGill, 1997)
Howson, B., *Houses of Noble Poverty*, (Bellevue Books, 1993)
Jones, Anthea, *A Thousand Years of the English Parish*, (Windrush, 2000)
Jones, E., *A Guide to the Architecture of London*, (Weidenfeld and Nicholson, 1983)
Kubler, George, *Building the Escorial*, (Princeton University Press, 1982)
Marshall, Dorothy, *English People in the Eighteenth Century*, (Greenwood Press, 1956)
Ordnance Survey, *Monastic Britain*, (Ordnance Survey, 1976)
Orme, N. & Webster, M., *The English Hospital 1070–1570*, (Yale, 1995)
Pallister D.M., *The Age of Elizabeth*, (Longmans, 1983)
Parker, Roy, *English Society in the Eighteenth Century*, (Allan Lane, 1982)
Pevsner, Nicholas, *The Buildings of England*, (Penguin, 1952)
R.C. Hist. Mon., *York, Historic Buildings in the Central Area*, (HMSO, 1981)
Raphael, Mary, *The Romance of English Almshouses*, (Mills and Boon, 1926)
Reed, Michael, *The Age of Exuberance 1500–1700*, (Paladin, 1987)
Scarisbrick, J.J., *The Reformation and the English People*, (Blackwell, 1984)
Scholfield, John, *The Buildings of London*, (British Museum Publications Ltd, 1984)
Taylor, Kate, *Wakefield District Heritage*, (Wakefield E.A.H.Y. Committee, 1976)
Temple, Nigel, *John Nash and the Village Picturesque*, (Alan Sutton, 1979)
Thompson, David, *England in the Nineteenth Century*, (Pelican, 1978)
Walsh, J.J., *The Catholic Encyclopedia*, (Robert Appleton, 1910)
Wearmouth, R.F., *The Working Class Movements of the Nineteenth Century*, (Epworth Press, 1963)
Willis, M., *Nineteenth Century Britain*, (Blackwell, 1990)
Wrighton, K., *English Society 1580–1680*, (Hutchinson, 1982)

## PAMPHLETS

City of Salisbury Guide
City of Wells Guide
City of Winchester
Evesham Abbey
Ford's Hospital, Coventry
Hospital of William Brown, Stamford, Lincolnshire
Lord Leycester's Hospital, Warwick
Maritime Greenwich
Mini-guide to Worcester
National Association of Almshouses Yearbook
St John's Hospital, Canterbury
The Commandery, Worcester
The Holy Jesus Hospital and Joicey Museum, Newcastle-upon-Tyne
The Hospital of St Cross
The Royal Hospital, Chelsea
The Royal Hospital, Kilmainham, Dublin
The Vale of Evesham

# Appendix

Transcript of Indenture setting up Wentworth Hospital, Wentworth Barrow, South Yorkshire, February 1697:

THIS INDENTURE made the four and twentieth day of February in the tenth year of the Reign of our Sovereign Lord William the Third by the Grace of God of England, Scotland, France and Ireland, King, Defender of the Faith, and in the year of our Lord Christ 1697 BETWEEN the Honourable Thomas Wentworth alias Watson of Wentworth Woodhouse in the County of York Esquire, Nephew of the Right Honourable William late Earl of Stratford deceased of the one part and Doctor William Spencer Rector of Thurnscoe in the County of York Thomas Edumundo junior of Worsbrough in the said County of York Gentleman, William Green of Thunner Cliff Grange in the Parish of Ecclesfield in the County of York, Gentleman, Charles Newby of Hooton Roberts in the said County of York, Gentleman, Ralph Eaton of the Parish of Darfield in the said County of York and James Greenhaigh of Wentworth Woodhouse aforesaid Clerk of the other part WITNESSETH that the said Thomas Wentworth alias Watson having in pursuance of the Last Will and Testament of the said late Earl erected two hospitals in Wentworth aforesaid for the convenient dwelling of twelve poor people, six men in one and six women in the other to be chosen by the owners of the said late Earl's Estate Wentworth Woodhouse aforesaid for the time being out of the ancientest and poorest inhabitants there and placed poor people in the same accordingly and to the end three pounds per annum a price for every such poor man and woman may be for ever secured and paid half yearly out of the lands tenements and hereditaments hereinafter mentioned part of the said late Earl's Estate in Yorkshire according to the purport and intent of the said will in that behalf And for and in consideration of the sum of five shillings of lawful English money to the said Thomas Wentworth alias Watson in hand paid by the said William Spencer Thomas Edmundo, George Ellis, William Green, Charles Newby, Ralph Eaton and James Greenhaigh before the installing and deliver of these presents. (The Receipt whereof is hereby acknowledged) the said Thomas Wentworth alias Watson HATH granted bargained sold and confirmed and by these *presorts* doth grant bargain sell and confirm unto the said William Spencer Thomas Edmundo, George Ellis, William Green, Charles Newby, Ralph Eaton and James Greenhaigh, their heirs and assignees for ever the yearly rent or sum of six and thirty pounds of lawful English money to be issuing and payable out of ALL that messuage, Tenement and farm and all closes lands and hereditaments thereunto belonging or therewith held or enjoyed containing by Estimation One hundred and one acres three roods and one and twenty perches be the same more or less situate lying and being in West Melton in the Parish of Wath and County of York nor or late in the tenure or occupation of Francis Thickett his Assignee or Assigned at the yearly rent of Thirty six pounds fifteen shillings or thereabouts And also out of all that Messuage, Tenement or farm and all those lands and hereditaments thereunto belonging or therewith held or enjoyed containing by Estimation fifteen acres one rood and four perches be the same more or less situate lying and being in the West Melton aforesaid nor or late in the tenure of occupation of Thomas Gawtress and George Gawtress their or one of their under-tenants or assigned at the yearly rent of five pounds and twelve shillings or thereabouts the said yearly rent or sum of thirty six pounds to be paid unto the said William Spencer Thomas Edmundo George Ellis William Green Charles Newby, Ralph Eaton and James Greenhaigh their heirs and assigned All or in the Church Porch of Wentworth Woodhouse aforesaid half yearly on the first day of May and first day of November by even and equal portions without any defaultation or abatement for Taxes ordinary or extraordinary to be imposed or assessed on the said messuage farms lands and premises or any of them or on the said yearly rent or sum of six and thirty pounds or any part thereof by authority of Parliament or otherwise or for or by reason of any other matter cause or thing whatsoever Upon Trust to be disposed for the use and benefit of the said six poor men and six poor women according to the purport and intent of the said will in that behalf the first payment of the said Annuity or yearly rent to begin and be made on the first day of May now next coming AND THE SAID Thomas Wentworth alias Watson doth hereby for his and his heirs Grant that in case the said yearly rent or sum of six and thirty pounds or any part-thereof shall be behind and unpaid by the space of Thirty days next after either of the said days whereon the same ought and is limited to be paid as aforesaid Then and so often it shall and may be lawfull to and for the said William Spencer, Thomas Edmundo, George Ellis William Green, Charles Newby, Ralph Eaton and James Greenhaigh their heirs and assignees or any of them into and upon the said messuages, farms, closes, lands, tenements, hereditaments and premises or any part of parts thereof to Enter and distrain and the distress and distresses then and there from time to time found to take, lead, drive, carry away, detain and keep and also the rents issued and profits of the premises receive until the said yearly rent or sum of six and thirty pounds and all arrears thereof and all charities and damages sustained for or by reason of the non payment thereof or for the recovery thereof shall be fully satisfied and said AND TO THE INTENTS the Trust aforesaid may be for ever preserved and continued if is declared and agreed and the said Thomas Wentworth alias Watson doth hereby direct and appoint that when any five of aforesaid Trustees shall happen to depart this life so that there shall be only two of them surviving Then such two surviving Trustees shall within one month next after the decease of the aforesaid other five Trustees transfer and convey the said annuity or yearly sum of six and twenty pounds to the use of themselves and five such other persons as shall be by them nominated for that purpose and their heirs upon and under the same Trusts and confidentes as are in these presents before expressed and declared of and concerning the same and so from time to time as often as it shall happen that there shall be but only Two Trustees in being.

IN WITNESS whereof the parties above named have hereunto interchangeably set their hands and seals the day and year first above written.

2 February 1697
The Hon. Thomas Wentworth to Trustees

# Index

## A
Aachen, Council of, 15
Aberdeen, Scotland 75
Aberford, Yorkshire, 67
Abingdon, Oxfordshire, 57
Acre, 16
Act of Indemnity, 44
Act of Settlement and Removal 1662, 54
Act of Supremacy, 30
Adam, Robert, 48
Adolf of Holstein, 16
aelmysse, 17
Age Concern, 69
Aix en Provence, Synod, 17
Alexandria, Egypt, 14
Alexius, 14
almoner, 17
alms, 17
almsgiving, 17
almshouse, 14, 73
Almshouse Association, The, 72
Alnut's Hospital, Goring heath, Oxen, 57
Alyn, Edward, 40
Anderson, Tempest, 70
Andover, Berkshire, 60
Angiers, France, 83
annates, 30
Anne, Queen, 36, 51
Ansgar, Bishop, 15
Aragon, Catherine of, 30
Argyll, Earl of, 44
Arles, France, 14
asylum, 14
Athelstan, King, 20
Athis, France, 14
Augustinian Order, 88
Ausburg, Germany, 15
Autun, France, 14
Aylesbury, Buckinghamshire, 28

## B
Bablake's Hospital, Coventry, W. Midlands, 28, 93
bastilles, 60
Baumgarten, Germany, 15
Beamsley Hospital, Skipton, N. Yorkshire, 107
Beaufort, Cardinal, 96
Beaune, France, 74, 84
bedehouse, 23, 79
bedesmen, 23, 63
Beghards, 16
Beguines, 16
Bentham, Jeremy, 54
Berkeley Hospital, Worcester, 52
Bess of Hardwick, 32
Beverley, Humberside, 23
Birmingham, W. Midlands, 28, 68
Bishop Brassianus, 14
Bishop Bubwith, 78
Bishop Stichell, 38
Black Prince, 39
Blessed Virgin Mary, 27
Bodmin, Cornwall, 28
Bolyn, Ann, 30
Bond, Thomas, 93
Bond's Hospital, Coventry, W. Midlands 93
Boston, Lincolnshire, 28
Boston, MA. USA, 75
Bourchier, Bishop, 24
Bournville, West Midlands, 68
Bowes, Sir Martin, 32
Bradford, West Yorkshire, 67
Bradford Tradesmens' Homes, 67
Braunweiler, Germany, 15
Brehon Laws, the, 75
Bremen, Germany, 15, 16
Brephotrophium, 14
Brick Alley almshouses, Abingdon, Oxfordshire, 58
Bridgewater, Duke of, 38
Bristol, Avon, 23, 32
Brixham, Kent, 44
Browne's Hospital, Stamford, Lincs., 101
Bruant, Liberal, 46
Bruges, Belgium, 75, 83
Burgundy, France, 74, 84
Burleigh, Lord, 32
Burton Lazars, Leicestershire, 22
Butler, James, Duke of Ormond, 47

## C
Cadbury Brothers, 68
Caesarea, 14
Caesarius, 14
Cambridge, Cambridgeshire, 31, 44
Camden Town and Kentish Town Almshouses, London, 65
Castle Rising, Norfolk, 40
Celestine III, Pope, 16
chantries, 27, 88
Charitable Trusts Act of 1855, 61
Charitable Uses Act, 1601, 63
Charities Act 2006, 63
charity, 27
Charity Commission, The, 63

Charlemagne, Holy Roman Emperor, 15
Charles I, King, 37
Charles II, King, 26, 43
Charterhouse, Hull, 40
Charterhouse, The, London, 38, 98
Chartist, 64
Chelsea, London, 47
Chester, Cheshire, 28
Chester, William, 32
Chesterfield, 28
Chicago, USA, 76
Chichele, Henry, 79
Chichester, W. Sussex, 77
Children of the Almonry', 17
China, 13
Christ's Hospital, London, 92
Chuldebert, King, 14
Cistercian Order, 88
City Livery Companies, 32
Civil War, 42
Clement III, Pope, 16, 30
Clifford, Ann, 107
Clockmakers' Company, 32
Cloyne, Ireland, 75
Clun, Salop, 40
Cluny Abbey, France, 15
College Matrarum, Salisbury, Wilts. 51
Cologne, Germany, 15
Commandery The, 26
Commonwealth, 42, 44
confraternities, 15, 27
Coningsby's Hospital, Hereford, 40, 107
Conningsby, Sir Thomas, 40, 107
Constantine, Emperor, 14
Constantinople, Turkey, 14
Consuetudinarium The, 96
conversi, 20
Cook County Almshouse, the, USA 75
Corbie, France, 15
corporate almshouses, 69
Corpus Christi, 27, 93
corrody, 24
Cottage Homes, 71
Court of Chancery, the, 62
Court of Commissioners for Ecclesiastical Causes, 44
Court of High Commission, 31
courtyard design, 92
Coventry, W. Midlands, 28
Crecy, Battle of, 23
Croke, Thomas, 24
Cromwell, Oliver, 39
Cromwell, Thomas, 30
Crossley, Joseph, 67
Crossley, Sir Francis, 67
Crowther, Dr Caleb, 65
cruciform layout, 88
Cumberland, Countess of, 107

cy-pres, 64
Cyprus, 16

# D

David, King, 75
de Blois, Henry, 26, 95
de la Pole, William, 93
de Manny, Sir Walter, 39
de Molendis, William, 24
de Puiset, Hugh, 23
de Suffield, Walter, 88
de Toclyve, Richard, 96
Declaration of Indulgences, 44
Derby, Derbyshire, 28, 32
Deutz, Germany, 15
Disraeli, Benjamin, 68
Dissolution of the monasteries, 20, 27, 37, 39
Dolman, F.T., 77
*domus dieu*, 14
*domus pauporum*, 14
Dorchester, Dorset, 17, 42
dowries, 27
Drapers Company, 32
Dulwich College, 40, 63
Durham, Co. Durham, 17, 23
Durham Aged Mineworkers' Homes 69
Dylew, William, 24

# E

East India Company, 31, 36
Eberbach, Germany. 15
Edinburgh, Scotland, 75
Edward VI, King, 27, 88
Egan, Enrique, 91
eleemonsune, 17
Elizabeth I, Queen 30
Elizabeth the Queen Mother, 107
Elizabethan Settlement, 31
Enclosure Movement, 37
English Reformation, 27
Ephasus, Turkey, 14
evangelicalism, 65
Evelyn, John, 49
Evesham, H. & W. 17
Ewelme, Hospital, Oxfordshire, 93
Exeter, Devon, 23, 31
Exodus, 20

# F

farmery, 77
Fielding, Henry, 56
Filarate, Antonio, 90
Fishermen's Hospital Great Yarmouth, Norfolk, 52
Florence, Italy, 90
Follett Holt, Mrs Jean, 72
Forde's, Hospital, Coventry, W. Midlands, 101
Forus Tuarthe, 75
foundling home, 14

Fountaine, Richard, 56
Fountaine's Hospital at Linton-in-Craven, North Yorkshire, 56
Fountains Abbey, 77
Fox, Sir Stephen, 48
fraternities, 27
Free Watermen and Lightermens Asylum, Penge, London, 68
friendly societies, 27
Frieston Hospital, Wakefield, W. Yorkshire, 107

# G
Galatia, 14
Gascoigne Almshouses, Aberford, 67
Gascoigne sisters, 67
Geffrye Museum, 52
Geffrye, Sir Richard, 52
gentry, rise of, 34
George I, King, 34
Georgian Almshouses, 52
Gerhard, Abbot, 16
Gerontochium, 14
Gibbons, Grinling, 51
Glastonbury, Somerset, 81
Glorious Revolution, 48
Godalming, Surrey, 39
Godstone, Surrey, 67
Goldsmiths' Company the, 32
Granada, Spain, 75
Granger, Mrs Ellen, 70
Great Hall, 77
Great Hospital of St Giles, The, Norwich, 88
Greatham Hospital, Cleveland, 38
Greenwich, London, 32, 40
Gresham, Sir John, 32
guest house, 14
guilds, 27
guilds, parish, 27
Guinness, E.C., 69
Gundolph, Bishop, 22

# H
Haberdashers Company, 32
Hackett, Leonard, 72
Halifax, W. Yorkshire, 67
Hamilton, Duke of, 93
Hanoverians, 48, 52
Harbledown, Canterbury, Kent, 22
Harding, Revd Septimus, 61
Haswell, Co. Durham, 70
Hawksmoor, Nicholas, 51
Heilig-geist, 16
Help the Aged, 69
Henry VII, King, 91
Henry VIII, King, 26, 29, 31, 32, 88
Hewley Lady, 65
High Ackworth, West Yorkshire, 59
Higham Ferrers, Northamptonshire, 79

Hildesheim, Germany, 15
Hinemar, Germany, 14
Hinton, Somerset, 39
Hiram's Hospital, 61, 78
Hirschau, Germany, 15
Hoggs Mead, Kent, 71
Holy Ghost, 16
Holy Spirit, 16
'Homes fit for Heroes', 70
Hoo Union Workhouse, 60
Hopital de la Salpetriere, Paris, 46
Hopitaux-Generaux, 74
Hopper, Joseph, 70
hospes, 14
hospice, 14
hospital, 14, 73
Hospital Della Scala, Milan, Italy 21
Hospital of Forty Martyrs, 14
hospitum, 17
hostel, 14
hotel, 14
*Hotel-Dieu*, Beaune, Burgundy, France, 74
*Hotel-Dieu*, Paris, France, 15, 83
*Hotels-Dieu*, 74
Houghton, John, 39
Housing Associations, 69
Howard, Henry, 40
Huguenots, 31
Hull, Humberside, 28
'hundred mennes hall', 95
Hurst Green, Lancashire, 57

# I
Illinois, USA 75
indulgences, 27
Industrial Revolution the, 37
infirmary, 77, 92
Innocent III, Pope, 16
Interregnum the, 43
Ipswich, Suffolk, 31
Ireland, 44
Ironmongers' Almshouses, 52

# J
James I, King, 34, 37, 94
James II, King, 44
Jeffreys, Judge, 44
Jerusalem, Israel, 16
Jesus Hospital, Rothwell, Northants, 34
Job, 13
Johnson, Dr, 51
Jones, Inigo, 48
Julian the Apostate, 14

# K
Kells, Ireland, 75
Kilbixy, Ireland, 75
Kilmainham, Dublin, Ireland, 47, 75, 105

Kilmainham Hospital, 47, 75, 105
Kilsaran, Ireland, 75
King William IV Naval Asylum, 68
Kirkhill, Ireland 75
Kirkleatham, Cleveland, 32, 105
Kirkthorpe, Wakefield, W. Yorkshire, 107
Knatchbull Act of 1723, 54
Knights Hospitaller, 16
Knights Templar, 16

## L

Lancaster, Sir James, 32
Landry, Bishop of Paris, 15
Lanfranc, Archbishop, 22, 84
lazer-house, 20
Leather-sellers Company, 32
leper, 20
leproseries, 73
leprosy, 20
Les Invalides, 46, 74
Leviticus, 20, 21
Leycester, Lord, 34, 105
Licensed Victuallers' Benevolent Institution, 68
Lincoln, Lincolnshire, 31
Linen and Woollen Drapers' Homes, 71
Linen-armourers company, 32
Linlithgow, Scotland, 75
London, 23, 31
London Almshouse Committee, the, 72
London County Council, 52, 69
Long Alley Almshouses, Abingdon, Oxen, 57
Louis XIV, King, 44, 74
Louth, Lincolnshire, 28
Lovett, William, 65
Lowther, Mary, 50
Luther, Martin, 27, 29, 73
Lyons, France, 14

## M

MacNaughten, Lord, 63
maladreries, 73
Malcolm IV King, 75
Malta, 16, 21
Mapledurham, Oxfordshire, 42
Markland, Dr Abraham, 96
Marryat, Matthew, 56
Marshall and Snellgroves, 71
Marshall, James, 71
Mary Magdalene, 22
Mary Queen of Scots, 39
Mary, Queen, 44, 48, 49
Maryland USA, 75
Masona, Bishop, 15
mass penny, 27
Massachusetts USA, 75
Massachusetts Poorhouse, 75
Maudlin House, 22
McAuliffe, Miss R.G.M. Miss, 72

Merchant Adventurers Company, 31, 32
merchant classes, rise of, 31
Messina, Italy, 16
Metropolitan Beer and Wine Trades Society, 68
Mitton, Lancashire, 57
Mogul India, 17
monastery, 17
Monmouth, Duke of, 44
Morden College, Blackheath, London, 51
Morden, Sir John, 51
Moretonhampstead, Devon, 42
mortrel and wastel, 97
Morysyne, Richard, 26

## N

Napier, Sir Robert, 42
Napper's Mite, 42
National Assistance Act 1948, 72
National Union of Mineworkers, 70
Neville's Cross, Co. Durham, 23
New Earswick, York, 68
New Lanark, Scotland, 68
Newarke, The, Leicester, 82
Newcastle-on Tyne, Tyne and Wear, 23, 28
Niven, Agnes V., 98
North, Revd Francis, 61
Northampton, Northants, 86
Northampton, Lord, 32
North-East Railway Cottage Homes and Benefit Fund, 70
Northumberland Mineworkers' Aged Homes, 70
Norwich, Norfolk, 31
Nosocomium, 14
Notre Dame of St Carmel and St Lazare, Order of, 74

## O

oakum, 60
oblati, 20
orphanage, 14
orphanotrophium, 14
*Ospidale Maggiore*, Milan, Italy, 90
Owe, Sir Thomas, 32
Owen, George, 32
Owen, Robert, 68
Oxfam, 69
Oxford, Oxfordshire, 44, 91

## P

Palmer, Dr Jack, 71
panopticon system, 60
Papal See, The, 90
Parish Clerks, Almshouses, 32
Paxton, Joseph, 67
Peabody, George, 69
Pembroke, the Countess of, 107
Pilgrim Fathers, the, 75
poor farms, 75

poor house, 14
Poor Law Act of 1597, 30
Poor Law Act of 1834, 31
Poor Law Amendment Act of 1834, 60
Poor Law Board, 60
Poor Law Commission, 60
Poor Law Unions, 56
Portinary, Francis, 91
Powell, Sir William, 68
protestant, 44
ptochium, 14
Pugin, A.W.N., 67
Purgatory, 27
Puritans, 38, 42, 75

## Q
Quakers, 68

## R
Ragdale, Owen, 34
Ranelagh, Lord, 47
Reformation, the, 27, 73
Reims, France, 14
Restoration, The, 48
Revolutionary War, the, 75
Ridley, Bishop, 92
Ridolfi Plot, 39
Ripon, North Yorkshire, 23
Robinson, William, 47
Rochester Hospital, Kent, 22
Roman Empire, the, 13
Rome, Italy, 17
Rowntree, Joseph, 68
Royal Hospital, Chelsea, London, 47, 105
Royal Naval Hospital, Greenwich, London, 48, 56
Russia Company, 31, 36
Ryder, Sue, 69

## S
Salisbury, Wiltshie, 51
Salt, Sir Titus, 68
Saltaire, W. Yorkshire, 66, 68
Sancte Clere, William, 87
Santa Caterina da Siena, Italy, 21
Santa Maria della Scala, Rome, Italy, 16
Santiago de Compostela, Spain, 75, 91
Santo Spirito in Sassia, Rome, Italy, 16, 91
Save the Children, 69
Savoy Palace, London, 91
scheme, the, 63
Scotland, 75
Scott, David, 72
Scott, Sir George Gilbert, 67
Seamen's Houses, Whitby, 67
Sedgemoor, Devon, 44
Seven Corporal Works of Mercy, 17
Sherborne, Dorset, 82
Sherburn Hospital, Durham, 28

Shireburn, John, 57
Shireburn, Sir Michael, 57
Sibthorpe, R.W., 67
Sienna, Italy, 16, 90
Sigibert, King, 14
Silversmiths' Company, 32
Sint Jan's Hospitaal, Bruges, Belgium, 75, 83
Skinners Company, 32
Skipton, North Yorkshire, 107
slum parsons, 64
Soane, Sir John, 48
Society for Improvement of the Conditions of the Labouring Classes, the, 69
South Chailey, Haywards Heath, W. Sussex, 71
Speenhamland ruling, 54
Spence, Ferrand, 98
Spence's Hospital, Carleton-in-Craven, North Yorkshire, 98
St Albans, 23
St Andrea, 16
St Anne, 23
St Annes Bedehouse, Lincoln, 67
St Augustine, 16
St Bartholomew, 22, 39
St Basil, 14
St Benedict, 17
St Cross, Hospital, Winchester, Hants. 26, 56, 61, 95
St Elizabeth of Thuringia, 21
St Francis of Assisi, 21
St Gregory of Tours, 21
St James, 15
St John at Canterbury, Kent, Hospital, 84
St John Chrysostan, 14
St John the Almsgiver, 14
St John the Baptist, 27, 82, 87
St John the Baptist, Winchester, Hants. 78
St John the Evangelist, 23, 27, 82
St John's Hospital, Bruges, 75, 83
St Lazarus, 22
St Leonard, 20, 22, 23
St Matthew, 15
St Maria Latina Abbey, 16
St Martin-in-the-Fields Almshouses, London, 65
St Mary Magdalene, 23, 84
St Mary's Hospital, Chichester, 77
St Mary's Homes, Godstone, Surrey, 67
St Maximus, 15
St Nicholas, Salisbury, Wilts., 78
St Pancras Almshouses, London, 65
St Peter's, Rome, Italy 27, 90
St Pulcheria, 14
St Saviour, Wells, Somerset, 78
St Simeon, 15
St Stephens Hospital, Dublin, Ireland, 75
St Wulston, 23
Stamford, Lincolnshire, 32
Stephen V, Pope, 17

Stephen, King, 20, 22, 26, 95
Stidd-under-Langridge, Lancashire, 57
Stuarts, The, 34
Sudely Almshouses, 67
Sun King, The, 46
Sutton, Thomas, 38, 39, 69
Swing Riots, 60

## T
Tailors Company, 32
Talmud, the, 14
Taunton, Devon, 28
Tavera, Spain, 91
Test Acts, 44
Teutonic Knights, 16
Tewksbury Almshouse, Mass. USA, 76
Theodosius II, 14
Thorne, Robert, 32
Thornhill, James, 51
Toledo, Spain, 75, 91
Tomkin, Benjamin, 58
Tonnerre, France, 83
Trinity Almshouses, Mile End Road, London, 52, 107
Trinity Hospital, Leicester, 82
Trinity Hospital, Salisbury, Wilts., 51
Trollope, Anthony, 61
Turkey, 14
Turner, Sir William, 32, 105
Twist, Oliver, 60
Twitty, Charles, 58
Tyne Master Mariners' Asylum, Tynemouth, Tyne and Wear, 66
Tyrconnel, Earl of, 44

## V
Vagabond Act of 1547, 31
Valor Ecclesiasticus, 30
Vanbrugh, Sir John, 48, 49
Vechio, Italy, 16
Vendidad, 14
Vetusta Monumenta, 84
Vicar General, 30

Villefranche, 16
Volkenrode, Germany, 15
Voltaire, Francois-Marie, 21

## W
Wakefield, West Yorkshire, 62, 106
Waldren's Almshouses, Tiverton, Devon, 34
Walkenreid, Germany, 15
Wandesford, Mary, 59
Warden, The, 61
Warwick, W. Midlands, 28, 60
Wayneflete William of, 96
Webb, John, 48
Wells, Somerset, 81
Westminster Abbey, London, 107
Wexford, Ireland 75
Whitby, North Yorkshire, 67
Whiteley Village, Surrey, 71
Whitgift's Hospital, Croydon, London, 107
William and Mary, 44, 48, 49
William of Orange, 42, 44, 49
William Rufus, King, 20
Winchester, Hampshire, 95
Witham, Somerset, 39
Wittenberg, Saxony, Germany, 27
Woodfield Report, 64
Worcester, Hereford and Worcester, 23, 26
Workhouse, the, 56, 59
Workhouse Test, the, 60
Workhouse Union, 60
Wren, Sir Christopher, 32, 47, 51
Wright, Elizabeth, 67
Wyatville, James, 38
Wykeham, William, 96

## X
xenodochium, 14

## Y
York, 23

## Z
Zoticus, 14

If you are interested in purchasing other books published by The History Press,
or in case you have difficulty finding any of our books in your local bookshop,
you can also place orders directly through our website

www.thehistorypress.co.uk